Praise for *Tozer on the Almighty God*

Tucked away in the opening chapter of the book of Exodus is a provocative statement: *Now a new king arose over Egypt who did not know Joseph.*

It is possible for present generations to forget the spiritual giants of the past. It is a great sadness when we forget the men who have gone before us and walked with God. That's why so often the best books are the old books.

A.W. Tozer was a man who walked with God and drank deeply from the well of Scripture. Tozer was a pastor, but his emphasis and focus was not on church growth. His emphasis was always on the majesty and holiness of God.

Ron Eggert has done a great service for us all in taking the great insights of Tozer and setting them into a devotional that can be read throughout the year. You can be sure that your inner man will be nourished, strengthened, and encouraged by his insights from God's Word as you face each new day.

STEVE FARRAR | Men's Leadership Ministries, author of *Point Man, King Me,* and *How to Ruin Your Life by 30*

A.W. Tozer was ever at his delightful, passionate best! For many years I have read his thoughtful, provocative, incisive words. They always demand my serious contemplation. His plainly expressed comments, penetrating and direct, challenge me to study, pray over and try to live out Christ in my life. Tozer drives me to the Word of God.

Ron Eggert, in his three compilations of Tozer's works, has seriously and affirmatively facilitated my study of Tozer. I owe a debt to Eggert for his studious expertise in making his selections from the writings of Tozer.

EDMUND R. YATES | deacon First Baptist Church, Dallas

Tozer has ministered to all of us. As we read his works, we find so many nuggets of wisdom that we want to share with others. Ron Eggert's new book *Tozer on the Almighty God* makes those nuggets more readily available. For those who teach or preach or just want to ponder in amazement the first Person of the Trinity, this is a "must" book.

CHARLES MORRIS | president and speaker, Haven Today, author of *Missing Jesus*

In *Tozer on the Almighty God,* Ron Eggert captures the visceral quality of Tozer's reflections on the Lord. The selections in this devotional guide reveal the immediacy of Tozer's vision of God and describe a searing intimacy that makes us long to know the One with whom the author shares such a vital relationship.

Through Tozer's dynamic metaphors, *Tozer on the Almighty God* invites us to worship God with all of our senses. Then, when we are fully engaged, we can begin to appreciate our majestic Lord in His fullness and to magnify Him in ours.

DR. REG GRANT | pastoral ministries department Dallas Theological Seminary

I am delighted to recommend Ron Eggert's *Tozer on the Almighty God* as a daily devotional. I have come to greatly appreciate the work Ron has done with the writings of A.W. Tozer. This volume will add considerably to the enjoyment and benefit that are to be derived from a systematic and thorough reading of Tozer. No matter the subject matter, Tozer's words, coupled with the Holy Spirit's inspiration, will help us plumb the depths of the majesty of God.

BRUCE STEVENSON | minister of worship Stonebriar Community Church, Frisco, Texas

TOZER

ON THE ALMIGHTY GOD

A 365-DAY DEVOTIONAL

MOODY PUBLISHERS
CHICAGO

Originally compiled by Ron Eggert
Interior Design: Brandi Davis
Cover design and illustration: Faceout Studio, Tim Green

Library of Congress Cataloging-in-Publication Data

Names: Tozer, A. W. (Aiden Wilson), 1897-1963, author.
Title: Tozer on the almighty God : a 365-day devotional.
Description: Chicago : Moody Publishers, 2020. | Includes index. | Summary:
    "Spend a year dwelling on the awesomeness of God with A. W. Tozer. He
    will expand your faith in a God so great that words fall short to
    describe Him. He will nourish you with truth. Encounter Tozer's heart
    and wisdom like never before in this newly revised edition"-- Provided
    by publisher.
Identifiers: LCCN 2020020179 (print) | LCCN 2020020180 (ebook) | ISBN
    9780802419682 (paperback) | ISBN 9780802498649 (ebook)
Subjects: LCSH: God--Meditations. | Devotional calendars.
Classification: LCC BT101 .T69 2020 (print) | LCC BT101 (ebook) | DDC
    242/.2--dc23
LC record available at https://lccn.loc.gov/2020020179
LC ebook record available at https://lccn.loc.gov/2020020180

Originally delivered by fleets of horse-drawn wagons, the affordable paperbacks from D. L. Moody's publishing house resourced the church and served everyday people. Now, after more than 125 years of publishing and ministry, Moody Publishers' mission remains the same—even if our delivery systems have changed a bit. For more information on other books (and resources) created from a biblical perspective, go to www.moodypublishers.com or write to:

Moody Publishers
820 N. LaSalle Boulevard
Chicago, IL 60610

1 3 5 7 9 10 8 6 4 2

Printed in the United States of America

To Tristan

I pray that you will very early come to know God personally, to love Him intimately, to obey Him consistently, and to serve Him willingly. I pray that you will follow Him faithfully throughout your life (even later in your teen and college years!) just as your grandpa has sought to do, by the grace of God.

Preface

A iden Wilson Tozer was born April 21, 1897, on a small farm among the spiny ridges of Western Pennsylvania. Within a few short years, Tozer, as he preferred to be called, would earn the reputation and title of "twentieth-century prophet."

When he was fifteen years old, Tozer's family moved to Akron, Ohio. One afternoon as he walked home from his job at Goodyear, he overheard a street preacher say, "If you don't know how to be saved . . . just call on God." When he got home, he climbed the narrow stairway to the attic where, heeding the preacher's advice, Tozer was launched into a lifelong pursuit of God.

In 1919, without formal education, he was called to pastor a small storefront church in Nutter Fort, West Virginia. That humble beginning thrust him and his wife, Ada, into a forty-four-year ministry with The Christian and Missionary Alliance.

Thirty-one of those years were spent at Chicago's Southside Alliance Church. The congregation, captivated by Tozer's preaching, grew from eighty to 800.

His humor, both written and spoken, has been compared to that of Will Rogers—honest and homespun. Congregations could one moment be swept by gales of laughter and the next sit in a holy hush.

But Tozer's forte was his prayer life, which often found him walking the aisles of a sanctuary or lying face down on the floor. Tozer biographer James L. Snyder notes that "his preaching as well as his writings were but extensions of his prayer life." An earlier biographer and confidante, David J. Fant, wrote, "He spent more time on his knees than at his desk."

Tozer's final years of pastoral ministry were at Avenue Road Church in Toronto, Canada. On May 12, 1963, his pursuit of God was realized when he died of a heart attack at age sixty-six. In a small cemetery near Akron, Ohio, his tombstone bears this simple epitaph: "A Man of God."

Tozer once prayed, "O God, the Triune God, I want to want Thee; I long to be filled with longing; I thirst to be made more thirsty still. Show me Thy glory, I pray Thee, so that I may know Thee indeed."

May that be your prayer this year as you come daily to grow in your knowledge of the Almighty God.

—RON EGGERT

Please note:

Each passage cited from Tozer's writings is followed by a code and number representing the name of the book and the page from which the excerpt was adapted. A list of the reference codes and a Scripture index are provided in the back of the book.

Ron Eggert holds a Th.M. from Dallas Theological Seminary and served in pastoral and youth ministries for thirty years. He is currently a regional representative for Mastermedia International, a ministry of evangelism and discipleship with executives in the film and television industry. Ron lives with his wife Dianna in Garland, Texas. They have three grown children and one with the Lord.

God's Awesomeness

Oh, the depth of the riches of the wisdom and knowledge of
God! How unsearchable his judgments, and his paths beyond
tracing out!
—ROMANS 11:33

Webster's Unabridged Dictionary lists 550,000 words. And it is a solemn and beautiful thought that in our worship of God there sometimes rush up from the depths of our souls feelings that all this wealth of words is not sufficient to express. To be articulate at certain times we are compelled to fall back upon "Oh!" or "O!"—a primitive exclamatory sound that is hardly a word at all and that scarcely admits of a definition.

Vocabularies are formed by many minds over long periods and are capable of expressing whatever the mind is capable of entertaining. But when the heart, on its knees, moves into the awesome Presence and hears with fear and wonder things not lawful to utter, then the mind falls flat, and words, previously its faithful servants, become weak and totally incapable of telling what the heart hears and sees. In that awful moment the worshiper can only cry "Oh!" And that simple exclamation becomes more eloquent than learned speech and, I have no doubt, is dearer to God than any oratory. BAM084-085

Lord, I come, with my heart on its knees, into Your awesome presence this first day of the year. I long to know You better and to sense that awesomeness that leaves me speechless before You. Amen.

Oh!

"Alas, Sovereign Lord," I said, "I do not know how to speak;
I am too young."
—JEREMIAH 1:6

In theology there is no "Oh!" and this is a significant if not an ominous thing. Theology seeks to reduce what may be known of God to intellectual terms, and as long as the intellect can comprehend, it can find words to express itself. When God Himself appears before the mind—awesome, vast, and incomprehensible—then the mind sinks into silence and the heart cries out "O Lord God!" There is the difference between theological knowledge and spiritual experience, the difference between knowing God by hearsay and knowing Him by acquaintance. And the difference is not verbal merely; it is real and serious and vital.

We Christians should watch lest we lose the "Oh!" from our hearts. . . .

When we become too glib in prayer we are most surely talking to ourselves. When the calm listing of requests and the courteous giving of proper thanks take the place of the burdened prayer that finds utterance difficult, we should beware the next step, for our direction is surely down whether we know it or not. BAM085-087

Lord, don't ever let me lose the "Oh!" from my heart. May I truly experience You so that my knowledge of You will inspire my cries of admiration. Amen.

A Thirst for God

As the deer pants for streams of water, so my soul pants for you, my God.
—PSALM 42:1

In this hour of all-but-universal darkness one cheering gleam appears: within the fold of conservative Christianity there are to be found increasing numbers of persons whose religious lives are marked by a growing hunger after God Himself. They are eager for spiritual realities and will not be put off with words, nor will they be content with correct "interpretations" of truth. They are athirst for God, and they will not be satisfied till they have drunk deep at the Fountain of Living Water.

This is the only real harbinger of revival which I have been able to detect anywhere on the religious horizon. It may be the cloud the size of a man's hand for which a few saints here and there have been looking. It can result in a resurrection of life for many souls and a recapture of that radiant wonder which should accompany faith in Christ, that wonder which has all but fled the Church of God in our day. POG007

O Lord, I pray that a thirst for You may build and grow, may prove unquenchable and may indeed result in a recapturing of "that radiant wonder," both in my own faith and in that of the church. Amen.

Show Me Your Glory

If you are pleased with me, teach me your ways so I may know you and continue to find favor with you.
—EXODUS 33:13

Come near to the holy men and women of the past, and you will soon feel the heat of their desire after God. They mourned for Him, they prayed and wrestled and sought for Him, day and night, in season and out, and when they had found Him the finding was all the sweeter for the long seeking. Moses used the fact that he knew God as an argument for knowing Him better. "Now therefore, I pray thee, if I have found grace in thy sight, shew me now thy way, that I may know thee, that I may find grace in thy sight" (Ex. 33:13); and from there he rose to make the daring request, "I beseech thee, shew me thy glory" (33:18). God was frankly pleased by this display of ardor, and the next day called Moses into the mount, and there in solemn procession made all His glory pass before him.

David's life was a torrent of spiritual desire, and his psalms ring with the cry of the seeker and the glad shout of the finder. Paul confessed the mainspring of his life to be his burning desire after Christ. "That I may know him" (Phil. 3:10), was the goal of his heart, and to this he sacrificed everything. POG015-016

Lord, make Your glory known to me and let me learn from Moses, David, Paul, and others that deep longing that results in intimate knowledge of You. Amen.

Justified Sinners

If we confess our sins, he is faithful and just and will forgive us
our sins and purify us from all unrighteousness.

1 JOHN 1:9

When God justifies a sinner, everything in God is on the sinner's side. All the attributes of God are on the sinner's side. It isn't that mercy is pleading for the sinner and justice is trying to beat him to death, as we preachers sometimes make it sound. All of God does all that God does. When God looks at a sinner and sees him there unatoned for (he won't accept the atonement; he thinks it doesn't apply to him), the moral situation is such that justice says he must die. And when God looks at the atoned-for sinner, who in faith knows he's atoned for and has accepted it, justice says he must live! The unjust sinner can no more go to heaven than the justified sinner can go to hell. O friends, why are we so still? Why are we so quiet? We ought to rejoice and thank God with all our might!

I say it again: Justice is on the side of the returning sinner. . . . Justice is over on our side now because the mystery of the agony of God on the cross has changed our moral situation. So justice looks and sees equality, not inequity, and we are justified. That's what justification means. AOG071

Father, thank for You justifying me and being on my side, for loving me and making me Your child. May I walk as a child of the light this day. Amen.

Spiritual Receptivity

My heart says of you, "Seek his face!" Your face, LORD, I will seek.
—PSALM 27:8

Pick at random a score of great saints whose lives and testimonies are widely known. Let them be Bible characters or well-known Christians of post-biblical times. . . .

I venture to suggest that the one vital quality which they had in common was spiritual receptivity. Something in them was open to heaven, something which urged them Godward. Without attempting anything like a profound analysis, I shall say simply that they had spiritual awareness and that they went on to cultivate it until it became the biggest thing in their lives. They differed from the average person in that when they felt the inward longing, they *did something about it.* They acquired the lifelong habit of spiritual response. They were not disobedient to the heavenly vision. As David put it neatly, "When thou saidst, Seek ye may face; my heart said unto thee, Thy face, LORD, will I seek" (Ps. 27:8). POG062-063

Lord, give me open ears, a quiet mind, a receptive heart, and a willingness to obey. I commit before You my desire to acquire a "lifelong habit of spiritual response." Amen.

He Wants Us to Come

The Spirit and the bride say, "Come!" And let the one who hears say, "Come!" Let the one who is thirsty come; and let the one who wishes take the free gift of the water of life.
—REVELATION 22:17

God takes great pleasure in having a helpless soul come to Him simply and plainly and intimately. He takes pleasure in having us come to Him. This kind of Christianity doesn't draw big crowds. It draws only those who have their hearts set on God, who want God more than they want anything else in the world. These people want the spiritual experience that comes from knowing God for Himself. They could have everything stripped away from them and still have God.

These people are not vastly numerous in any given locality. This kind of Christianity doesn't draw big crowds, but it is likely to draw the hungriest ones, the thirstiest ones, and some of the best ones. And so God takes great pleasure in having helpless people come to Him, simply and plainly and intimately. He wants us to come without all that great overlording of theology. He wants us to come as simply and as plainly as a little child. And if the Holy Spirit touches you, you'll come like that. AOG030-031

Thank You, Lord, for this warm invitation. I come to You humbly, deeply grateful for Your compassionate desire to meet with me and fill me. Amen.

The Sum Total of Our Hungers

My soul thirsts for God, for the living God.
When can I go and meet with God?
—PSALM 42:2

One of the big milk companies makes capital of the fact that their cows are all satisfied with their lot in life. Their clever ads have made the term "contented cows" familiar to everyone. But what is a virtue in a cow may be a vice in a man. And contentment, when it touches spiritual things, is surely a vice. . . .

Religious complacency is encountered almost everywhere among Christians these days, and its presence is a sign and a prophecy. For every Christian will become at last what his desires have made him. We are all the sum total of our hungers. The great saints have all had thirsting hearts. Their cry has been, "My soul thirsteth for God, for the living God: when shall I come and appear before God?" Their longing after God all but consumed them; it propelled them onward and upward to heights toward which less ardent Christians look with languid eye and entertain no hope of reaching.

Orthodox Christianity has fallen to its present low estate from lack of spiritual desire. Among the many who profess the Christian faith, scarcely one in a thousand reveals any passionate thirst for God.

ROR059-061

Oh, Lord, deliver me from the complacency that is so prevalent both around me and within me. Give me an unquenchable thirst for You that I may cry out for You along with the saints of long ago. Amen.

Seeking for More of God

Then Moses said, "Now show me your glory."
—EXODUS 33:18

When Moses saw the glory of God, he begged that he might see more. When God revealed to him that he had found grace, he wanted more grace. Remember this: The man that has the most of God is the man who is seeking the most ardently for more of God. . . .

I have been greatly and deeply concerned that you and I do something more than listen, that we dare to go to God like the Lady Julian and dare to ask Him to give us a faithful, fatherly wound—maybe three of them, if you please: to wound us with a sense of our own sinful unworthiness that we'll never quite get over; to wound us with the sufferings of the world and the sorrows of the Church; and then to wound us with the longing after God, a thirst, a sacred thirst and longing that will carry us on toward perfection. . . .

Almost every day of my life I am praying that "a jubilant pining and longing for God" might come back on the evangelical churches. We don't need to have our doctrine straightened out; we're as orthodox as the Pharisees of old. But this longing for God that brings spiritual torrents and whirlwinds of seeking and self-denial—this is almost gone from our midst. MDP116-117

Lord, I pray that You will bring about a renewed, intense longing for You in my heart. Begin the work in my own heart, and let it spread also to all of Your Church! Amen.

Daily Glimpses of His Glory

Since ancient times no one has heard, no ear has perceived, no
eye has seen any God besides you, who acts on behalf of those
who wait for him.

—ISAIAH 64:4

Every emotion has its reaction, and every pleasurable experience
will dim after a while. The human organism is built that way,
and there is nothing we can do about it. It is well known that the
second year of marriage is often the most critical, for then the first
excitement has worn off the relationship, and the young couple has
not had time to acquire a new set of common interests and to learn
to accept a more stable if less emotional kind of life.

Only engrossment with God can maintain perpetual spiritual enthusiasm because only God can supply everlasting novelty. In God
every moment is new and nothing ever gets old. Of things religious
we may become tired; even prayer may weary us; but God never. He
can show a new aspect of His glory to us each day for all the days of
eternity, and still we shall have but begun to explore the depths of the
riches of His infinite being. . . .

The sum of all this is that nothing can preserve the sweet savor
of our first experience except to be preoccupied with God Himself.
Our little rill is sure to run dry unless we keep it replenished from
the fountain. GTM127-129

*Lord, every day there is indeed some new glimpse of Your glory.
May I enter the day today with a holy anticipation! Amen.*

A Genuine Encounter with God

There the angel of the LORD *appeared to him in flames of
fire from within a bush. Moses saw that though the bush was on
fire it did not burn up.*
—EXODUS 3:2

Is it not true that for most of us who call ourselves Christians there is no real experience? We have substituted theological ideas for an arresting encounter; we are full of religious notions, but our great weakness is that for our hearts there is no one there.

Whatever else it embraces, true Christian experience must always include a genuine encounter with God. Without this, religion is but a shadow, a reflection of reality, a cheap copy of an original once enjoyed by someone else of whom we have heard. It cannot but be a major tragedy in the life of any man to live in a church from childhood to old age and know nothing more real than some synthetic god compounded of theology and logic, but having no eyes to see, no ears to hear, and no heart to love. . . .

We who experience God in this day may rejoice that we have in Him all that Abraham or David or Paul could have; indeed the very angels before the throne can have no more than we, for they can have no more than God and can want nothing apart from Him. And all that He is and all that He has done is for us and for all who share the common salvation. POM010, 013

---

*Lord, may I experience Your presence in such a real way today
that I'll feel like taking off my shoes, because I'll know I'm
on holy ground. Amen.*

Made for Higher Worlds

Set your minds on things above, not on earthly things.
—COLOSSIANS 3:2

God has revealed Himself many times and in many ways to assure men and women made in His image that there is another and a better world than this vale of tears we refer to as home....

When people around us learn that we are involved in a spiritual kingdom not yet visible, they think we are prime candidates for a mental institution. But this we know: Those same people around us are subject to the cruel tyranny of material and temporal things—things that will decay and pass away. No world dictator ever ruled his cowering subjects with any more fierce and compulsive domination than the material, visible things that rule the men and women of this world.

Of all the calamities that have been visited upon this world and its inhabitants, the willing surrender of the human spirit to materialistic values is the worst! We who were made for higher worlds are accepting the ways of this world as the ultimate. That is a tragedy of staggering proportions.

We who were meant to commune with the Creator God, with the angels, archangels, and seraphim, have decided instead to settle down here. As well might the eagle leave his lofty domain to scratch in the barnyard with the common hens. MMG101-102

It's so easy, Lord, to become enamored with and ensnared by the things of this barnyard. Help me to be loftier in my affections today. Amen.

The Secret Garden

Then the man and his wife heard the sound of the Lord God as
he was walking in the garden in the cool of the day, and they
hid from the Lord God among the trees of the garden.
—GENESIS 3:8

However we may explain this mysterious "ground" within us, we will not have been long in the Christian way until we begin to experience it. We will find that we have within us a secret garden where no one can enter except ourself and God. This secret inner chamber is the secret trysting place for Christ and the believing soul; no one among all our dearest friends has the open sesame that will permit him to enter there. If God is shut out, then there can be only everlasting loneliness and numb despair.

Where God is not known in the inner shrine, the individual must try to compensate for his sense of aloneness in whatever way he can. Most persons rush away to the world to find companionship and surround themselves with every kind of diversionary activity. All devices for killing time, every shallow scheme for entertainment, are born out of this inner loneliness. It is a significant and revealing fact that such things have in these last days grown into billion-dollar enterprises! So much will men pay to forget that they are a temple without a God, a garden where no voice is heard in the cool of the day. NCA114-115

---

*What a privilege, Lord, to fellowship with the God of the universe.
Slow me down today, that I might know this intimate inner
fellowship. Amen.*

Give Me Thyself

The LORD said to Aaron, "You will have no inheritance in their land, nor will you have any share among them; I am your share and your inheritance among the Israelites."
—NUMBERS 18:20

Above all gifts, God desires most to give Himself to His people. Our nature being what it is, we are the best fitted of all creatures to know and enjoy God. . . .

When God told Aaron, "Thou shalt have no inheritance in their land, neither shalt thou have any part among them: I am thy part and thine inheritance among the children of Israel," He in fact promised a portion infinitely above all the real estate in Palestine and all the earth thrown in (Num. 18:20). To possess God—this is the inheritance ultimate and supreme. . . .

To give God back to us was the chief work of Christ in redemption. To impart Himself to us in personal experience is the first purpose of God in salvation. To bring acute God-awareness is the best help the Spirit brings in sanctification. All other steps in grace lead up to this.

Were we allowed but one request, we might gain at a stroke all things else by praying one all-embracing prayer:

Thyself, Lord! Give me Thyself and I can want no more. WTA071-072

Lord, may I be truly satisfied today with nothing but the best gift of all—You. Amen.

Less Than the Best

Blessed are those who hunger and thirst for righteousness,
for they will be filled.
—MATTHEW 5:6

It is disheartening to those who care, and surely a great grief to the Spirit, to see how many Christians are content to settle for less than the best. Personally I have for years carried a burden of sorrow as I have moved among evangelical Christians who somewhere in their past have managed to strike a base compromise with their heart's holier longings and have settled down to a lukewarm, mediocre kind of Christianity utterly unworthy of themselves and of the Lord they claim to serve. And such are found everywhere. . . .

Every man is as close to God as he wants to be; he is as holy and as full of the Spirit as he wills to be. Our Lord said, "Blessed are they which do hunger and thirst after righteousness: for they shall be filled." If there were but one man anywhere on earth who hungered and was not filled, the word of Christ would fall to the ground.

Yet we must distinguish wanting from wishing. By "want" I mean wholehearted desire. Certainly there are many who wish they were holy or victorious or joyful but are not willing to meet God's conditions to obtain it. TIC064

Lord, may I settle for nothing less than the best when it comes to my relationship with You. Give me a wholehearted thirst for You, that I may partake of the incredible privilege of intimate fellowship with You. Amen.

The Imperative of Meeting God

In my thirtieth year, in the fourth month on the fifth day, while I was among the exiles by the Kebar River, the heavens were opened and I saw visions of God.
—EZEKIEL 1:1

Sometimes preachers get carried away and start sermonizing on the great calamities posed by communism and secularism and materialism. But our greatest calamity is the closed heaven, the silent heaven. God meant for us to be in fellowship with Him. When the heavens are closed, men are left to themselves. They are without God.

Ezekiel and all the rest of God's faithful servants learned something that we must learn. If there is anything worth having, it will have to be something that we get from God Himself. The heavens have been closed since mankind began reasoning God out of our world. What used to be the hand and providence of God is now just natural law. . . .

But in the Christian faith it is imperative that the individual meet God. We are not talking about just the possibility of meeting God. We are not saying just that it would be a good thing to meet God. *Meeting God is imperative!* MMG119-120

Lord, deliver me from Your absence today; open the doors of heaven and bestow upon me Your presence. Make this imperative in my life, both now and always. Amen.

Only Him

Because you are my help, I sing in the shadow of your wings.
I cling to you; your right hand upholds me.
—PSALM 63:7–8

It is part of my belief that God wants to get us to a place where we would still be happy if we had only Him! We don't need God and something else. God does give us Himself and lets us have other things, too, but there is that inner loneliness until we reach the place where it is only God that we desire.

Most of us are too social to be lonely. When we feel lonely, we rush to the telephone and call Mrs. Yakkety. So we use up thirty minutes, and the buns are burned in the oven. With many, it is talk, talk, talk, and we rush about looking for social fellowship because we cannot stand being alone.

If you will follow on to know the Lord, there comes a place in your Christian life when Mrs. Yakkety will be a pest instead of being a consolation. She won't be able to help you at all. There will not be a thing that she can do for you. It is loneliness for God—you will want God so badly you will be miserable. This means you are getting close, friend. You are near the kingdom, and if you will only keep on, you will meet God. God will take you in and fill you, and He will do it in His own blessed and wonderful way. COU078-079

Lord, bring me to that place of inner loneliness that David knew, so that when all else is stripped away, I might find satisfaction in You—only You. Amen.

A Mighty Man Was David

My soul yearns, even faints, for the courts of the LORD; my heart
and my flesh cry out for the living God.
—PSALM 84:2

Perhaps David's greatness and his significance for mankind lie in his complete preoccupation with God. He was a Jew, steeped in the Levitical tradition, but he never got lost in the forms of religion. "I have set the LORD always before me" (Ps. 16:8), he said once, and again he said, or rather cried, for his words rise from within like a cry, "My soul thirsteth for God, for the living God: when shall I come and appear before God?" (42:2).

David was acutely God-conscious. To him God was the one Being worth knowing. Where others saw nature, he saw God. He was a nature poet indeed, but he saw God first and loved nature for God's sake. Wordsworth reversed the order and, while he is great, he is not worthy to untie the shoelaces of the man David.

David was also a God-possessed man. He threw himself at the feet of God and demanded to be conquered, and Jehovah responded by taking over his personality and shaping it as a potter shapes the clay.

Because he was God-possessed, he could be God-taught. . . .

He sent his heart to school to the Most High God, and soon he knew Him with an immediacy of knowing more wonderful than is dreamed of in our philosophies. WOS033-035

Lord, may I be as God-possessed as David. Give me a heart that cries out to You; then teach me and enable me to know You with immediacy and intimacy. Amen.

JANUARY 19

We Begin with God

For in him all things were created: things in heaven and
on earth, visible and invisible. . . . He is before all things,
and in him all things hold together.
—COLOSSIANS 1:16–17

Now, I know that some have said about me: "That man is always talking about God!" I can only say in reply that if that is
the only charge that anyone can properly bring against me, I will be
quite a happy man. I know that I talk a lot about God—about the
triune God, because I still believe in God. I believe in Him as God
Almighty, the Father, and Jesus Christ, His Son and our Lord, and
the Holy Spirit, the Comforter.

We do begin with God here, where all truth begins, for God is the
one true and absolute reality. Back of all, and underneath and supporting all things, He girds the universe and holds it up and guides it.

God does that. That is the only explanation for the universe and
the only explanation of human life, for as Creator He gives to human
life its meaning and significance.

He is the sacred meaning that gives validity to all meaning. Ex-
clude God from your thinking, and you will find yourself with no
sense of moral values—you will have no standard of right or wrong.
EFE040

*Lord, may I also talk "too much" about You. May I keep You first
in everything I do, think, or say today. Enable me by Your Spirit,
I pray, in Jesus' name. Amen.*

The Business of the Church Is God

Now this is eternal life: that they know you, the only true God,
and Jesus Christ, whom you have sent.
—JOHN 17:3

The Church is born out of the gospel, and that gospel has to do with God and man's relation to God. Christianity engages to bring God into human life, to make men right with God, to give them a heart knowledge of God, to teach them to love and obey God, and ultimately to restore in them the lost image of God in full and everlasting perfection.

Our Lord, in defining eternal life, summed up the supreme goal of human existence: "That they might know thee, the only true God, and Jesus Christ, whom thou hast sent." And Paul revealed the one overpowering interest of his life when he wrote, "That I may know him" (Phil. 3:10).

The business of the Church is God. She is purest when most engaged with God, and she is astray just so far as she follows other interests, no matter how "religious" or humanitarian they may be.

SOS079-080

Lord, may I make You my business today, and may the lost image of Your perfection be revealed to me in all its fullness. Amen.

According to Who He Is

Every good and perfect gift is from above, coming down
from the Father of the heavenly lights, who does not change
like shifting shadows.
—JAMES 1:17

Compassion flows from goodness, and yet goodness without justice is not goodness. You couldn't be good and not be just, and if God is good, He has to be just. When God punishes the wicked, it is a just thing to do, because it is consistent with the wicked man's deserts. But when God pardons a wicked man, it is a just thing to do as well, because it is consistent with God's nature. So we have God the Father, Son, and Holy Ghost always acting like God. Your wife may be grouchy, your best friend may be cold, foreign wars may be going on, but God is always the same. Always God acts according to His attributes of love, justice, and mercy. . . .

There is the parable of the man who appeared without a wedding garment. And after he got in, they said, "What is he doing here?" and they threw him out—bound him hand and foot, lugged him out, and threw him into outer darkness (see Matt. 22:11–13). There'll be nothing like that in God's kingdom because God the All-Wise One knows all that can be known. He knows everybody—He knows you. And God the All-Just One will never permit the unequal man in there. "Why walk ye along on two unequal legs?" said Elijah (1 Kings 18:21, author's paraphrase). That's unequal, iniquity. And the man who is iniquitous will never get in. Never! AOG072-074

Lord, bring me into a communion with You that only grows richer and more splendid the longer it lasts. Enable me to hear the Holy Spirit, and through Him to know You more deeply. Amen.

Curious to Know God

The LORD replied, "My Presence will go with you, and I will give you rest." Then Moses said to him, "If your Presence does not go with us, do not send us up from here."
—EXODUS 33:14–15

In what I have to say I may not be joined by any ground swell of public opinion, but I have a charge to make against the Church. We are not consciously aware of God in our midst. We do not seem to sense the tragedy of having almost completely lost the awareness of His presence.

I do not say that to condemn. I say it with a grieving spirit. I pray that the churches in this day may yet reap the joys and fruits of gracious revival and the deep inward awareness of God's presence.

Revival and blessing come to the Church when we stop looking at a picture of God and look at God Himself. Revival comes when, no longer satisfied just to know about a God in history, we meet the conditions of finding Him in living, personal experience. . . .

Modern mankind can go everywhere, do everything, and be completely curious about the universe. But only a rare person now and then is curious enough to want to know God. MMG121-122, 127

Lord, increase my curiosity and help me to know You so intimately that I am especially, specifically, consciously aware of Your Presence throughout the day. Help me to know You that intimately. Amen.

God Is Wise

> By wisdom the LORD laid the earth's foundations,
> by understanding he set the heavens in place.
> —PROVERBS 3:19

The English language, you will notice, has succeeded in creating new words by uniting one word to another. For instance, we take the word *science,* meaning "knowledge," and we unite it to the word *omni,* meaning "all" to create *omniscience.* We take the word *potent* and unite it to the word *omni* to create *omnipotence.* But when we come to the word wisdom, the word-makers never got around to making such a word. . . . So I will not make a new word, but I will simply say that God is wise! And if God is infinite, then God is infinitely wise.

It tells us in Proverbs 3:19 and Jeremiah 10:12 that the Lord founded the earth, established and stretched out the heavens by wisdom, understanding and discretion. Those are two of many verses in the Bible that tell us about the wisdom of God.

The wisdom of God is something to be taken on faith. Anselm tells us, as I have said before, that we do not reason in order that we might believe, but we reason because we already believe. If I have to reason myself into faith, then I can be reasoned back out of it again. But faith is an organ of knowledge; if I know something by faith, I will reason about it. AOGII132

Lord, give me a glimpse of Your wisdom, and then help me to live in the light of that wisdom, exhibiting a transformed life and representing a renewed Church. Amen.

Both Easy and Difficult

To the only God our Savior be glory, majesty, power and
authority, through Jesus Christ our Lord, before all ages,
now and forevermore! Amen.
—JUDE 25

It is a great consolation to me that God knows instantly, effortlessly, and perfectly all matter and all matters, all law and all laws, all space and all spaces, all principles and every principle, all minds, all spirits and all souls. God knows all causes and all relations, all effects and all desires, all mysteries and all enigmas, all things unknown and hidden. There are no mysteries to God.

There are many things that are mysteries to you and me. "And without controversy great is the mystery of godliness: God was manifest in the flesh" (1 Tim. 3:16). Theologians throughout the centuries have reverently tried to discover how the infinite, inimitable God could condense Himself into the form of a man. It's a great mystery. We don't know, but God knows and God isn't worried about it. That's why I can live a good and peaceful Christian life, even though I am not a man that takes things very easy. AOGII126

*Lord, deliver me from viewing You as simply a utilitarian God,
and give to me the spiritual wisdom that defies my obstinacy and
leads me to true knowledge of You. Amen.*

A Vast Difference

What we have received is not the spirit of the world, but
the Spirit who is from God, so that we may understand what
God has freely given us.
—1 CORINTHIANS 2:12

It is possible to grow up in a church, learn the catechism, and have everything done to us that they do to us, within reason. But after we have done all that, we may not know God at all, because God isn't known by those external things. We are blind and can't see, because the things of God no man knows but by the Spirit of God. . . .

We imagine that we can handle it by the flesh, and we do handle it by the flesh—the Lord lets us do it. We can hold the creed and not know God in His person at all. We can know the doctrine and not know spiritual things at all. The fearful consequence is that many people know about God but don't know God Himself. There is a vast difference between knowing about God and knowing God—a vast difference! . . .

So it is that the human being can know about God, can know about Christ's dying for him, can even write songs and books, can be the head of religious organizations and hold important church offices—and still never have come to the vital, personal knowledge of God at all. Only by the Holy Spirit can he know God. COU019, 025-026

*Lord, it is humbling to consider the possibility that I could know
all about You, and yet not know You personally. Impart Your Spirit,
Lord, that I may truly know You. Amen.*

God Is a Person

But whose delight is in the law of the LORD, and who meditates
on his law day and night.
—PSALM 1:2

We have almost forgotten that God is a person and, as such, can be cultivated as any person can. It is inherent in personality to be able to know other personalities, but full knowledge of one personality by another cannot be achieved in one encounter. It is only after long and loving mental intercourse that the full possibilities of both can be explored. . . .

God is a person, and in the deep of His mighty nature, He thinks, wills, enjoys, feels, loves, desires, and suffers as any other person may. In making Himself known to us, He stays by the familiar pattern of personality. He communicates with us through the avenues of our minds, our wills, and our emotions. The continuous and unembarrassed interchange of love and thought between God and the soul of the redeemed man is the throbbing heart of New Testament religion.

POG013-014

Lord, how careless I am with the privilege of deep and intimate interaction with You! May I learn to delight in constant, loving communication with You, that I may more fully know You. Amen.

Not Mere Words Alone

*The unfolding of your words gives light; it gives understanding
to the simple.*
—PSALM 119:130

Thanks to our splendid Bible societies and to other effective agencies for the dissemination of the Word, there are today many millions of people who hold "right opinions," probably more than ever before in the history of the Church. Yet I wonder if there was ever a time when true spiritual worship was at a lower ebb.

Sound Bible exposition is an imperative *must* in the Church of the Living God. Without it no church can be a New Testament church in any strict meaning of that term. But exposition may be carried on in such a way as to leave the hearers devoid of any true spiritual nourishment whatever. For it is not mere words that nourish the soul, but God Himself, and unless and until the hearers find God in personal experience, they are not the better for having heard the truth. The Bible is not an end in itself, but a means to bring men to an intimate and satisfying knowledge of God, that they may enter into Him, that they may delight in His Presence, may taste and know the inner sweetness of the very God Himself in the core and center of their hearts. POG009

---

*Lord, as I study Your Word, may I not merely read the words on
the page but personally experience their truths, that I may know
You and genuinely delight in Your presence. Amen.*

Cultivating Knowledge of God

I meditate on your precepts and consider your ways. I delight
in your decrees; I will not neglect your word.
—PSALM 119:15–16

Probably the most widespread and persistent problem to be found among Christians is the problem of stagnated spiritual progress. Why, after years of Christian profession, do so many persons find themselves no farther along than when they first believed? . . .

The causes of retarded growth are many. It would not be accurate to ascribe the trouble to one single fault. One there is, however, which is so universal that it may easily be the main cause: *failure to give time to the cultivation of the knowledge of God.* . . .

The Christian is strong or weak depending upon how closely he has cultivated the knowledge of God. . . .

Progress in the Christian life is exactly equal to the growing knowledge we gain of the triune God in personal experience. And such experience requires a whole life devoted to it and plenty of time spent at the holy task of cultivating God. God can be known satisfactorily only as we devote time to Him. ROR007-009

In a busy life, Lord, it's so easy to neglect the important time we need to cultivate our knowledge of You. I devote myself to furthering my spiritual progress by seeking knowledge of You. Amen.

Take Your Cowboy God

LORD, our Lord, how majestic is your name in all the earth!
You have set your glory in the heavens.
—PSALM 8:1

Christianity at any given time is strong or weak depending upon her concept of God. And I insist upon this and I have said it many times, that the basic trouble with the Church today is her unworthy conception of God. I talk with learned and godly people all over the country, and they're all saying the same thing.

Unbelievers say, "Take your cowboy god and go home," and we get angry and say, "They're vile heathen." No, they're not vile heathen—or at least that's not why they say that. They can't respect our "cowboy god." And since evangelicalism has gone overboard to "cowboy religion," its conception of God is unworthy of Him. Our religion is little because our god is little. Our religion is weak because our god is weak. Our religion is ignoble because the god we serve is ignoble. We do not see God as He is. . . .

A local church will only be as great as its conception of God. An individual Christian will be a success or a failure depending upon what he or she thinks of God. It is critically important that we have a knowledge of the Holy One, that we know what God is like.

AOG041-042

Lord, help me to know You in all Your majesty and in all Your excellence. Help me then to portray to the world a God worth worshiping! Amen.

God Is God

*Who has measured the waters in the hollow of his hand,
or with the breadth of his hand marked off the heavens?*
—ISAIAH 40:12

We must be concerned with the person and character of God, not the promises. Through promises we learn what God has willed to us, we learn what we may claim as our heritage, we learn how we should pray. But faith itself must rest on the character of God.

Is this difficult to see? Why are we not stressing this in our evangelical circles? Why are we afraid to declare that people in our churches must come to know God Himself? Why do we not tell them that they must get beyond the point of making God a lifeboat for their rescue or a ladder to get them out of a burning building? How can we help our people get over the idea that God exists just to help run their businesses or fly their airplanes?

God is not a railway porter who carries your suitcase and serves you. God is God. He made heaven and earth. He holds the world in His hand. He measures the dust of the earth in the balance. He spreads the sky out like a mantle. He is the great God Almighty. He is not your servant. He is your Father, and you are His child. He sits in heaven, and you are on the earth. FBR044-045

God, I fall on my face before You in worship today. Forgive me for those times I have treated You as if You were my servant. I am Your servant, Lord, and I humbly bow before You today. Amen.

To Push into the Presence

When Moses came down from Mount Sinai . . . he was not aware
that his face was radiant because he had spoken with the Lord.
—EXODUS 34:29

Such worship as Faber knew (and he is but one of a great company
which no man can number) can never come from a mere doctrinal knowledge of God. Hearts that are "fit to break" with love for the
Godhead are those who have been in the Presence and have looked
with opened eye upon the majesty of Deity. Men of the breaking hearts
had a quality about them not known to nor understood by common
men. They habitually spoke with spiritual authority. They had been in
the presence of God, and they reported what they saw there.

They were prophets, not scribes, for the scribe tells us what he has
read, and the prophet tells what he has seen. The distinction is not
an imaginary one. Between the scribe who has read and the prophet
who has seen there is a difference as wide as the sea. We are overrun
today with orthodox scribes, but the prophets, where are they? The
hard voice of the scribe sounds over evangelicalism, but the Church
waits for the tender voice of the saint who has penetrated the veil and
has gazed with inward eye upon the wonder that is God. And yet,
thus to penetrate, to push in sensitive living experience into the holy
Presence, is a privilege open to every child of God. POG040-041

*Take me into the Presence, Lord, that I might tell others what I
have seen and be a prophet for today, not merely another scribe.
Amen.*

FEBRUARY

A Living Person Is Present

And without faith it is impossible to please God, because anyone
who comes to him must believe that he exists and that he re-
wards those who earnestly seek him.

—HEBREWS 11:6

A loving personality dominates the Bible, walking among the
trees of the garden and breathing fragrance over every scene.
Always a living Person is present, speaking, pleading, loving, working, and manifesting Himself whenever and wherever His people
have the receptivity necessary to receive the manifestation. . . .

But why do the very ransomed children of God themselves know
so little of that habitual, conscious communion with God which
Scripture offers? The answer is because of our chronic unbelief. Faith
enables our spiritual sense to function. Where faith is defective the
result will be inward insensibility and numbness toward spiritual
things. This is the condition of vast numbers of Christians today. No
proof is necessary to support that statement. We have but to con-
verse with the first Christian we meet or enter the first church we
find open to acquire all the proof we need.

A spiritual kingdom lies all about us, enclosing us, embracing us,
altogether within reach of our inner selves, waiting for us to recognize it. God Himself is here awaiting our response to His presence.
This eternal world will come alive to us the moment we begin to
reckon upon its reality. POG048-050

---

*Lord, give me faith to believe, to see, to know Your awesome
Presence and bring Your spiritual kingdom alive in my life. Amen.*

God Is Right

When I saw him, I fell at his feet as though dead. Then he placed
his right hand on me and said: "Do not be afraid. I am the First
and the Last."
—REVELATION 1:17

A long with John, every redeemed human being needs the humility of spirit that can only be brought about by the manifest presence of God.

This mysterious yet gracious Presence is the air of life eternal. It is the music of existence, the poetry of the Christian life. It is the beauty and wonder of being one of Christ's own—a sinner born again, regenerated, created anew to bring glory to God. To know this Presence is the most desirable state imaginable for anyone. To live surrounded by this sense of God is not only beautiful and desirable, but it is imperative!

Know that our living Lord is unspeakably pure. He is sinless, spotless, immaculate, stainless. In His person is an absolute fullness of purity that our words can never express. This fact alone changes our entire human and moral situation and outlook. We can always be sure of the most important of all positives: God is God and God is right. He is in control. Because He is God, He will never change!

I repeat: God is right—always. That statement is the basis of all we are thinking about God. JAF092

---

*Lord, I bow at Your feet and acknowledge Your sovereignty.
I know You will do what is best for me because You
are always right. Amen.*

We Are Not Alone

Have I not commanded you? Be strong and courageous. Do not be afraid; do not be discouraged, for the Lord your God will be with you wherever you go.

—JOSHUA 1:9

We are each like a little child lost in a crowded market, who has strayed but a few feet from his mother, yet because she cannot be seen, the child is inconsolable. So we try by every method devised by religion to relieve our fears and heal our hidden sadness; but with all our efforts we remain unhappy still, with the settled despair of men alone in a vast and deserted universe.

But for all our fears we are not alone. Our trouble is that we *think* of ourselves as being alone. Let us correct the error by thinking of ourselves as standing by the bank of a full flowing river; then let us think of that river as being none else but God Himself. We glance to our left and see the river coming full out of our past; we look to the right and see it flowing on into our future. *But we see also that it is flowing through our present.* And in our today it is the same as it was in our yesterday, not less than, nor different from, but the very same river, one unbroken continuum, undiminished, active and strong as it moves sovereignly on into our tomorrow. POM006-007

Thank You, Lord, that I can have confidence in Your unchanging Presence. Yesterday, today, and tomorrow, I know I am not alone. Amen.

A Sense of the Present God

About midnight Paul and Silas were praying and singing
hymns to God, and the other prisoners were listening to them.
—ACTS 16:25

Wherever faith has been original, wherever it has proved itself to be real, it has invariably had upon it a sense of the *present God.* The holy Scriptures possess in marked degree this feeling of actual encounter with a real Person. The men and women of the Bible talked with God. They spoke to Him and heard Him speak in words they could understand. With Him they held person-to-person interaction, and a sense of shining reality is upon their words and deeds. . . .

It was this that filled with abiding wonder the first members of the Church of Christ. The solemn delight which those early disciples knew sprang straight from the conviction that there was One in the midst of them. They knew that the Majesty in the heavens was confronting them on earth: They were in the very Presence of God. And the power of that conviction to arrest attention and hold it for a lifetime, to elevate, to transform, to fill with uncontrollable moral happiness, to send men singing to prison and to death, has been one of the wonders of history and a marvel of the world. POM007-008

*Lord, may I respond like Paul and Silas to whatever I will face
today, knowing that Your Presence is always with me. Amen.*

God Speaks to Men

In the past God spoke to our ancestors through the prophets at
many times and in various ways, but in these last days he has
spoken to us by his Son, whom he appointed heir of all things,
and through whom also he made the universe.

—HEBREWS 1:1–2

I think it may be accepted as axiomatic that God is constantly trying to speak to men. He desires to communicate Himself, to impart holy ideas to those of His creatures capable of receiving them.

This divine impulse toward self-expression may account for the creation, particularly for God's having made intelligent and moral beings who could hear and understand truth. Among these beings man stands at the top, having been created in the image of God and so possessing purer and finer organs for the apprehension of whatever can be known of God. The Second Person of the Godhead is called the Word of God, that is, the mind of God in expression. . . .

That the creative voice of God is constantly sounding throughout the creation is a truth forgotten by modern Christianity. Yet it was by His word that He called the world into being and it is by His word that all things are held together. It is the still voice of God in the heart of every human being that renders everyone culpable before the bar of God's judgment and convicts of sin even those who have never been exposed to the written word. GTM007, 009

---

*Lord, may I make use of the intellect You have given me and open
my ears to hear Your voice today. Amen.*

Be Still to Know

He says, "Be still, and know that I am God; I will be exalted
among the nations, I will be exalted in the earth."
—PSALM 46:10

Our fathers had much to say about stillness, and by stillness they meant the absence of motion or the absence of noise or both.

They felt that they must be still for at least a part of the day, or that day would be wasted. God can be known in the tumult of the world if His providence has for the time placed us there, but He is known best in the silence. So they held, and so the sacred Scriptures declare. Inward assurance comes out of the stillness. We must be still to know.

There has hardly been another time in the history of the world when stillness was needed more than it is today, and there has surely not been another time when there was so little of it or when it was so hard to find. GTM012-013

Lord, in today's world stillness is so rare but so needed. Quiet my world even for these few moments and speak to me in the stillness, I pray. Amen.

A Voice Out of the Silence

After the wind there was an earthquake, but the LORD was
not in the earthquake. After the earthquake came a fire, but
the LORD was not in the fire. And after the fire came a gentle
whisper.
—1 KINGS 19:11–12

It is significant that the psalm in which the words "Be still" occur
is filled with noise and commotion. The earth shakes, the waters
roar and are troubled, the mountains threaten to tumble into the
midst of the sea, the nations rage, the kingdoms are moved, and the
sound of war is heard throughout the land. Then a voice is heard out
of the silence saying, "Be still, and know that I am God" (Ps. 46:10).

So today we must listen till our inner ears hear the words of God.
When the Voice is heard, it will not be as the excited shouting of the
nervous world; rather it will be the reassuring call of One of whom it
was said, "He shall not cry, nor lift up, nor cause his voice to be heard
in the street" (Isa. 42:2).

It cannot be heard in the street, but it may be heard plainly enough
in the heart. And that is all that matters at last. GTM018

---

*Quiet the storms around me and still my heart, Lord, that I may
hear the call of Your still small voice. Amen.*

Men and Women Who Have Met God

This was the appearance of the likeness of the glory of the Lord.
When I saw it, I fell facedown, and I heard the voice of one
speaking.
—EZEKIEL 1:28

These are elements that are always the same among men and women who have had a personal meeting with God.

First, these great souls always have a compelling sense of God Himself, of His person and of His presence. While others would want to spend their time talking about a variety of things, these godly men and women, touched by their knowledge of God, want to talk about Him. They are drawn away from a variety of mundane topics because of the importance of their spiritual discoveries.

Second, it is plain that the details and the significance of their personal experiences remain sharp and clear with true spiritual meaning. . . .

The third element is the permanent and life-changing nature of a true encounter with God. The experience may have been brief, but the results will be evident in the life of the person touched as long as he or she lives. MMG016-017

Lord, may I too experience You in a way that overwhelms me with a clear sense of Your presence and changes my life so I never want to stop speaking of You. Amen.

An Empty, Hungry Heart

Abram believed the LORD, and he credited it to him
as righteousness.
—GENESIS 15:6

I happen to believe that Abraham's encounters with the living God nearly 4,000 years ago leave modern men and women without excuse.

Abraham stands for every believer. His eager and willing faith becomes every Christian's condemnation. On the other hand, his fellowship with God becomes every believer's encouragement.

If there is a desire in your heart for more of God's blessing in your life, turn your attention to the details of Abraham's encounters with God. You will find yourself back at the center, at the beating heart of living religion. . . .

Remember, too, that at that point in history, almost 2,000 years before the coming of Jesus Christ into our world, Abraham had no Bible and no hymnal. He had no church and no godly religious traditions for guidance. He could not turn to a minister or an evangelist for spiritual help.

Abraham had only his own empty, hungry heart. That and the manifestation of the God who reveals Himself to men and women who desire to find Him and know Him! MMG019-020

Like Abraham, Lord, I come to You today with an empty, hungry heart, ready to listen for Your voice. Amen.

On His Face Listening

Abram fell facedown, and God said to him, "As for me, this is my
covenant with you: You will be the father of many nations.

—GENESIS 17:3–4

Think about the reality of Abraham's experience. Abraham was
consciously aware of God, His presence, and His revelation. He
was aware that the living God had stepped over the threshold into
personal encounter with a man who found the desire within himself
to know God, to believe God, and to live for God.

See the effect of this encounter on Abraham. He was prepared
to pay any price for the privilege of knowing God. For certain he
recognized the lofty, holy character of the Creator and Revealer God.

The Scriptures declare, "Abram fell on his face" as the Lord talked
with him (Gen. 17:3). Abraham was reverent and submissive. Probably there is no better picture anywhere in the Bible of the right place
for mankind and the right place for God. God was on His throne
speaking, and Abraham was on his face listening!

Where God and man are in relationship, this must be the ideal.
God must be the communicator, and man must be in the listening,
obeying attitude. If men and women are not willing to assume this
listening attitude, there will be no meeting with God in living, personal experience. MMG020-021

*Oh, Lord, give me an attitude like Abraham's, that I might have a
living, personal experience of You. Amen.*

A Fellowship within a Fellowship

All your robes are fragrant with myrrh and aloes and cassia;
from palaces adorned with ivory the music of the strings
makes you glad.

—PSALM 45:8

There is a fellowship within a fellowship—a sort of wheel in the middle of a wheel—which gathers to itself all who are of its spirit in every church in every land and every age. Its members are the God-smitten, those who have heard the Voice speaking within them and have caught a glimpse, however fleeting, of the glory of God. . . .

They who compose this fellowship have never been herded into any one organization; they have no earthly head, pay no dues, hold no conventions, and keep no minutes, yet they recognize each other instantly when they meet by a kind of secret sign which the Spirit has placed within their hearts.

These have been in the Presence and will never be the same again. They know a holy reverence, a wondrous sense of sacredness that rises at times to transports of delight. Their garments smell of myrrh and aloes and cassia, a gift from their Bridegroom and King who came walking out of the Ivory Palaces, trailing clouds of glory, to win them for Himself. TET067-068

---

*Lord, allow me to enter that sacred fellowship—give me a
"glimpse, however fleeting," of Your glory. I'm willing to never
be the same again, and I want to be permeated with that sweet
fragrance that comes from being in Your Presence. Amen.*

Practice Spiritual Concentration

Fixing our eyes on Jesus, the pioneer and perfecter of faith.
For the joy set before him he endured the cross, scorning its
shame, and sat down at the right hand of the throne of God.
—HEBREWS 12:2

Retire from the world each day to some private spot, even if it is only the bedroom (for a while I retreated to the furnace room for want of a better place). Stay in the secret place till the surrounding noises begin to fade out of your heart and a sense of God's presence envelops you. Deliberately tune out the unpleasant sounds and come out of your closet determined not to hear them. Listen for the inward Voice till you learn to recognize it. Stop trying to compete with others. Give yourself to God, and then be what and who you are without regard to what others think. Reduce your interests to a few. Don't try to know what will be of no service to you. Avoid the digest type of mind—short bits of unrelated facts, cute stories and bright sayings. Learn to pray inwardly every moment. After a while you can do this even while you work. Practice candor, childlike honesty, humility. Pray for a single eye. Read less, but read more of what is important to your inner life. Call home your roving thoughts. Gaze on Christ with the eyes of your soul. Practice spiritual concentration.
OGM128-129

---

*Lord, lift my gaze from the clutter and distractions around me
and give me a "single eye" for that which is eternal. Amen.*

The Deeper Life

I want to know Christ—yes, to know the power of his
resurrection and participation in his sufferings,
becoming like him in his death.
—PHILIPPIANS 3:10

I almost shrink from hearing the expression "the deeper life" because so many people want to talk about it as a topic—but no one seems to want to know and love God for Himself!

God is the deeper life! Jesus Christ Himself is the deeper life, and as I plunge on into the knowledge of the triune God, my heart moves on into the blessedness of His fellowship. This means that there is less of me and more of God—thus my spiritual life deepens, and I am strengthened in the knowledge of His will.

I think this is what Paul meant when he penned that great desire, "That I may know him!" He was expressing more than the desire for acquaintance—he was yearning to be drawn into the full knowledge of fellowship with God which has been provided in the plan of redemption. ITB017-018

*Lord, I want to know You more, that I might enter into lasting
fellowship with You. May that be my deep desire and not just
a topic for spiritual discussion. Amen.*

We Have All the Rest

But seek first his kingdom and his righteousness, and all these things will be given to you as well.

—MATTHEW 6:33

Again, part of the answer we are looking for is the fact that so many professing Christians just want to get things from God. Anyone can write a book now that will sell—just give it a title like *Seventeen Ways to Get Things from God!* You will have immediate sales. Or, write a book called *Fourteen Ways to Have Peace of Mind*—and away they go by the ton. Many people seem to be interested in knowing God for what they can get out of Him.

They do not seem to know that God wants to give Himself. He wants to impart Himself with His gifts. Any gift that He would give us would be incomplete if it were separate from the knowledge of God Himself. . . .

I feel that we must repudiate this great, modern wave of seeking God for His benefits. The sovereign God wants to be loved for Himself and honored for Himself, but that is only part of what He wants. The other part is that He wants us to know that when we have Him, we have everything—we have all the rest. Jesus made that plain when He said, "But seek ye first the kingdom of God, and his righteousness; and all these things shall be added unto you" (Matt. 6:33). ITB024-025

Lord, I know that in having You I will have everything I could ever need. Just give me Yourself today, Lord, and that's enough. Amen.

Beyond Our Power of Thought

Dear friends, let us love one another, for love comes from God.
Everyone who loves has been born of God and knows God.
—1 JOHN 4:7

If you are longing after God with the expectation that you are go-ing to be able to think your way through to Him, you are com-pletely mistaken. . . .

The promise is that God will fill the heart, or man's innermost being. The Word of God makes it very plain that the Church of Jesus Christ will never operate and minister and prosper by the stock of knowledge in the heads of Christian believers but by the warmth and urgency of God's love and compassion flowing through their beings.

Now, don't throw your head away—you are going to need it! I am convinced that God has made it plain that man alone, of all the crea-tures on earth, is created so that he can have fullness of knowledge about the earth and all the wonders and glories that it holds. I believe that through grace man can have a fullness of knowledge even about the works of God—but this certainly does not mean that we find Him and know Him and love Him through thought processes and human wisdom.

It is utterly and completely futile to try to think our way through to knowing God, who is beyond our power of thought or visualiza-tion. ITB100-101

Lord, it's great to know Your works through the intellect,
but it is infinitely more wonderful to know Your Person through
a relationship with You. Fill my heart today, I pray. Amen.

More Than to Know About

All things have been committed to me by my Father. No one
knows the Son except the Father, and no one knows the Father
except the Son and those to whom the Son chooses to reveal him.
—MATTHEW 11:27

The inability of the human mind to know God in a true and final
sense is taken for granted throughout the Bible . . . . God's nature
is of another kind from anything with which the mind is acquainted;
hence, when the mind attempts to find out God, it is confronted by
obscurity. It is surrounded with mystery and blinded by the light no
man can approach unto. . . .

The Spirit of God is able to make the spirit of man know and
experience the awful mystery of God's essential being. It should be
noted that the Spirit reveals God to the spirit of man, not to his intellect merely. The intellect can know God's attributes because these
constitute that body of truth that can be known *about* God. The
knowledge *of* God is for the spirit alone. Such knowledge comes not
by intellection but by intuition.

To know God in the scriptural meaning of the term is to enter
into experience of Him. It never means to know about. It is not a
knowledge mediated by the intellect, but an unmediated awareness
experienced by the soul on a plane too high for the mind to reach.

SOS047-048

---

*Thank You, Father, for the ministry of the Spirit in revealing You
to Your children. May I no longer simply know about You,
but come to know You personally. Amen.*

More Than by Hearsay

After he had dismissed them, he went up on a mountainside by himself to pray. Later that night, he was there alone.
—MATTHEW 14:23

There are many in the churches of our day who talk some of the Christian language but who know God only by hearsay. Most of them have read some book about God. They have seen some reflection of the light of God. They may have heard some faint echo of the voice of God, but their own personal knowledge of God is very slight. . . .

When Jesus was here upon the earth, the record shows that He had work to do and He also knew the necessity for activity as He preached and healed, taught and answered questions, and blessed the people. He also knew the fellowship of His brethren, those who followed Him and loved Him. But these were the incidental things in Jesus' life compared to His fellowship with and personal knowledge of the Father. When Jesus went into the mountain to pray and wait on God all night, He was not alone, for He knew the conscious presence of the Father with Him.

In our modern Christian service, we are constantly pressed to do this and to do that, and to go here and go there. How often we miss completely the conscious presence of God with the result that we know God only by hearsay! ITB023-024

Lord, draw me away today to spend time alone with You, that I might have a conscious sense of Your presence, knowing you by experience and not by words alone. Amen.

A Naked Intent unto God

We must pay the most careful attention, therefore, to what we have heard, so that we do not drift away.
—HEBREWS 2:1

Now here is a strange thing. If you talk about mysticism in our day, every fundamentalist throws his hands high in the air with disgust to let you know that he considers the mystics dreamers, those who believe in the emotion and feeling. But all of those old saints and the fathers of whom I have read taught that you must believe God by a naked, cold intent of your will and then the other things follow along.

A naked intent unto God—those old saints were practical men. They have exhorted us to press on in faith whether we feel like it or not. They have exhorted us to pray—when we feel like it and when we don't. They never taught that we would always be lifted emotionally to the heights. They knew that there are times when your spiritual progress must be by a naked intent unto God.

Oh that we would have this naked intent to know God, to know Jesus Christ! To be able to put the world and things and people beneath our feet and to open our hearts to only one lover, and that the Son of God Himself! ITB075

Lord, give me today a new passion for knowing You, a "naked intent" that compels me to seek You always, no matter what I feel. Amen.

So Rich a Treasure

*But one thing I do: Forgetting what is behind and straining
toward what is ahead, I press on toward the goal to win the
prize for which God has called me heavenward in Christ Jesus.*
—PHILIPPIANS 3:13–14

The experiential knowledge of God is eternal life (John 17:3), and increased knowledge results in a correspondingly larger and fuller life. So rich a treasure is this inward knowledge of God that every other treasure is as nothing compared with it. We may count all things of no value and sacrifice them freely if we may thereby gain a more perfect knowledge of God through Jesus Christ our Lord. This was Paul's testimony (Phil. 3:7–14), and it has been the testimony of all great Christian souls who have followed Christ from Paul's day to ours. . . .

To enjoy this growing knowledge of God will require that we go beyond the goals so casually set by modern evangelicals. We must fix our hearts on God and purposefully aim to rise above the dead level and average of current Christianity.

If we do this Satan will surely tempt us by accusing us of spiritual pride, and our friends will warn us to beware of being "holier than thou." But as the land of promise had to be taken by storm against the determined opposition of the enemy, so we must capture new spiritual heights over the sour and violent protests of the devil. TIC083-085

*Lord, I'll set my sights higher and seek a greater experience
of You. I'll not let the enemy stop me. Amen.*

Instant Christianity

Only let us live up to what we have already attained.
—PHILIPPIANS 3:16

It is hardly a matter of wonder that the country that gave the world instant tea and instant coffee should be the one to give it instant Christianity. And it cannot be denied that it was American Fundamentalism that brought instant Christianity to the gospel churches. . . .

Instant Christianity tends to make the faith act terminal and so smothers the desire for spiritual advance. It fails to understand the true nature of the Christian life, which is not static but dynamic and expanding. It overlooks the fact that a new Christian is a living organism as certainly as a new baby is, and must have nourishment and exercise to assure normal growth. It does not consider that the act of faith in Christ sets up a personal relationship between two intelligent moral beings, God and the reconciled man, and no single encounter between God and a creature made in His image could ever be sufficient to establish an intimate friendship between them. . . .

Instant Christianity is twentieth-century orthodoxy. I wonder whether the man who wrote Philippians 3:7–16 would recognize it as the faith for which he finally died. I am afraid he would not. TIC023-025

Lord, keep me from falling into the patterns of instant Christianity. I want to participate in an ever-changing, ever-expanding relationship with You. Amen.

Stop Lamenting and Look Up

Whoever has my commands and keeps them is the one who
loves me. The one who loves me will be loved by my Father,
and I too will love them and show myself to them.
—JOHN 14:21

In seeking to know God better, we must keep firmly in mind that we need not try to persuade God. He is already persuaded in our favor, not by our prayers but by the generous goodness of His own heart. "It is God's nature to give Himself to every virtuous soul," says Meister Eckhart. "Know then that God is bound to act, to pour Himself out into thee as soon as ever He shall find thee ready." As nature abhors a vacuum, so the Holy Spirit rushes in to fill the nature that has become empty by separating itself from the world and sin. This is not an unnatural act and need not be an unusual one, for it is in perfect accord with the nature of God. He must act as He does because He is God. . . .

If only we would stop lamenting and look up. God is here. Christ is risen. The Spirit has been poured out from on high. All this we know as theological truth. It remains for us to turn it into joyous spiritual experience. And how is this accomplished? There is no new technique; if it is new it is false. The old, old method still works. Conscious fellowship with Christ is by faith, love, and obedience. And the humblest believer need not be without these. TIC065-067

*Lord, impart to me a fresh measure of faith, love and obedience,
that I might know You as perfectly as possible. Amen.*

I Know the One Who Made This!

"But let the one who boasts boast about this: that they have the understanding to know me, that I am the LORD, who exercises kindness, justice and righteousness on earth, for in these I delight," declares the LORD.

—JEREMIAH 9:24

I just listened today while we had our dinner to a sonata by Beethoven, and it was beautiful. But I suppose it would have been more wonderful if I could have shaken hands with the great Beethoven and said, "It's an honor to shake your hand, sir. I consider you one of the greatest composers that ever lived—a genius!". . . It would have been wonderful.

And so with Michaelangelo, the greatest artist of his day. . . .

Perhaps he would have called me by my first name and I could have called him by his first name. I would introduce him to my friends and say, "I'd like to have you meet the great Michaelangelo." That would have been better than knowing his works. I have seen his tremendous sculpture of Moses, but it would have been better if I could have seen the man himself.

So let men turn their telescopes on the heavens and their microscopes on the molecules. Let them probe and search and tabulate and name and find and discover. I can dare to say to them, "I know the One who made all this. I'm personally acquainted with the One who made it." AOG081-082

I bow before You, great God, realizing the awesome privilege that is mine: the privilege of knowing You personally. Amen.

Our God Is Too Small

In the beginning God created the heavens and the earth.
—GENESIS 1:1

I am positively sure after many years of observation and prayer that the basis of all of our trouble today, in religious circles, is that our God is too small.

When he says magnify the Lord, he doesn't mean that you are to make God big, but you are to see Him big. When we take a telescope and look at a star, we don't make the star bigger, we only see it big. Likewise you cannot make God bigger, but you are only to see Him bigger. . . .

What is the most important verse in the Bible? It is not the one you think it is: "Jesus Christ the same yesterday, and to day, and for ever" (Heb. 13:8). Nor is it the other one you think it is: John 3:16, "For God so loved the world . . ." The most important verse in the Bible is this one: "In the beginning God . . ." (Gen. 1:1). That is the most important verse, because that is where everything must begin. God is the mountain out of which everything springs, and He is the foundation upon which everything rests. God is all in all. SAT036-037

Lord, I fall to my knees in worship before the God who is all in all, the great Creator and Foundation upon which everything rests. May I see you bigger today, I pray. Amen.

All Eloquence Is Done

Who can proclaim the mighty acts of the Lᴏʀᴅ or fully declare
his praise?
—PSALM 106:2

O ld Novatian said, "That in the contemplation of God's majesty,
all eloquence is done," which is to say that God is always greater
than anything that can be said about Him. No language is worthy of
Him. He is more sublime than all sublimity, loftier than all loftiness,
more profound than all profundity, more splendid than all splendor,
more powerful than all power, more truthful than all truth. Greater
than all majesty, more merciful than all mercy, more just than all justice, more pitiful than all pity. Nothing anybody can say about Him
is enough. . . .

If God is not the biggest thing in the world to you, not all your
talk will ever impress me. We ought to be where God is everything,
where we walk into a meeting and see God and think God and feel
God. We ought to see God all around us, where He comes down over
us and we see Him in a vision, in the cool of the day. We ought to see
Him in a mountain, in thunder and fire. We ought to see Him on the
cross in blood and tears, and coming down through the sky, riding a
white horse, and sitting on a throne judging the nations. But always,
we see God, and God is everything. SAT039-041

---

*Lord, You are worthy of praise, though words are inadequate to
express Your majesty. Today I bow in silence, for what have I
to say about the God who is everything? Amen.*

Truths for You and Me

For the LORD is the great God, the great King above all gods. . . .
Come, let us bow down in worship, let us kneel before
the LORD our Maker.
—PSALM 95:3, 6

Do you see how the attributes of God are not ivory-towered theology that only scholars can get ahold of, but truths for you and me? What's your trouble? . . . Got a temper you can't control? God will take care of that if you let Him. There isn't anything God can't handle. There isn't a situation that God can't take care of. Nothing is too hard for Jesus, and no man can work like Him.

His is an effortless power, because effort means I'm expending energy, but when God works, He doesn't expend energy. He *is* energy! With effortless power, God did and is doing His redeeming work. We stand in awe and speak in hushed tones of His incarnation. How could it be that the great God Almighty could be conceived in the womb of a virgin? I don't know how it could be, but I know that the Great God who is omnipotent, the Great God Almighty, could do it if He wanted to. The incarnation was easy for God. It may be hard for us to understand—a mystery of godliness—but it is not hard for God.

AOGII091-092

*Lord, establish in me a proper conception of You, our great King,
that I will have a strong foundation for my life of faith. Amen.*

If We've Lost Majesty

They tell of the glory of your kingdom and speak of your might,
so that all people may know of your mighty acts and the glorious
splendor of your kingdom.

—PSALM 145:11–12

If you want to pray strategically, in a way which would please God, pray that God might raise up men who would see the beauty of the Lord our God and would begin to preach it and hold it out to people, instead of offering peace of mind, deliverance from cigarettes, a better job, and a nicer cottage. . . .

What good is all our busy religion if God isn't in it? What good is it if we've lost majesty, reverence, worship—an awareness of the divine? What good is it if we've lost a sense of the Presence and the ability to retreat within our own hearts and meet God in the garden? If we've lost that, why build another church? Why make more converts to an effete Christianity? Why bring people to follow after a Savior so far off that He doesn't own them?

We need to improve the quality of our Christianity, and we never will until we raise our concept of God back to that held by apostle, sage, prophet, saint, and reformer. When we put God back where He belongs, we will instinctively and automatically move up again; the whole spiral of our religious direction will be upward. AOG194-195

---

*Lord, may I learn to see You not as a functional God who fulfills
my requests but as a beautiful God of glorious majesty. May
I hold that concept out for others to see, that they might also
behold Your majesty. Amen.*

The Common Man and the Common God

They speak of the glorious splendor of your majesty—and I will meditate on your wonderful works. They tell of the power of your awesome works—and I will proclaim your great deeds.

—PSALM 145:5–6

We also seem to have gotten away from the concept of majesty altogether. This is the age of the common man and along with the common man has come the common god. . . .

The modern Christian has lost a sense of worship along with the concept of majesty, and of course, reverence as well. He has lost his ability to withdraw inwardly and commune in the secret place with God in the shrine of his own hidden spirit. It is this that makes Christianity, and we have all but lost it. Added numbers, yes, but lost fear. Multiplied schools, yes, but lost awareness of the invisible. Tons of literature being poured out, of course, but no consciousness of the divine Presence. Better communication, certainly, but nothing to communicate. Evangelistic organizations, yes, but the concept of majesty and worship and reverence has almost left us. AOG180-181

Oh, God, restore to Your Church a sense of majesty, worship, and reverence that sends us to our secret closets in awe. Amen.

True to His Nature

I keep asking that the God of our Lord Jesus Christ, the glorious
Father, may give you the Spirit of wisdom and revelation, so that
you may know him better.

—EPHESIANS 1:17

If we make Him a god of grace and nothing else, as gospel churches
have over the past fifty years, we have a god who cannot see moral
distinctions. This is why the church has been unable to see moral distinctions. Instead of a separated, holy church, we have a church that's
so geared into the world, you can't tell one from the other. It was said
of a certain great English preacher that he preached grace in such a
manner as to lower the moral standards of England. It's entirely possible to preach grace in the church until we become as arrogant and
brazen as can be, forgetting that grace is one of the attributes of God,
but not all. While God is a God of grace, He is also a God of justice,
holiness, and truth. Our God will always be true to His nature because
He is a faithful God.

Faithlessness is one of the greatest sources of heartache and
misery in all the world. God will never be faithless; He cannot be.
AOGII179-180

---

*Lord, give Your church and its leaders a spirit of wisdom and
revelation, that we might indeed have an adequate appreciation
of who You are. Amen.*

The Perfections of God

Praise the LORD. Praise the LORD, my soul. I will praise
the LORD all my life; I will sing praise to my God as long as I live.
—PSALM 146:1–2

My conviction has been growing for years that we must recapture the concept of the perfections of God. We must see again how awful (awe-full) God is, how beautiful and how perfect. And we must begin to preach it, sing it, write about it, promote it, talk it, tell and pray it until we have recaptured the concept of majesty, until the awareness of the divine is back in our religion again, until we have regained the ability and desire to retire within our own hearts and worship God in the silence of our own spirits.

If we continue as we are, spreading our impaired religion, our weakened Christianity, over a wider area until the Lord comes, the Lord will break through the clouds and will show Himself majestic and wonderful in heaven above and earth beneath and under the sea, and everywhere they shall bow and own Him as Lord and King. But I'd like to see it brought back to the Church before that dramatic hour comes. I'd like to see us know it now. AOG181-182

*Lord, I too long to see Your Church recapture a sense of Your
majesty. I commit to spreading the knowledge of Your perfection
to those in my own life. Amen.*

MARCH

Man-Centered Christianity

Yours, LORD, is the greatness and the power and the glory and
the majesty and the splendor, for everything in heaven and earth
is yours. Yours, LORD, is the kingdom; you are exalted as head
over all.
—1 CHRONICLES 29:11

Christianity today is man-centered, not God-centered. God is
made to wait patiently, even respectfully, on the whims of men.
The image of God currently popular is that of a distracted Father,
struggling in heartbroken desperation to get people to accept a Savior
of whom they feel no need and in whom they have very little interest.
To persuade these self-sufficient souls to respond to His generous offers, God will do almost anything, even using salesmanship methods
and talking down to them in the chummiest way imaginable. This view
of things is, of course, a kind of religious romanticism, which, while
it often uses flattering and sometimes embarrassing terms in praise of
God, manages nevertheless to make man the star of the show. MDP027

*Lord, take me to my knees in worship. Then let me go to share
You, our great and majestic God Who deserves our worship. Amen.*

Wisdom in Creation and Redemption

Oh, the depth of the riches of the wisdom and knowledge of
God! How unsearchable his judgments, and his paths beyond
tracing out!
—ROMANS 11:33

The wisdom of God is seen in His creation and in His redemption, in that God has planned the highest good for the highest number for the longest time. . . . God, on the other hand, always thinks of the highest good, for the greatest number, for the longest time. God always thinks in terms of eternity. When God plans to bless a man, He takes that poor, little, time-cursed creature in His hand and says, "My son, I breathe into you eternity and immortality; I let you share in my endlessness." If you really knew how long you were privileged to live and to be with God, you would rejoice! God Almighty has planned that you shall not only enjoy Him now, but for all the eternities to come. And it's for the greatest number and the highest good. AOGII141

*Lord, we've forgotten how to be still and witness Your wisdom.
May I rediscover You in a way that affects my entire life. Amen.*

Nothing Can Stop God

You are worthy to take the scroll and to open its seals, because you were slain, and with your blood you purchased for God persons from every tribe and language and people and nation.

—REVELATION 5:9

But you can be absolutely certain that the God who is perfectly free, anywhere, all the time, to do everything He wills to do, will carry out His purposes. And one of His purposes is to bring forth a ransomed people from every tongue, people, tribe, nation, color, race, and ethnic origin around the world (Rev. 5:9). He will make them to be like His holy Son, and they will be the bride of His Son. Jesus Christ, the Son of God, will introduce them to the Father—ransomed, redeemed, and purified—for they were virgins and they walked with the Lamb. I believe in this.

Nothing and nobody can stop God. You may say, "God means well, and He has power and authority, but some unforeseen circumstance may derail His plans." But for God there are no unforeseen circumstances! When you start out on a walk down the block, a black cat may run in front of you; a police-man may call you aside; you may drop dead; a car may run up on the sidewalk and break your leg. You never can tell. Unforeseen circumstances are everywhere around you and me—but the Sovereign God knows nothing about unforeseen circumstances. He has seen the end from the beginning. He never needs to ask what is in a man; He knows every man. So there can be no unforeseen circumstances. AOGII170-171

Lord, when do I ever get that sense of sinfulness and guilt, fear and dismay in my encounters with You? Forgive me for my casual approach to You and renew in me a fear and wonder in Your presence. Amen.

Lord God, You Know!

He asked me, "Son of man, can these bones live?" I said,
"Sovereign LORD, you alone know."
—EZEKIEL 37:3

To those who have (unintentionally) degraded their conception of God to the level of their human understanding, it may appear frightening to admit that there are many things in the Scriptures and more things about the Godhead that transcend the human intellect. But a few minutes on our knees looking into the face of Christ will teach us humility, a virtue whose healing qualities have been known by God's elect from time out of mind.

Coleridge gave it as his considered belief that the profoundest sentence ever uttered by human lips was the spontaneous cry of the prophet Ezekiel in the valley of dry bones when asked by the Lord whether those bones could live: "And I answered, O Lord GOD, thou knowest." Had Ezekiel answered yes or no, he would have closed off his heart to the mighty mystery which confronted him and would have missed the luxury of wonder in the presence of the Majesty on high. For never forget that it is a privilege to wonder, to stand in delighted silence before the Supreme Mystery and whisper, "O Lord GOD, thou knowest!" ROR088-089

Lord, today I stand in wonder as I contemplate Your person and Your working. I delight in Your mystery and cry with Ezekiel, "O Lord GOD, thou knowest!" Amen.

A Royal Display

In his hand are the depths of the earth, and the mountain peaks belong to him. The sea is his, for he made it, and his hands formed the dry land.

—PSALM 95:4–5

A new rich mine would be opened in our consciousness if we could learn to recognize God in nature as well as in grace. For the God of nature is also the God of grace. . . .

Because sin has injured us so deeply, and because the whole transaction of repentance and deliverance from the guilt and power of iniquity makes such a mighty impression upon us emotionally, we naturally tend to appreciate the work of God in redemption more than in nature. But everything God does is praiseworthy and deserves our deepest admiration. Whether He is making or redeeming a world, He is perfect in all His doings and glorious in all His goings forth. . . .

If we miss seeing God in His works, we deprive ourselves of the sight of a royal display of wisdom and power so elevating, so ennobling, so awe-inspiring as to make all attempts at description futile. Such a sight the angels behold day and night forever and ask nothing more to make them perpetually satisfied. OGM145-147

Lord, I so often look at the grandeur and the infinite variety of Your creation, and I bow in worship before the great Creator. Thank You for providing this natural world for us as a glimpse of Your majestic nature. Amen.

God's Stamp

The heavens declare the glory of God; the skies proclaim
the work of his hands.
—PSALM 19:1

Consider why we think like we do in today's society. We are partici-pants in a new age—a scientific age, an atomic age, a space age. We have been conditioned by our sciences. No longer have we any great sense of wonder or appreciation for what God continues to do in His creation. Amid our complex engineering and technological accomplishments, it is difficult for us to look out on God's world as we should.

As believers in God and in His plan for mankind, we must not yield to the philosophies that surround us. We have a God-given message to proclaim to our generation: *The world was made by Almighty God.* It bears the stamp of deity upon it and within it.

An architect leaves his stamp upon the great buildings he has designed. A notable artist leaves his mark and personality on his paintings. The same principle applies to the visible and invisible worlds.

JMI050

*Great Creator, Your stamp is so evident, yet I so often credit
Your work to less noble sources. I bow in wonder and in worship
before my Creator God. Amen.*

The Garden of God

Sing to the LORD with grateful praise; make music to our God on
the harp. He covers the sky with clouds; he supplies the earth
with rain and makes grass grow on the hills.
—PSALM 147:7–8

The heavens and the earth were intended to be a semitransparent
veil through which moral intelligences might see the glory of
God (Ps. 19:1–6; Rom. 1:19–20), but for sin-blinded men this veil
has become opaque. They see the creation but do not see through
it to the Creator; or what glimpses they do have are dim and out of
focus. It is possible to spend a lifetime admiring God's handiwork
without acknowledging the presence of the God whose handiwork
it is. . . .

With what joy the Christian turns from even the purest nature
poets to the prophets and psalmists of the Scriptures. These saw God
first. . . . Their love of natural objects was deep and intense, but they
loved them not for their own sakes but for the sake of Him who created them. They walked through the world as through the garden of
God. Everything reminded them of Him. They saw His power in the
stormy wind and tempest; they heard His voice in the thunder; the
mountains told them of His strength; and the rocks reminded them
that He was their hiding place. The sun by day and the moon and
stars by night recited the story of their divine birth. OGM139-140

*Lord, may I be reminded of Your role as Creator by every created
thing I encounter. Amen.*

The Wonders of Creation

Who created all these? He who brings out the starry host one by
one and calls forth each of them by name. Because of his great
power and mighty strength, not one of them is missing.
—ISAIAH 40:26

If you will really give yourself to study, you will discover that the
Old Testament is a marvelous rhapsody on the natural creation.
Start with Moses, and when you get beyond the Levitical order, you
will find him soaring in his acute consciousness of the presence of
God in all of creation.

Go on to the book of Job, and in the closing sections, you will be
amazed at the sublimity of the language describing the world around
us.

Then go on to the Psalms, and you will find David literally dancing
with ecstatic delight as he gazes out upon the wonders of God's world.

Begin reading in Isaiah, and you will find the loftiest imagery. It
is neither fanciful nor flighty but a presentation of the wonders of
creation as the prophet observed them.

These men, who were some of the holiest and godliest men of that
ancient time, revealed in their writings that they were intensely in love
with every natural beauty around them. But always they saw nature as
the handiwork of an all-powerful, all-wise, glorious Creator. WHT043

---

*Lord, I desire to glory in Your creation, not for nature's sake but
because it is the work of a majestic Creator. I bow in wonder
before Your mighty hand. Amen.*

The Ability to Wonder

When I consider your heavens, the work of your fingers,
the moon and the stars, which you have set in place, what is
mankind that you are mindful of him, human beings that you
care for them?
—PSALM 8:3–4

God made the world; it is a beautiful thing and something to venerate. It's a great loss—a tragic loss—that we've suffered in the last generation. We have lost the ability to wonder. We know so everlasting much, and we're so sure of ourselves. But David stood and wondered in the presence of God's creation; he raised his eyes and said, "What is man, that thou art mindful of him?" (Ps. 8:4). And Isaiah and Jeremiah and Ezekiel and all the rest of them stood and wondered in the presence of God Almighty's creation. . . .

The footprints of God are everywhere about us. And while we can't see Him, we can see His luminous trail like a bird that sings while hidden in a tree. As Middleton said, "The bird sings darkling." We can't see the bird, but we can hear her sing. God sings among His branches and sings in His universe. You and I cannot gaze upon Him, for no man can see God and live. But we can hear Him sing His song of creation and redemption. And we can feel the pressure of His breath upon us as we move through the world. We'll never see things rightly till we see them as the garments of God. SAT104-105

---

*I'll watch for Your footprints, God. I'll listen for Your song and be
sensitive to Your breath. I will stand in wonder at what I see. Amen.*

I See the Glory of God

Surely as I live and as surely as the glory of the Lord fills the whole earth.
—NUMBERS 14:21

Let us learn to admire God in all things, great and small—in the soft play of a kitten on the rug as well as in the vast and breathtaking sweep of some galaxy around a point so remote as to stun the imagination and make language dumb. . . .

Two men stood on the shore watching the sun come up out of the sea. One was a merchant from London; the other was the poet, William Blake. As the bright yellow disk of the sun emerged into view, gilding the water and painting the sky with a thousand colors, the poet turned to the merchant and asked, "What do you see?" "Ah! I see gold," replied the merchant. "The sun looks like a great gold piece. What do you see?" "I see the glory of God," Blake answered, "and I hear a multitude of the heavenly host crying 'Holy, Holy, Holy is the Lord God Almighty. The whole earth is full of His glory'" (see Isa. 6:5). OGM147-148

Lord, as I go about my day, may I not just see nature for what it is, but as a majestic expression of Your holiness. Amen.

God Made Color

The heavens praise your wonders, Lord, your faithfulness too,
in the assembly of the holy ones.
—PSALM 89:5

Some people are afraid of color. They think that spirituality consists in being drab. But God made color! He made all shades of colors. Look at the sunset—what is it, just something scientific? Do you think that God splashed the lovely, beautiful sky with rose, cerise, blue, and white and wasn't smiling when He did that? Is that just an accident of nature, scientifically explained? Then you've got too much learning for your own good! Go empty your head and get your heart filled and you'll be better off. The Holy Spirit wrote 150 psalms, and in those psalms He celebrates the wonders of God's creation. . . .

We ought to stop thinking like scientists and think like psalmists.

This infinite God is enjoying Himself. Somebody is having a good time in heaven and earth and sea and sky. Somebody is painting the sky. Somebody is making trees to grow where only gashes were a year ago. Somebody is causing the ice to melt out of the river and the fish to swim and the birds to sing and lay their blue eggs and build their nests and hatch their young. Somebody's running the universe.

AOG011-013

Indeed, Lord, the heavens shall praise Your wonders! Thank You for running the universe with beauty, variety, intricacy, and color. Amen.

Divine Purpose

The LORD Almighty has sworn, "Surely, as I have planned, so it
will be, and as I have purposed, so it will happen."
—ISAIAH 14:24

Now, I think that God first makes things orderly for utility. Whenever He made something in this universe it was because He had a purpose for it. I do not believe there is anything in the universe that just got here by accident. Everything in the universe has a meaning.

My father was philosophical about many things, and I remember that he used to sit during the summertime and ponder why God made the mosquitoes. I still do not have the answer, but I am just a human being, and just because I do not have that answer, I am not going to accuse the Creator of making a cosmic blunder. I know the mosquito is not a blunder—it is just a pest. But God made it.

The same principle is true of a great many other things. I do not know why God does some things, but I am convinced that nothing is accidental in His universe. The fact that we do not know the reason behind some things is not basis enough for us to call them divine accidents. WPJ120-121

---

*Lord, as I go about my day, help me to remember that nothing
happens by accident, but that everything is divinely controlled by
Your eternal purpose. Amen.*

Just Humble Yourself

LORD, what are human beings that you care for them,
mere mortals that you think of them? They are like a breath;
their days are like a fleeting shadow.

—PSALM 144:3-4

Far better than the attempt to understand is the humility that admits its ignorance and waits quietly on God for His own light to appear in His own time. We will be better able to understand when we have accepted the humbling truth that there are many things in heaven and earth that we shall never be able to understand. It will be good for us to accept the universe and take our place in the mighty web of God's creation, so perfectly known to Him and so slightly known to even the wisest of men. . . .

Probably David lying on his back on the green meadow at night, brooding over the mystery of the moon and the stars and the littleness of man in the total scheme of things, worshiping the God who had made him only a little lower than the angels, was a truer man than the astronomer who in his high pride weighs and measures the heavenly bodies. Yet the astronomer need not despair. If he will humble himself and confess his deep inward need, the God of David will teach him how to worship, and by so doing will make him a greater man than he could ever have been otherwise. ROR088, 090

Lord, I can't even begin to understand all the vastness of Your universe, but I see Your hand in it. I humble myself before You today, that I might learn to worship You better. Amen.

The Study of Theology

We know also that the Son of God has come and has given us understanding, so that we may know him who is true. And we are in him who is true by being in his Son Jesus Christ. He is the true God and eternal life.

—1 JOHN 5:20

That theology probably receives less attention than any other sub-ject tells us nothing about its importance or lack of it. It indicates rather that men are still hiding from the presence of God among the trees of the garden and feel acutely uncomfortable when the matter of their relation to God is brought up. . . .

It is precisely because God *is,* and because man is made in His im-age and is accountable to Him, that theology is so critically import-ant. Christian revelation alone has the answer to life's unanswered questions about God and human destiny. To let these authoritative answers lie neglected while we search everywhere else for answers and find none is, it seems to me, nothing less than folly.

No motorist would be excused if he neglected to consult his road map and tried instead to find his way across the country by looking for moss on logs, or by observing the flight of wild bees or watching the movement of the heavenly bodies. If there *were* no map, a man *might* find his way by the stars; but for a traveler trying to get home, the stars would be a poor substitute for a map. TIC093, 095

Lord, there are so many questions in this life that cry out for answers. Be my road map, Lord, that I might find You and know You more. Amen.

Full Comprehension Is Yet to Come

The glory of the LORD settled on Mount Sinai. For six days
the cloud covered the mountain, and on the seventh day
the LORD called to Moses from within the cloud.
—EXODUS 24:16

We know very well that the human mind cannot comprehend or encompass the person of God. We can know what God is not, but in this earthly life it is impossible for us to say, "I know what God is." We never can know because God belongs to a realm entirely different from ours. The great God exists in awesome wonder. He is uncreated holiness, high above all the things that the hands of mankind have made. . . .

There is neither preacher nor teacher anywhere in the world who can say, "Let me tell you all about God!" God told Moses and Israel, and He tells us: "Always there will be the cloud about Me. Always there will be a veil covering My person. While you are on My earth, you will sense this obscurity, for I Am who I Am!". . .

And I can say this from personal experience: After you have known God and walked with Him by faith for fifty years, growing daily in His grace and the knowledge of Him, you will still see a cloud on Mount Sinai. You will still sense the obscurity. Your mind and your spirit will still bow before Him. Your day of full comprehension is yet to come. MMG082-083

---

*I long for that day, Lord, when the cloud is completely removed,
and I shall know You completely. Amen.*

God Is Ineffable

For who knows a person's thoughts except their own spirit within them? In the same way no one knows the thoughts of God except the Spirit of God.

—1 CORINTHIANS 2:11

We can best conceive of God by conceiving of what He is not. We can always know what God is not, but we can never know quite what God is. The greatness of God's mind leaves all our soaring thoughts behind. God is ineffable (incapable of being expressed in words), inconceivable, and unimaginable. . . .

As I said, we are driven to the use of negative statements when speaking about God. When we speak of the self-existence of God, we say God has no origin. When we speak of God's eternity, we say God has no beginning. When we speak of the immutability of God, we say God has no change. When we speak of the infinity of God, we say that God has no limits. When we speak of the omniscience of God, we say that God has no teachers and cannot learn. . . .

Well now, the Scripture takes this negative method too. Scripture says the Lord "fainteth not, neither is weary" (Isa. 40:28) and that He "cannot lie" (Titus 1:2). It says, "I am the LORD, I change not" (Mal. 3:6). It says, "with God nothing shall be impossible" (Luke 1:37).

AOGII107, 109-110

Teach me, Lord, that I might know all of You that I can within the limits of my humanity. I await the day when I will more completely know who You are. Amen.

I Fell on My Face

For our "God is a consuming fire."
—HEBREWS 12:29

Just because God cannot tell us *what He is*, He very often tells us *what He is like*. By these "like" figures, He leads our faltering minds as close as they can come to that "light which no man can approach unto" (1 Tim. 6:16). Through the more cumbersome medium of the intellect, the soul is prepared for the moment when it can, through the operation of the Holy Spirit, know God as He is in Himself. God has used a number of these similitudes to hint at His incomprehensible being, and judging from the Scriptures, one would gather that His favorite similitude is fire. In one place the Spirit speaks expressly, "For our God is a consuming fire" (Heb. 12:29). This accords with His revelation of Himself as recorded throughout the Bible. As a fire He spoke to Moses from the burning bush; in the fire He dwelt above the camp of Israel through all the wilderness journey; as fire He dwelt between the wings of the cherubim in the Holy of Holies; to Ezekiel He revealed Himself as a strange brightness of "a fire infolding itself. . . . This was the appearance of the likeness of the glory of the LORD. And when I saw it, I fell upon my face, and I heard a voice of one that spake." (Ez. 1:4, 28) POM098-099

Great God, if I really saw You in all Your majesty, I too would fall on my face before You. And this is only a glimpse of what You are! Show me Your glory, I pray. Amen.

Emotion on a High Plane

The LORD your God is with you, the Mighty Warrior who saves.
He will take great delight in you; in his love he will no longer
rebuke you, but will rejoice over you with singing.
—ZEPHANIAH 3:17

Now the Bible teaches that there is something in God which is like emotion. He experiences something which is like our love, something that is like our grief, that is like our joy. And we need not fear to go along with this conception of what God is like. Faith would easily draw the inference that since we were made in His image, He would have qualities like our own. But such an inference, while satisfying to the mind, is not the ground of our belief. God has said certain things about Himself, and these furnish all the grounds we require.

> The LORD thy God in the midst of thee is mighty; he will save, he will rejoice over thee with joy; he will rest in his love, he will joy over thee with singing. (Zeph. 3:17)

This is but one verse among thousands which serve to form our rational picture of what God is like, and they tell us plainly that God feels something like our love, like our joy, and what He feels makes Him act very much as we would in a similar situation. He rejoices over His loved ones with joy and singing.

Here is emotion on as high a plane as it can ever be seen, emotion flowing out of the heart of God Himself. POM110-111

Oh, Lord, do You really rejoice over me with singing? I often give You more cause for grief than for joy. Help me live in a way that is worthy of Your love. Amen.

Three Persons, One God

Hear, O Israel: The LORD our God, the LORD is one.
—DEUTERONOMY 6:4

I am a unitarian in that I believe in the unity of God. I am a trinitarian in that I believe in the trinity of God. And they're not contrary one to the other. . . .

Now that's what we believe, my brethren: we believe in the three Persons, but one God.

The three persons are three, but the one God is One. And this we believe. So when I talk about God, I mean the three Persons of the Trinity. You can't separate them—"not dividing the substance," said these old fathers. You can't have God the Father except you have God the Son; you can't have God the Spirit unless you have the Father and the Son, "for the Spirit proceedeth from the Father and the Son" (see John 15:26). So when I'm talking about God, I'm talking about the Father, the Son, and the Holy Spirit—not confusing their Persons, for there are three Persons. But everything that is true of the Father is true of the Son and the Holy Spirit. And everything that is true of the Son and the Holy Spirit is true of the Father. Let's get that settled before we go any further. AOGII019-021

Lord, I don't completely understand the Trinity, but it is clearly taught in Scripture, and I will accept it because Your Word is truth. How awesome that You can be both three persons and yet one God! Amen.

Without Change

I the LORD do not change.
—MALACHI 3:6

God cannot change from better to worse or from worse to better. . . . A creature can go from one kind of being to another. That beautiful butterfly that you squeal over in the springtime—why, just a little while ago it was a miserable, hairy worm; you wouldn't have touched it. But now you say, "Isn't it beautiful!" There was a change from one kind of creature to another.

Moral changes can also take place. A good man can change and be a bad man. And then, thank God, a bad man can, by the grace of God, change and be a good man. . . . Did you know that the apostle Paul was, by his own testimony, the chiefest of sinners (1 Tim. 1:15)? But these men became saints of God.

They changed. It's possible to change. There may have been a time in your life when you would have been bored to tears listening to all this talk about God. But you've changed! There's been mutation. Thank God, you are not immutable; you are able to change. You changed from worse to better. You went from one kind of creature to another kind of creature. But you can't think that about God. God cannot do that; it's unthinkable. The perfect and the absolute and the infinite God cannot become anything else but what He is. AOGII102-103

With my mind I struggle, Lord, but with my heart I rest. I am awed by Your unchanging Trinity in unity, and I long to know You not through reason but through love and faith. Amen.

On God's Side

I have chosen the way of faithfulness; I have set my heart
on your laws.
—PSALM 119:30

A man who is with God can't lose because God can't lose. God is
the sovereign God who is having His way in the whirlwind and
the storm. And when the storm is over and the whirlwind of history
has blown itself out, the God who sat on the throne with the rainbow
round about it will still be seated on that throne. Beside Him will be
a ransomed company who chose to go His way; heaven will not be
filled with slaves.

There will be no conscripts marching in the armies of heaven.
Everyone will be there because he exercised his sovereign freedom to
choose to believe in Jesus Christ and surrender to the will of God. . . .

Are you on God's side—completely, wholly, forever? Have you
given Him everything—your home, your business, your school, your
choice of a partner in life? Choose Christ's way, because Christ is
Lord and the Lord is sovereign. It's foolish to choose any other way.
It's folly to try to outsmart God, to try to fight against Him. "Why
dost thou strive against him?" (Job 33:13). AOGII173-174

---

*Lord, I long to show myself to be on Your side, not just with my
words, with my heart and deeds as well. Help me to choose
Christ's way. Amen.*

Infinite Excellence

Let them praise the name of the LORD, for his name alone is
exalted; his splendor is above the earth and the heavens.
—PSALM 148:13

I once heard Dr. George D. Watson, one of the great Bible teachers of his generation, point out that men can have two kinds of love for God—the love of gratitude or the love of excellence. He urged that we go on from gratefulness to a love of God just because He is God and because of the excellence of His character.

Unfortunately, God's children rarely go beyond the boundaries of gratitude. I seldom hear anyone in worshipful prayer admiring and praising God for His eternal excellence.

Many of us are strictly "Santa Claus" Christians. We think of God as putting up the Christmas tree and putting our gifts underneath. That is only an elementary kind of love.

We need to go on. We need to know the blessing of worshiping in the presence of God without thought of wanting to rush out again. We need to be delighted in the presence of utter, infinite excellence.

WHT087

Lord, quiet my heart and minister to my spirit. I'll take time to unhurriedly meditate on Your infinite excellence and worship You without asking for a thing! Amen.

He Always Will Be God

But the LORD is the true God. . . . When he is angry, the earth trembles; the nations cannot endure his wrath.
—JEREMIAH 10:10

Men and women who think they have all the answers about this life and the next have been mouthing their brave words for generations. They are big, challenging words, but they come from puny, empty hearts and minds. These infidels are too blind to recognize or acknowledge that God does have . . . a divine plan in which mankind is never permitted to utter the first word or the last. . . .

Humans try to ignore God, continuing to make their own ambitious, selfish plans. In the years before World War I, Germany's Kaiser Wilhelm was exceedingly headstrong. At a chapel service attended by the kaiser, a faithful German minister preached on the coming again of Jesus Christ to establish God's kingdom of righteousness and peace throughout the earth. Wilhelm was greatly offended and spoke to the minister at the close of the service.

"I never want to hear that kind of a sermon again," he warned the preacher. "Such an event is not at all in keeping with the plans we have for the future and the glory of our Fatherland!"

But Kaiser Wilhelm and, a generation later, Adolph Hitler are merely fading memories—illustrations of that vain human propensity to make ourselves big and God small. JIV016-018

Lord, I acknowledge that You have the first and last word on all things. I bow before Your wisdom. Amen.

Knowing God

For since the creation of the world God's invisible qualities—
his eternal power and divine nature—have been clearly seen . . .
so that people are without excuse.

—ROMANS 1:20

When we talk about God's knowledge of everything, we're talking about a rational approach to God. There are two ways to approach God: theologically and experientially. You can know God experientially and not know much theology, but it's good to know both. The more you know about God theologically, the better you can know Him experientially.

A rational approach to God is what I can get into my head. You can't get too much into your head, really. And what I can get into my head about God isn't very much at all. But that's one way to approach God—through theology, through your intellect, through doctrine. But the purpose of doctrine is to lead you to see and to know God experientially, to know God for Himself, for yourself. But until we know God theologically, we're not likely to know God very well experientially.

AOGII115-116

I can't comprehend You entirely, God, but I thank You for what You have revealed. Help me to learn all I can about You through an understanding of Your attributes. Amen.

Oh God, Thou Art

God said to Moses, "I Am Who I Am. This is what you are to say
to the Israelites: 'I Am has sent me to you.'"
—EXODUS 3:14

We must remember that the "attributes" of God are not component parts of the blessed Godhead nor elements out of which He is composed. A god who could be composed would not be God at all but the work of something or someone greater than he, great enough to compose him. We would then have a synthetic god made out of the pieces we call attributes, and the true God would be another being altogether, One indeed who is above all thought and all conceiving.

The Bible and Christian theology teach that God is an indivisible unity . . . from whom nothing can be taken and to whom nothing can be added. Mercy, for instance, immutability, eternity—these are but names which we have given to something which God has declared to be true of Himself. All the "of God" expressions in the Bible must be understood to mean not what God has but what God is in His undivided and indivisible unity. Even the word "nature" when applied to God should be understood as an accommodation to our human way of looking at things and not as an accurate description of anything true of the mysterious Godhead. God has said, "I Am That I Am" (Ex. 3:14), and we can only repeat in reverence, "O God, Thou art."

POM086-087

---

*Lord, it is because You are beyond all conceiving that I worship
You in wonder and bow before You today. Amen.*

God Does Not Change

God is not human, that he should lie, not a human being, that he should change his mind. Does he speak and then not act? Does he promise and not fulfill?
—NUMBERS 23:19

Only God does not change. "And all things, as they change, proclaim the Lord eternally the same." That's a theological fact. That's something you can build on. That is revealed truth—it needs no support of poetry or reason. But once a truth has been declared and established, I like to reason it out. To quote Anselm, "I do not seek to understand that I may believe, but I believe in order to understand." And so I'd like to show you, as briefly as I can, three reasons why God cannot change. That's reasoning within the Scriptures.

Now for God to alter or change at all, to be different from Himself, one of three things has to take place: 1. God must go from better to worse, or 2. He must go from worse to better, or 3. He must change from one kind of being to another.

Therefore, if God is to change, then God either has to get better or worse or different. But God can't go from better to worse, because God is a holy God. Because God is eternal holiness, He can never be any less holy than He is now. And of course, He never can be any more holy than He is now, because He is perfect just as He is. There will never be a change in God—no change is necessary! AOGII98-100

What confidence that inspires, Lord! Thank You for Your faithfulness, love, and unchanging nature. Amen.

What a Sea to Swim In!

There is no one holy like the LORD; there is no one besides
you; there is no Rock like our God.
—1 SAMUEL 2:2

What a broad world to roam in, what a sea to swim in is this
God and Father of our Lord Jesus Christ. He is *eternal*. He
antedates time and is wholly independent of it. Time began in Him
and will end in Him. To it He pays no tribute and from it He suffers
no change.

He is *immutable*. He has never changed and can never change in
any smallest measure. To change He would need to go from better to
worse or from worse to better. He cannot do either, for being perfect,
He cannot become more perfect, and if He were to become less perfect, He would be less than God.

He is *omniscient*. He knows in one free and effortless act all matter, all spirit, all relationships, all events. He has no past and He has
no future. He is, and none of the limiting and qualifying terms used
of creatures can apply to Him.

Love and mercy and righteousness are His, and *holiness* so ineffable that no comparisons or figures will avail to express it. POG037

*I'm overwhelmed when I even try to comprehend Your attributes,
Father. I worship You, for there is indeed no God like You. Amen.*

God Rises Above Rationality

These are but the outer fringe of his works; how faint the
whisper we hear of him! Who then can understand the thunder
of his power?

—JOB 26:14

Now the holy man of God said, "Lo, these are parts of his ways:
but how little a portion is heard of him?" (Job 26:14). All that
we can think or say is rational. But God rises above rationality. He
rises as high above the rational as He does above the physical. God
is of an essence and substance the like of which nothing else exists in
the universe. He is above it all—and yet we can know a little portion
of God's ways. When I preach on the being of God, the attributes of
God, when I talk about what God is like, and what kind of God He
is, I approach it respectfully, from afar. I point with a reverent finger
to the tall mountain peak which is God, which rises infinitely above
my power to comprehend. But that is only a little portion. The paths
of His ways cannot be known; the rest is super-rational. . . .

How terrible it is that, in the presence of this awesome, awful
God, some people are untouched by it all! How frightful, how awesome, how awful it is! We don't want to hear about God. We want to
hear about something that can tickle our fancy, that can satisfy our
morbid curiosity or our longing after romance. AOGII040-041

---

*I see such a little portion, Lord, of who You are, and yet how
awesome are Your ways! May I never be untouched by what I see
of You. Amen.*

Speechless Humility

While he was saying this to me, I bowed with my face toward the ground and was speechless. . . . "My strength is gone and I can hardly breathe."
—DANIEL 10:15, 17

When we meet God, we also have a sense of weakness. I don't think you will ever be strong until you know how utterly weak you are. And you will never know how utterly weak you are until you have stood in the presence of that great plenitude of strength, that great fullness of infinite power that we call God. When for an awful, happy, terrible, wonderful moment the eyes of our hearts have gazed upon the transcendent God, high and lifted up with His train filling the temple, then we will know how weak we are. . . .

I've been preaching since I was nineteen years old, and now I'm sixty-three. And yet, after all these years of preaching, I come into the pulpit shaking inside—not because I fear the people, but because I fear God. It's the fear and trembling of knowing that I stand to speak of God and if I don't speak rightly about God, what a terrible error it will be. If I speak evilly of God, what a frightful crime! It is only when I speak well of God that I dare sleep at night without asking forgiveness. AOGII046

Most of us have never had a true vision of Your power, Lord, and so have not experienced a real sense of our own weakness. May I fear You in speechless humility. Amen.

God Is There First

"I am the Alpha and the Omega," says the Lord God, "who is,
and who was, and who is to come, the Almighty."
—REVELATION 1:8

The unconditioned priority of God in His universe is a truth celebrated both in the Old Testament and in the New. The prophet
Habakkuk sang it in ecstatic language, "Art thou not from everlasting,
O LORD my God, mine Holy One?" (1:12). The Apostle John set it
forth in careful words deep with meaning,

> In the beginning was the Word, and the Word was with God,
> and the Word was God. The same was in the beginning with
> God. All things were made by him; and without him was not
> any thing made that was made. (1:1–3)

Here we acknowledge (and there is fear and wonder in the thought)
the essential unity of God's nature, the timeless persistence of His
changeless being throughout eternity and time. . . . Begin where we
will, God is there first. He is Alpha and Omega, the beginning and the
ending. . . . If we grope back to the farthest limits of thought where
imagination touches the pre-creation void, we shall find God there.
In one unified present glance. He comprehends all things from everlasting, and the flutter of a seraph's wing a thousand ages hence is seen
by Him now without moving His eyes. POM001, 003-004

*Your timelessness is a truth that is beyond my comprehension,
Lord, but it leads me to fall before You in awe. Amen.*

God Is Infinite!

Great is the LORD and most worthy of praise; his greatness
no one can fathom.
—PSALM 145:3

God is infinite! That's the hardest thought I will ask you to grasp. You cannot understand what infinite means, but don't let it bother you—I don't understand it and I'm trying to explain it! "Infinite" means so much that nobody can grasp it, but reason nevertheless kneels and acknowledges that God is infinite. We mean by infinite that God knows no limits, no bounds, and no end. What God is, He is without boundaries. All that God is, He is without bounds or limits.

We've got to eliminate all careless speech here. You and I talk about unlimited wealth, but there's no such thing; you can count it. We talk about boundless energy—which I don't feel I have at the moment—but there's no such thing; you can measure a man's energy. We say an artist takes infinite pains with his picture. But he doesn't take infinite pains; he just does the best he can and then throws up his hands and says, "It isn't right yet, but I'll have to let it go." That's what we call infinite pains.

But that is a misuse of the words "boundless," "unlimited," and "infinite." These words describe God—they don't describe anything but God. AOG004

Lord, Your greatness extends beyond the limitations of my human ability to comprehend. You are boundless, unlimited, and infinite, and You are greatly to be praised. Amen.

Infinite Understanding

Great is our LORD and mighty in power; his understanding has no limit.
—PSALM 147:5

If there were a point where God stopped, then God wouldn't be perfect. For instance, if God knew almost everything, but not quite everything, then God wouldn't be perfect in knowledge. His understanding wouldn't be infinite, as it says in Psalm 147:5.

Let us take all that can be known—past, present and future, spiritual, psychic, and physical—everywhere throughout the universe. And let us say God knows all of it except one percent—He knows ninety-nine percent of all that can be known. I'd be embarrassed to go to heaven and look into the face of a God that didn't know everything. He has to know it all, or I can't worship Him. I can't worship that which is not perfect.

What about power? If God had all the power there is except a little bit, and if somebody else had a little bit of power hoarded that God couldn't get to, then we couldn't worship God. We couldn't say that this God is of infinite power because He wouldn't be of infinite power; He'd just be close to it. While He would be more powerful than any other being and perhaps even more powerful than all the beings in the universe lumped together, He still would have a defect, and therefore He couldn't be God. Our God is perfect—perfect in knowledge and power. AOG006

Lord, how wonderful it is to know that I can worship a God who is perfect. I praise You for Your infinite understanding and power. Amen.

This Little Cheap God

Now to the King eternal, immortal, invisible, the only God,
be honor and glory for ever and ever. Amen.
—1 TIMOTHY 1:17

If God had goodness, but there was one spot in God that wasn't good, then He wouldn't be our God and Father. If God had love but didn't have all the love, just ninety-nine and nine-tenths percent of the love—or even a higher percentage—God still wouldn't be God. God, to be God, must be infinite in all that He is. He must have no bound and no limit, no stopping place, no point beyond which He can't go. When you think of God or anything about God, you'll have to think infinitely about God.

You may have a charley horse in your head for two weeks after trying to follow this, but it's a mighty good cure for this little cheap god we have today. This little cheap god we've made up is one you can pal around with—"the Man upstairs," the fellow who helps you win baseball games. That god isn't the God of Abraham, Isaac, and Jacob. He isn't the God who laid the foundations of the heaven and the earth; he's some other god. AOG006-007

Lord, forgive me for assuming such a cheap familiarity with such an awesome God. You are worthy of so much more. May I begin to learn to think infinitely about You today. Amen.

A Journey into God

I pray that the eyes of your heart may be enlightened in order
that you may know the hope to which he has called you,
the riches of his glorious inheritance in his holy people.
—EPHESIANS 1:18

The Church will come out of her doldrums when we find out that salvation is not a lightbulb only, that it is not an insurance policy against hell only, but that it is a gateway into God and that God is all that we would have and can desire. Again I quote [Lady] Julian: "I saw that God is to us everything that is good and comfortable. He is our clothing; His love wrappeth us and claspeth us and all encloseth us for His tender love, that He may never leave us, being to us all that is good."

Christianity is a gateway into God. And then when you get into God, "with Christ in God," then you're on a journey into infinity, into infinitude. There is no limit and no place to stop. There isn't just one work of grace, or a second work or a third work, and then that's it. There are numberless experiences and spiritual epochs and crises that can take place in your life while you are journeying out into the heart of God in Christ. AOG003-004

Lord, whether we've been Your children for five months or fifty years, many of us are just beginning our journey through the gateway of Christianity. Open my eyes to all that You are and can be to me. Amen.

The Immanence of God

"Who can hide in secret places so that I cannot see them?"
declares the LORD. "Do not I fill heaven and earth?"
declares the LORD.
—JEREMIAH 23:24

G od is immanent, which means you don't have to go distances to find God. He is in everything. He is right here.

God is above all things, beneath all things, outside of all things and inside of all things. God is above, but He's not pushed up. He's beneath, but He's not pressed down. He's outside, but He's not excluded. He's inside, but He's not confined. God is above all things presiding, beneath all things sustaining, outside of all things embracing, and inside of all things filling. That is the immanence of God.

God doesn't travel to get anywhere. We may say in prayer, "Oh God, come and help us," because we mean it in a psychological way. But actually God doesn't have to "come" to help us because *there isn't any place where God is not.* AOG022

What an encouragement, Lord, to know that You are here with me as I seek to meet with You. Give me a clear sense of Your presence, both now and as I move through the day. Amen.

The Immensity of God

Who has measured the waters in the hollow of his hand, or with
the breadth of his hand marked off the heavens? Who has held
the dust of the earth in a basket, or weighed the mountains on
the scales and the hills in a balance?

—ISAIAH 40:12

Imagine going out millions of light years into space and finding a body so vast that you could throw all our solar system into it. Like throwing a shovelful of coal into a furnace, it would simply swallow up our solar system and go on. After you've thought of all that, remember that God contains all that. Remember that God is outside of all things and inside of all things and around all things. Remember that our God made it. That is the immensity of God. . . .

We have here in Isaiah that which is vaster and more awesome than anything that ever came out of the mind of Shakespeare. It is the thought of the great God . . . moving through His universe . . . with its worlds so big that our whole solar system would look like a grain of sand by comparison. And God stands out yonder and calls all of these millions of worlds as His sheep; He calls them all by name and leads them out across the vast sky.

I'd say this is the highest thought I know of, in the Bible or out. And God does this "by the greatness of his might, for that he is strong in power; not one faileth" (Isa. 40:26). AOG023, 025

---

*Lord, You are more immense than I can imagine, yet You are
a personal God who knows me by name. I bow before You
in awe. Amen.*

Play with Your Little Ball

He sits enthroned above the circle of the earth, and its people
are like grasshoppers. He stretches out the heavens like
a canopy, and spreads them out like a tent to live in.
—ISAIAH 40:22

I don't know where heaven is. I read that the people in the space
program shot a gold-plated arrow sixty-some thousand miles into
the air, and some are wondering if it might not be reaching heaven
at last. I have to smile at that, because God does not dwell in space;
space is nothing to God. The great infinite heart of God gathers up
into Himself all space.

Our space program is like a baby playing with a rubber ball in
Wrigley Field. He can't do anything but bat it around and crawl after it. If he bats it away two feet, he squeals with delight as if he hit
a home run. But way out there, 400 feet long, stretches the field. It
takes a strong man to knock a ball over the fence.

When man sends up his little arrow, and it reaches the moon and
goes into orbit round it, he boasts about it for years to come. Go on,
little boy, play with your rubber ball. But the great God who carries
the universe in His heart smiles. He is not impressed. He is calling
mankind to Himself, to His holiness, beauty, love, mercy, and goodness. He has come to reconcile us and call us back. AOG193

*It's so easy, Lord, for us to think too highly of our worldly intellect.
Help me to see You anew in all Your glory, that I might see my
comparative smallness and my need for You. Amen.*

Longing for God

As the deer pants for streams of water, so my soul pants for you, my God. My soul thirsts for God, for the living God. When can I go and meet with God?

—PSALM 42:1–2

O God, I have tasted Thy goodness, and it has both satisfied me and made me thirsty for more. I am painfully conscious of my need of further grace. I am ashamed of my lack of desire. O God, the triune God, I want to want Thee; I long to be filled with longing; I thirst to be made more thirsty still. Show me Thy glory, I pray Thee, that so I may know Thee indeed. Begin in mercy a new work of love within me. Say to my soul, "Rise up, my love, my fair one, and come away." Then give me grace to rise and follow Thee up from this misty lowland where I have wandered so long. In Jesus' name. Amen. POG020

"I want to want You; I long to be filled with longing; I thirst to be made more thirsty still." Amen.

God Is Always Cordial

*If you, then, though you are evil, know how to give good gifts
to your children, how much more will your Father in heaven
give good gifts to those who ask him!*
—MATTHEW 7:11

I have for over thirty years spoken about God's goodness. It is most important that we know about God's goodness and know what kind of God He is. What is God like? It is a question that must be answered if we're going to be any kind of Christians at all. Don't take that for granted and say, "I already know." . . .

God is kindhearted, gracious, good-natured, and benevolent in intention. And let us remember that God is cordial. We only think we believe, really. We are believers in a sense, and I trust that we believe sufficiently to be saved and justified before His grace. But we don't believe as intensely and as intimately as we should. If we did, we would believe that God is a cordial God, that He is gracious and that His intentions are kind and benevolent. . . .

There are never any times when God won't be cordial. Even the best Christian doesn't always feel cordial. Sometimes he didn't sleep well, and though he's not mad and he's living like a Christian, he doesn't feel like talking in the mornings. He doesn't feel cordial; he's not overflowing; he's not enthusiastic. But there's never a time when God isn't. Because what God is, He is perfectly. AOG040, 042-043

---

*Oh, Lord, may I believe in your goodness more intensely. Give
me a deep confidence that You are a gracious God and that Your
intentions are always benevolent. Amen.*

The Kindness of God

The LORD is gracious and righteous; our God is full
of compassion. The LORD protects the unwary;
when I was brought low, he saved me.
—PSALM 116:5–6

Satan's first attack upon the human race was his sly effort to destroy Eve's confidence in the kindness of God. Unfortunately for her and for us, he succeeded too well. From that day, men have had a false conception of God, and it is exactly this that has cut out from under them the ground of righteousness and driven them to reckless and destructive living. . . .

The God of the Pharisee was not a God easy to live with, so his religion became grim and hard and loveless. It had to be so, for our notion of God must always determine the quality of our religion. . . .

It is most important to our spiritual welfare that we hold in our minds always a right conception of God. If we think of Him as cold and exacting, we shall find it impossible to love Him, and our lives will be ridden with servile fear. If, again, we hold Him to be kind and understanding, our whole inner life will mirror that idea.

The truth is that God is the most winsome of all beings and His service one of unspeakable pleasure. . . .

The fellowship of God is delightful beyond all telling. ROR011-013

Lord, I've already seen much of Your majesty. How phenomenal
that You are also so gracious and kind, so winsome and delightful
in fellowship! I thank You. Amen.

Only God's Goodness

How priceless is your unfailing love, O God!
People take refuge in the shadow of your wings.
—PSALM 36:7

Why were we created? Was it that we deserved to be created? How can nothing deserve something? There was a time when there was no human race. How therefore could a human race that hadn't existed deserve something? How could a man that wasn't yet created earn anything or pile up any merit? It couldn't be so. God out of His goodness created us. Why were we not destroyed when we sinned? The only answer is that God, out of His goodness, spared us. The cordial, kind-intentioned God spared us.

Why would God the Eternal Son bleed for us? The answer is, out of His goodness and lovingkindness. "Therefore the children of men put their trust under the shadow of thy wings" (Ps. 36:7). Why would God forgive me when I've sinned and then forgive me again and again? Because God out of His goodness acts according to that goodness and does what His loving heart dictates that He do. AOG046

Loving Father, I bow today in humble dependence on Your goodness, undeserving as I am. Amen.

If My Account Were Closed Tomorrow

Praise the LORD, my soul; all my inmost being, praise his holy name. Praise the LORD, my soul, and forget not all his benefits.
—PSALM 103:1–2

Increasing knowledge of God's ways and works, especially His wise and tender treatment of His redeemed children, fills me with ever-mounting degrees of admiration and praise. It is becoming every day easier to understand experientially the hosannas and hallelujahs which make up such a large portion of the sacred Scriptures. They are the normal response of the heart to the manifold goodness of God, and it would, in fact, be hard to understand their omission if they were not found there.

While I have no doubt that the grace which has followed me since my boyhood will continue with me while I live on earth and for an eternity after, I have enjoyed already enough of God's benefits to supply me with matter for constant praise for at least a thousand years to come. If God were to close my account tomorrow and refuse any longer to honor me with His favors, the circumstances of His grace to me so far would require that I should still thank Him unceasingly with tears of honest gratitude. TET071-072

Lord, don't ever let me take for granted the many blessings You send my way. Give me a thankful heart today, and be pleased with my offering of praise. Amen.

The Sum of All Patience

Because the Lord disciplines the one he loves, and he chastens
everyone he accepts as his son.
—HEBREWS 12:6

How good it would be if we could learn that God is easy to live with. He remembers our frame and knows that we are dust. He may sometimes chasten us, it is true, but even this He does with a smile, the proud, tender smile of a Father who is bursting with pleasure over an imperfect but promising son who is coming every day to look more and more like the One whose child he is.

Some of us are religiously jumpy and self-conscious because we know that God sees our every thought and is acquainted with all our ways. We need not be. God is the sum of all patience and the essence of kindly good will. We please Him most, not by frantically trying to make ourselves good, but by throwing ourselves into His arms with all our imperfections, and believing that He understands everything and loves us still. ROR014

Thank You, Loving Father, for Your incredible patience. Help me indeed to look more and more like You each and every day. Amen.

God's Justice

And I heard the altar respond: "Yes, Lord God Almighty,
true and just are your judgments."
—REVELATION 16:7

Y ou sometimes hear it said, "Justice requires God to do this." I've probably used this expression myself, though it is semantically improper. The human language staggers when we try to use it to describe God. The prophets of the Old Testament and the apostles of the New put such pressure on language that words groan and squeak under the effort to tell the story. We must remember that justice is not something outside of God to which God must conform. Nothing ever requires God to do anything. If you have a god who is required to do anything, then you have a weak god who has to bow his neck to some yoke and yield himself to pressure from the outside. Then justice is bigger than God. But that is to think wrongly.

All God's reasons for doing anything lie inside of God. They do not lie outside of God to be brought to bear upon Him. They lie inside of God—that is, they are what God is. And God's reasons for doing what He does spring out of what God is. . . .

God is justice, and God will always act justly—not by compulsion from the outside but because that's the way He is Himself. Justice must always prevail because God is the sovereign God who will always prevail. AOG061-063

Lord, may we remember that You are not compelled to do anything, but that You will always be fair because You are justice itself. Amen.

Why Are We So Still?

All are justified freely by his grace through the redemption that
came by Christ Jesus.
—ROMANS 3:24

When God justifies a sinner, everything in God is on the sinner's side. All the attributes of God are on the sinner's side. It isn't that mercy is pleading for the sinner and justice is trying to beat him to death, as we preachers sometimes make it sound. All of God does all that God does. When God looks at a sinner and sees him there unatoned for (he won't accept the atonement; he thinks it doesn't apply to him), the moral situation is such that justice says he must die. And when God looks at the atoned-for sinner, who in faith knows he's atoned for and has accepted it, justice says he must live! The unjust sinner can no more go to heaven than the justified sinner can go to hell. Oh friends, why are we so still? Why are we so quiet? We ought to rejoice and thank God with all our might! AOG071

With all my might I praise You, gracious God, that I have been justified freely by Your grace in Christ Jesus. Why are we so still, indeed! Amen.

God Is Also Holy and Just

Your eyes are too pure to look on evil; you cannot tolerate wrongdoing.
—HABAKKUK 1:13

A lot of people have talked about the goodness of God and then gotten sentimental about it and said, "God is too good to punish anybody," and so they have ruled out hell. But the man who has an adequate conception of God will not only believe in the love of God, but also in the holiness of God. He will not only believe in the mercy of God, but also in the justice of God. And when you see the everlasting God in His holy, perfect union, when you see the One God acting in judgment, you know that the man who chooses evil must never dwell in the presence of this holy God.

But a lot of people have gone too far and have written books and poetry that gets everybody believing that God is so kind and loving and gentle. God is so kind that infinity won't measure it. And God is so loving that He is immeasurably loving. But God is also holy and just. AOG107

We praise You for your love and mercy, Lord, but may we never take lightly Your awesome holiness and Your fearful justice. Amen.

The Fear of God

The fear of the Lord is the beginning of wisdom, and knowledge
of the Holy One is understanding.
—PROVERBS 9:10

A truth fully taught in the Scriptures and verified in personal experience by countless numbers of holy men and women through the centuries might be condensed thus into a religious axiom: No one can know the true grace of God who has not first known the fear of God. . . .

We have but to read the Scriptures with our eyes open, and we can see this truth running like a strong cable from Genesis to Revelation. The presence of the divine always brought fear to the hearts of sinful men. . . .

I do not believe that any lasting good can come from religious activities that do not root in this quality of creature-fear. The animal in us is very strong and altogether self-confident. Until it has been defeated, God will not show Himself to the eyes of our faith. Until we have been gripped by that nameless terror which results when an unholy creature is suddenly confronted by that One who is the holiest of all, we are not likely to be much affected by the doctrine of love and grace as it is declared by the New Testament evangel. The love of God affects a carnal heart not at all; or if at all, then adversely, for the knowledge that God loves us may simply confirm us in our self-righteousness. ROR039-040

Lord, may I not see only Your love without the balance of Your awesome holiness. Grip me with holy fear, that I may truly experience Your grace. Amen.

The Wrath of God

The wrath of God is being revealed from heaven against all the
godlessness and wickedness of people, who suppress the truth
by their wickedness,
—ROMANS 1:18

There is a strong tendency among religious teachers these days to disassociate anger from the divine character and to defend God by explaining away the Scriptures that relate it to Him. This is understandable, but in the light of the full revelation of God it is inexcusable. . . .

Whatever is stated clearly but once in the Holy Scriptures may be accepted as sufficiently well established to invite the faith of all believers and when we discover that the Spirit speaks of the wrath of God about 300 times in the Bible, we may as well make up our minds either to accept the doctrine or reject the Scriptures outright. . . .

To understand God's wrath we must view it in the light of His holiness. God is holy and has made holiness to be the moral condition necessary to the health of His universe. . . .

Since God's first concern for His universe is its moral health, that is, its holiness, whatever is contrary to this is necessarily under His eternal displeasure. . . .

The holiness of God, the wrath of God, and the health of the creation are inseparably united. Not only is it right for God to display anger against sin, but I find it impossible to understand how He could do otherwise. MDP119-122

Lord, deal with me in grace as I fall before You in repentance and worship. Amen.

I Hate the Sin You Love

Lord, I have heard of your fame; I stand in awe of your deeds, Lord. Repeat them in our day, in our time make them known; in wrath remember mercy.
—HABAKKUK 3:2

God's wrath is His utter intolerance of whatever degrades and destroys. He hates iniquity as a mother hates the diphtheria or polio that would destroy the life of her child.

God's wrath is the antisepsis by which moral putrefaction is checked and the health of the creation maintained. When God warns of His impending wrath and exhorts men to repent and avoid it, He puts it in a language they can understand: He tells them to "flee from the wrath to come" (Luke 3:7). He says in effect, "Your life is evil, and because it is evil you are an enemy to the moral health of My creation. I must extirpate whatever would destroy the world I love. Turn from evil before I rise up in wrath against you. I love you, but I hate the sin you love. Separate yourself from your evil ways before I send judgment upon you."

"O LORD . . . in wrath remember mercy" (Hab. 3:2). MDP122

Lord, I'm grieved to see the evil in the world all around me. Help me to be a light today to lead someone away from Your wrath and into an experience of Your mercy. Amen.

Knowing God

This is eternal life: that they know you, the only true God,
and Jesus Christ, whom you have sent.
—JOHN 17:3

I might know all about the Prime Minister of Canada, but I don't know him—I've never met him. From what I hear and read and the speeches I've heard him make, I suppose he's a fine gentleman. If I were to live with him awhile—travel with him, eat with him, talk with him—I suppose I'd get to know him. But now I only know *about* him, that's all. I know about him—his age, background, etc.—but I don't know him.

And so, when we talk about the attributes of God, we're talking about His essential essence, of which He says, "I Am." But we're talking only about that which the intellect can grasp. Thank God, there are some things the intellect can know about God. And even though we can't know, except by the Holy Spirit, about God, yet the mind is never better employed than when it is seeking to know this great God Almighty.

And if even the imperfect knowledge that you and I can have of our Father which art in heaven raises us to such rapture, and satisfies so deeply the roots of our being, then what must it be in that day when we look on His face! What will it be in the day when we no longer depend upon our minds, but when, with pioneer eyes of our souls, we look without mediation upon the face of God Himself! Wonderful! It's good to get acquainted with God now so that at the end of time you won't be embarrassed in His presence. AOGII018-019

Father, help me not to be content with simply knowing about You,
and grant me the desire to know You more and more. Only in
knowing You relationally am I satisfied. Amen.

Infinite Mercy

But from everlasting to everlasting the LORD's love is with those who fear him, and his righteousness with their children's children.

—PSALM 103:17

There is an old story . . . about the Jewish rabbi centuries ago who consented to take a weary traveler into his house for a night's rest. After they had eaten together, the rabbi said, "You are a very old man, are you not?"

"Yes," the traveler replied, "I am almost a century old."

As they talked, the rabbi brought up the matter of religion and asked the visitor about his faith and about his relation to God.

"Oh, I do not believe in God," the aged man replied. "I am an atheist."

The rabbi was infuriated. He arose and opened the door and ordered the man from his house.

"I cannot keep an atheist in my house overnight," he reasoned. . . .

But then the voice of God said, "Son, I have endured him for almost 100 years—don't you think you could endure him for one night?"

ICH054-055

Lord, You have endured and continue to endure so much from Your creation. Your mercy is indeed from everlasting to everlasting. Amen.

A Boundless and Fathomless Flood

The LORD said, "I will cause all my goodness to pass in front
of you, and I will proclaim my name, the LORD, in your presence.
I will have mercy on whom I will have mercy.
—EXODUS 33:19

There has been a lot of careless teaching that implies that the Old Testament is a book of severity and law, and the New Testament is a book of tenderness and grace. But do you know that while both the Old Testament and the New Testament declare the mercy of God, the word mercy appears in the Old Testament over four times more often than in the New? . . .

God's infinite goodness is taught throughout the entire Bible. Goodness is that in God which desires the happiness of His creatures and that irresistible urge in God to bestow blessedness. The goodness of God takes pleasure in the pleasure of His people. I wish I could teach the children of God to know this. For a long time it has been drummed into us that if we are happy, God is worried about us. We believe He's never quite pleased if we are happy. But the strict, true teaching of the Word is that God takes pleasure in the pleasure of His people, provided His people take pleasure in God. . . .

"The mercy of God is an ocean divine, / A boundless and fathomless flood" (A. B. Simpson). Let us plunge out into the mercy of God and come to know it. AOG077-079, 095

Thank You, Lord, for your mercy, that out of Your goodness You delight in the happiness of Your children. Amen.

All Are Recipients

Because of the LORD's great love we are not consumed,
for his compassions never fail.
—LAMENTATIONS 3:22

All men are recipients of God's mercy. Don't think for a minute that when you repented and came back from the swine pen to the Father's house that mercy then began to operate. No, mercy had been operating all the time. . . . So, remember that if you hadn't had the mercy of God all the time, stooping in pity, withholding judgment, you'd have perished long ago. The cruel dictator is a recipient of the mercy of God. The wicked murderer is a recipient of the mercy of God. And the blackest heart that lies in the lowest wallow in the country is a recipient of the mercy of God. . . .

All men are recipients of the mercy of God, but God has postponed the execution, that is all. When the justice of God confronts human guilt, then there is a sentence of death, but the mercy of God—because that also is an attribute of God, not contradicting the other but working with it—postpones the execution.

Mercy cannot cancel judgment apart from atonement. When justice sees iniquity, there must be judgment. But mercy brought Christ to the cross. I don't claim to understand that. I'm so happy about the things I do know and so delightedly happy about things I don't know.

AOG085-087

Lord, when I realize how much we deserve Your judgment, I am once again in awe of Your great mercy. Thank You for the message of the cross. Amen.

Isaeah 40:28-31
Psalm 24:7-8
Exodus 9:13
Phillip. 3:20-21
Romans 1:16
I Cor. 2:2-5
Exodus 14:14
I Chron. 29:11
2 Chronicles 20:6
Job 26:14
Psalm 62:10-11
Psalm 147:4-5

APRIL 23

Leaning Toward Heresy

The Mighty One, God, the LORD, speaks and summons
the earth from the rising of the sun to where it sets.
—PSALM 50:1

When large numbers of adherents in the Christian churches come to believe that God is different from what He actually is, that concept becomes heresy of the most insidious and deadly kind!

When the Christian church surrenders her once lofty concept of God and substitutes for it ideas so low, so ignoble as to be utterly unworthy, her situation is tragic indeed. Into the life and the practices of the church comes a whole new philosophy, and the sense of the divine Presence and the majesty of God is no longer known.

Although "morality" is no longer a popular word in our world, it is apparent that such low and unworthy concepts of God's Person actually constitute a moral calamity for professed believers in great segments of Christianity. The records of both sacred and secular history show that low views of God will surely destroy the appeal of the Christian for all who hold them!

To all sinners, Jesus said, "You must be born again—from above!" (see John 3:3). He knew that the gods begotten in the shadowy thoughts of the fallen sons and daughters of Adam will quite naturally be no true likeness of the true and living God! MWTAPRIL10

---

*Dear Lord, prevent me from ever diminishing Your greatness.
I pray that You will reveal a glimpse of Your mighty power to all
those in the world who hold You in low esteem.*

Grace Abounds

The law was brought in so that the trespass might increase.
But where sin increased, grace increased all the more.
—ROMANS 5:20

Grace is God's goodness, the kindness of God's heart, the good will, the cordial benevolence. It is what God is like. God is like that all the time. You'll never run into a stratum in God that is hard. You'll always find God gracious, at all times and toward all peoples forever. You'll never run into any meanness in God, never any resentment or rancor or ill will, for there is none there. God has no ill will toward any being. God is a God of utter kindness and cordiality and good will and benevolence. And yet all of these work in perfect harmony with God's justice and God's judgment. I believe in hell and I believe in judgment. But I also believe that there are those whom God must reject because of their impenitence, yet there will be grace. God will still feel gracious toward all of His universe. He is God and He can't do anything else. . . .

What God is, God is! When Scripture says grace does "much more abound," it means not that grace does much more abound than anything else in God but much more than anything in us. No matter how much sin a man has done, literally and truly grace abounds unto that man. AOG103-105

Lord, I am so horribly rebellious and sinful in the light of Your perfect holiness. Thank You that where sin abounds, Your grace abounds even more! Amen.

Everybody Receives Grace

All of us have become like one who is unclean, and all our
righteous acts are like filthy rags; we all shrivel up like
a leaf, and like the wind our sins sweep us away.

—ISAIAH 64:6

Everybody receives in some degree God's grace: the lowest woman in the world; the most sinful, bloody man in the world; Judas; Hitler. If it hadn't been that God was gracious, they would have been cut off and slain, along with you and me and all the rest. I wonder if there's much difference in us sinners after all.

When a woman sweeps up a house, some of the dirt is black, some is gray, some is light-colored, but it is all dirt, and it all goes before the broom. And when God looks at humanity, He sees some that are morally light-colored, some that are morally dark, some that are morally speckled, but it is all dirt, and it all goes before the moral broom.

So the grace of God is operated toward everybody. But the saving grace of God is different. When the grace of God becomes operative through faith in Jesus Christ, then there is the new birth. But the grace of God nevertheless holds back any judgment that would come until God in His kindness has given everyone a chance to repent.

AOG102-103

---

*Lord, each one of Your children has sinned and deserves to be
swept away. Thank You for Your saving grace that reaches out
to all of us in our sinfulness. Amen.*

Lord, thank you for continuing to remind me and teach me of your amazing grace. Thank you for being all knowing of the things I'm not meant to ever understand. Amen.

Amazing Grace

In order that in the coming ages he might show the incomparable
riches of his grace, expressed in his kindness to us
in Christ Jesus.
—EPHESIANS 2:7

For us who stand under the disapproval of God, who by sin lie under sentence of God's eternal, everlasting displeasure and banishment, grace is an incomprehensibly immense and overwhelming plenitude of kindness and goodness. If we could only remember it, we wouldn't have to be played with and entertained so much. If we could only remember the grace of God toward us who have nothing but demerit, we would be overwhelmed by this incomprehensibly immense attribute, so vast, so huge, that nobody can ever grasp it or hope to understand it.

Would God have put up with us this long if He had only a limited amount of grace? If He had only a limited amount of anything, He wouldn't be God. . . .

God's immensity, God's infinitude must mean that the grace of God must always be immeasurably full. We sing "Amazing Grace"— why, of course it's amazing! How can we comprehend the fullness of the grace of God? AOG105-106

Lord, how amazing it is that Your grace extends infinitely beyond the depths of my sin. May I remember that as I go about my day. Amen.

That's Just the Way God Is

And the angels who did not keep their positions of authority
but abandoned their proper dwelling—these he has kept
in darkness, bound with everlasting chains for judgment
on the great Day.

—JUDE 6

There are two ways to think about the grace of God: One is to look at yourself and see how sinful you were and say, "God's grace must be vast—it must be huge as space to forgive such a sinner as I am." That's one way and that's a good way—and probably that's the most popular way.

But there's another way to think of the grace of God. Think of it as the way God is—God being like God. And when God shows grace to a sinner He isn't being dramatic; He's acting like God. He'll never act any other way but like God. On the other hand, when that man whom justice has condemned turns his back on the grace of God in Christ and refuses to allow himself to be rescued, then the time comes when God must judge the man. And when God judges the man, He acts like Himself in judging the man. When God shows love to the human race, He acts like Himself. When God shows judgment to "the angels which kept not their first estate" (Jude 6), He acts like Himself.

Always God acts in conformity with the fullness of His own wholly perfect, symmetrical nature. AOG106

---

*Father, I'm thankful that You always act like Yourself—
with grace and justice. Your constancy produces great peace
within me. Amen.*

Near to Everything and Everyone

But will God really dwell on earth? The heavens, even the highest heaven, cannot contain you. How much less this temple I have built!

—1 KINGS 8:27

I want to explain briefly what omnipresence is and then show what it means in human experience. That God is omnipresent is of course believed by all churches who believe in the Bible. I am not introducing anything new. Omnipresence means that God is all-present. God is close to (for that is what the word means—"close to, near to, here") everywhere. He is near to everything and everyone. He is here; He is next to you wherever you may be. And if you send up the furious question, "Oh God, where art Thou?" the answer comes back, "I am where you are; I am here; I am next to you; I am close to everywhere." That's what the Bible says. . . .

We talk about God being close to us or about the problem of God being far away. We don't think right because we think geographically or astronomically; we think in light-years or meters or inches or miles or leagues. We're thinking of Him as dwelling in space, which He does not. Rather He contains space so that space is in God. There is never any problem about God being anywhere, for the fact is, as the texts say, God is everywhere. AOG118, 120

Lord, help me to take this truth out of the realm of theological concept and to realize the practical implication, today, of Your being right here with me. Amen.

But God Seems Remote

They are darkened in their understanding and separated from
the life of God because of the ignorance that is in them due
to the hardening of their hearts.

—EPHESIANS 4:18

The reason we sense that God is remote is because there is a dissimilarity between moral characters. God and man are dissimilar now. God made man in His image, but man sinned and became unlike God in his moral nature. And because he is unlike God, communion is broken. Two enemies may hate each other and be separated and apart even though they are for a moment forced to be together. There is an alienation there—and that is exactly what the Bible calls that moral incompatibility between God and man.

God is not far away in distance, but He seems to be because He is far away in character. He is unlike man because man has sinned and God is holy. The Bible has a word for this moral incompatibility, this spiritual unlikeness between man and God—alienation. AOG123

*Thank You, gracious Father, that You have provided the remedy
for the alienation between You and Your children. Thank You for
the blood of Jesus, whereby our blindness can be lifted and we
can be brought near to You. Amen.*

The Perfections of God

Ascribe to the LORD the glory due his name; worship the LORD
in the splendor of his holiness.
—PSALM 29:2

I hope that if I am remembered at all, it will be for this reason: I have spent my efforts and my energies trying to turn the direction of the people away from the external elements of religion to those that are internal and spiritual.

I have tried to take away some of the clouds in the hope that men and women would be able to view God in His glory. I would like to see this sense of glory recaptured throughout the church—too many Christians do not expect to experience any of the glory until they see Him face-to-face!

Within our Christian fellowship and worship, we must recapture the Bible concepts of the perfection of our God Most High! We have lost the sense and the wonder of His awe-fullness, His perfection, His beauty.

Oh, I feel that we should preach it, sing it, write about it, talk about it, and tell it until we have recaptured the concept of the Majesty of God!

Only that can be beautiful ultimately which is holy—and we who belong to Jesus Christ should know the true delight of worshiping God in the beauty of His holiness! MWTDecember31

Dear Lord, I pray for Your church, that it will be biblically faithful, Christ-centered, and fruitful in proclaiming Your majesty. Amen.

MAY

Sharing God's Nature

Through these he has given us his very great and precious
promises, so that through them you may participate in the
divine nature.

—2 PETER 1:4

O ur heavenly Father disciplines us for our own good, "that we
might be partakers of his holiness" (Heb. 12:10). God's motives
are always loving!

I have known people who seemed to be terrified by God's loving desire that we should reflect His own holiness and goodness. As
God's faithful children, we should be attracted to holiness, for holiness is Godlikeness—likeness to God!

God encourages every Christian believer to follow after holiness.
We know who we are and we know who God is. He does not ask us
to be God, and He does not ask us to produce the holiness that only
He Himself knows. Only God is holy absolutely: All other beings can
be holy only in relative degrees.

Actually, it is amazing and wonderful that God should promise
us the privilege of sharing in His nature. He remembers we were
made of dust. So He tells us what is in His being as He thinks of us:
"It is My desire that you grow in grace and in the knowledge of Me. I
want you to be more like Jesus, My eternal Son, every day you live!"

MWTFebruary2

---

*Lord, thank You for allowing us to share in Your divine nature.
I want to become even more like You, but I need Your Spirit's
help and encouragement.*

Divine Immanence

When Jacob awoke from his sleep, he thought, "Surely
the LORD is in this place, and I was not aware of it."
—GENESIS 28:16

What does the divine immanence mean in direct Christian
experience? It means simply that God is here. Wherever we
are, God is here. . . . There can be no place where He is not. . . .

Jacob had never been for one small division of a moment outside
the circle of that all-pervading Presence. But he knew it not. That
was his trouble, and it is ours. Men do not know that God is here.
What a difference it would make if they knew. . . .

Always, everywhere God is present, and always He seeks to discover Himself to each one. He would reveal not only that He is, but
what He is as well. He did not have to be persuaded to reveal Himself
to Moses. "And the LORD descended in the cloud, and stood with
him there, and proclaimed the name of the LORD" (Ex. 34:5). He
not only made a verbal proclamation of His nature but He revealed
His very Self to Moses so that the skin of Moses' face shone with the
supernatural light. It will be a great moment for some of us when we
begin to believe that God's promise of self-revelation is literally true,
that He promised much, but no more than He intends to fulfill.

Our pursuit of God is successful just because He is forever seeking to manifest Himself to us. POG058, 060-061

---

*Lord, You are indeed in this place, even when I am unaware
of You. I pray that I might know the reality of that truth and be
sensitive to Your presence today. Amen.*

Near or Far Away

But as for me, it is good to be near God. I have made the Sovereign LORD my refuge; I will tell of all your deeds.
—PSALM 73:28

To speak of being near to or far from God is to use language in a sense always understood when applied to our ordinary human relationships. A man may say, "I feel that my son is coming nearer to me as he gets older," and yet that son has lived by his father's side since he was born and has never been away from home more than a day or so in his entire life. What then can the father mean? Obviously he is speaking of experience. He means that the boy is coming to know him more intimately and with deeper understanding, that the barriers of thought and feeling between the two are disappearing, that father and son are becoming more closely united in mind and heart.

So when we sing, "Draw me nearer, nearer, nearer, blessed Lord," we are not thinking of the nearness of place, but of the nearness of relationship. It is for increasing degrees of awareness that we pray, for a more perfect consciousness of the divine Presence. We need never shout across the spaces to an absent God. He is nearer than our own soul, closer than our most secret thoughts. POG061-062

Lord, I long to be near to You in experience, in intimate awareness of our Father/child relationship. Draw me close, I pray. Amen.

God's Holiness

Who among the gods is like you, LORD? Who is like you—majestic in holiness, awesome in glory, working wonders?
—EXODUS 15:11

They say that when Leonardo DaVinci painted his famous Last Supper he had little difficulty with any of it except the faces. Then he painted the faces in without too much trouble except one. He did not feel himself worthy to paint the face of Jesus. He held off and kept holding off, unwilling to approach it but knowing he must. Then in the impulsive carelessness of despair, he just painted it quickly and let it go. "There is no use," he said. "I can't paint Him."

I feel very much the same way about explaining the holiness of God. I think that same sense of despair is on my heart. There isn't any use for anybody to try to explain holiness. The greatest speakers on this subject can play their oratorical harps, but it sounds tinny and unreal, and when they are through you've listened to music but haven't seen God.

I suppose the hardest thing about God to comprehend intellectually is His infinitude. But you can talk about the infinitude of God and not feel yourself a worm. But when you talk about the holiness of God, you have not only the problem of an intellectual grasp, but also a sense of personal vileness, which is almost too much to bear.

AOG157-158

Make me that sensitive to Your holiness, O God, that I might indeed be aware of my vileness and fall before You in humility and confession. Amen.

Language is Inadequate

"Do not come any closer," God said. "Take off your sandals,
for the place where you are standing is holy ground."
—EXODUS 3:5

I will endeavor to discuss the holiness of God, the Holy One. We cannot comprehend it, and we certainly cannot define it.

Holiness means purity, but "purity" doesn't describe it well enough. Purity merely means that it is unmixed, with nothing else in it. But that isn't enough. We talk of moral excellency, but that isn't adequate. To be morally excellent is to exceed someone else in moral character. But when we say that God is morally excellent, who is it that He exceeds? The angels, the seraphim? Surely He does—but that still isn't enough. We mean rectitude; we mean honor; we mean truth and righteousness; we mean all of these—uncreated and eternal. . . .

Language cannot express the holy, so God resorts to association and suggestion. He cannot say it outright because He would have to use words for which we know no meaning. . . .

He shows Moses at the burning bush before the holy, fiery Presence, kneeling down to take his shoes from his feet, hiding his face, for he was afraid to look upon God. AOG159-160

---

*Lord, I don't often stop to contemplate the reality of Your
holiness. Give me a glimpse of Your holiness today, even if
I have to hide my face in fear. Amen.*

Exalted Worship

Above him were seraphim. . . . They were calling to one another:
Holy, holy, holy, is the Lord Almighty; the whole earth is full
of his glory.
—ISAIAH 6:2–3

Now, because we are dealing with worship, let us consider the joys and delights of the heavenly creatures, the seraphim, around the throne of God. . . .

We know very little about these created beings, but I am impressed by their attitude of exalted worship. They are close to the throne, and they burn with rapturous love for the Godhead. They were engrossed in their antiphonal chants, "Holy, holy, holy!". . .

The key words then and the keynote still of our worship must be "Holy, holy, holy!"

I am finding that many Christians are really not comfortable with the holy attributes of God. In such cases I am forced to wonder about the quality of the worship they try to offer to Him.

The word "holy" is more than an adjective saying that God is a holy God—it is an ecstatic ascription of glory to the triune God.

WHT071-072

---

*Lord, I come before You this day and cry with the seraphim,
"Holy, holy, holy, is the Lord of hosts." May I always approach You
with such an attitude of worship. Amen.*

Struck with Awe

"Woe to me!" I cried. "I am ruined! For I am a man of unclean
lips, and I live among a people of unclean lips, and my eyes have
seen the King, the LORD Almighty."
—ISAIAH 6:5

It should help us to be concerned about the quality of our worship
when we consider that Isaiah's reaction was a feeling of absolute
profaneness in the presence of the moral purity of the divine Being.
Consider that Isaiah was a commendable young man—cultured, religious and a cousin of the king. He would have made a good deacon in
any church. Today he would be asked to serve on one of our mission
boards.

But here Isaiah was an astonished man. He was struck with awe,
his whole world suddenly dissolving into a vast, eternal brightness. He
was pinned against that brightness—red and black, the colors of sin.

What had happened? Isaiah, only human, had glimpsed One
whose character and nature signaled perfection. He could only manage the witness: "Mine eyes have seen the King." WHT072-073

*Lord, how can I help but fall on my face before You if I once get
a glimpse of Your great glory? Forgive my sinfullness as I fall
before You in worship. Amen.*

The Beauty of the Lord

One thing I ask from the LORD, this only do I seek: that I may dwell in the house of the LORD all the days of my life, to gaze on the beauty of the LORD and to seek him in his temple.
—PSALM 27:4

What does perfection mean? According to Webster, perfection means "the highest possible degree of excellence." That which is perfect lacks nothing it should have and has nothing it should not have. Perfection is fullness and completeness. Something that is perfect is not lacking in anything and doesn't have anything it shouldn't have. . . .

When we apply perfection to God, we mean that He has unqualified fullness and completeness of whatever He has. He has unqualified plenitude of power. He also has unqualified fullness of wisdom. He has unqualified knowledge. He has unqualified holiness.

When I say that a man is a perfect singer, I qualify that in my mind. I think, Well, he does the best a person can. But when I say that God is holy, I do not qualify it. I mean it fully and completely. God is what He is and that's it. God's power and being, His wisdom and knowledge, His holiness and goodness, His justice and mercy, His love and grace—all of these and more of the attributes of God— are in shining, full, uncreated perfection. They are called the beauty of the Lord our God. AOG182-183, 186

Lord, Your beauty is overwhelming in its perfection, and I wonder why we would ever want to look at anything else! Amen.

God Is an Artist!

So the Israelites did everything the LORD commanded Moses;
that is the way they encamped under their standards, and that is
the way they set out, each of them with their clan and family.
—NUMBERS 2:34

I remember as a young Christian when I got my first awful, wonderful, entrancing vision of God. I was in West Virginia in the woods, sitting on a log reading the Scriptures along with an old Irish evangelist by the name of Robert J. Cunningham, now long in heaven. I got up and wandered away to have prayer by myself. I had been reading one of the driest passages imaginable from the Scriptures where Israel came out of Egypt and God arranged them into a diamond-shaped camp. He put Levi in the middle and Reuben out in front and Benjamin behind. It was a diamond-shaped moving city with a flame of fire in the middle giving light. Suddenly it broke over me; God is a geometrician. He's an artist! When He laid out that city He laid it out skillfully, diamond-shaped with a plume in the middle, and it suddenly swept over me like a wave of the sea: how beautiful God is and how artistic and how poetic and how musical, and I worshiped God there under that tree all by myself. WMJ023-024

Lord, You've displayed Your artistry and poetry throughout all of Your great creation. Help us not to miss the beauty around us and in doing so miss such an important aspect of Your person. Amen.

The Uncreated One

How many are your works, Lord! In wisdom you made them
all; the earth is full of your creatures.
—PSALM 104:24

You may find this hard to believe, but God is just as far above an archangel as he is above a caterpillar. You know what a caterpillar is—it's a little worm the size of your finger, with a fur coat. And of course, it's not a very high-class thing. It's never been out in society. It doesn't amount to much—it's just a worm. And you have to watch it very carefully to know whether it's traveling west or east, because it looks the same all the way around. That's a caterpillar.

An archangel, on the other hand, is that holy creature that we see beside the sea of God, in the presence of God's throne. That mighty creature is a little higher than the angels, just as man was made for a time a little lower. That being can look upon the face of God with unveiled countenance. This is the archangel. It never was in sin, and no one knows how vast it might be. And yet God is just as far above that archangel as He is above the caterpillar.

Why? Because both the archangel and the caterpillar are creatures. And God is the uncreated One who had no beginning, the self-existent One who was never created, but who was simply God, who made all things. AOGII036-037

Lord, how awesome it is that You are infinitely far above me and yet You love me! I worship Your majesty and rest in Your love. Amen.

God Has No Origin

In the beginning you laid the foundations of the earth,
and the heavens are the work of your hands.
—PSALM 102:25

God is self-existent selfhood. Novation the church father said, "God has no origin." Just those four words, "God has no origin," would be an education to the average person. Origin, you see, is a creature word. Everything came from somewhere. One of the questions that every child asks is, "Where did I come from?" . . .

Everything has an origin. When you hear a bird sing, you know that once that bird was packed in a tiny little egg. It came from somewhere; it came from an egg. Where did the egg come from? It came from another little bird. And that bird came from another little egg, and that egg came from another bird, and so on, back, back, back to the heart of God, when God said, "Let the heavens bring forth, let the earth bring forth, let the dry land appear," as it says in Genesis 1.

Origin is a creature word. The trees had an origin, space had an origin, the mountains, the seas—all things have an origin. But when you come back to God, you come back to the One who has no origin. He is the Cause of all things, the uncaused Cause. AOGII021

I worship You today, Lord, as the great Creator, the uncaused
Cause behind my very existence. Amen.

God Is Sovereign

So that in all things God may be praised through Jesus Christ.
To him be the glory and the power for ever and ever.
—1 PETER 4:11

Basic beliefs about the Person and the nature of God have changed so much that there are among us now men and women who find it easy to brag about the benefits they receive from God—without ever a thought or a desire to know the true meaning of worship!

I have immediate reactions to such an extreme misunderstanding of the true nature of a holy and sovereign God, for I believe that the very last thing God desires is to have shallow-minded and worldly Christians bragging about Him.

Beyond that, it does not seem to be very well recognized that God's highest desire is that every one of His believing children should so love and so adore Him that we are continually in His presence, in spirit and in truth.

Something wonderful and miraculous and life changing takes place within the human soul when Jesus Christ is invited in to take His rightful place. That is what God anticipated when He wrought the plan of salvation. He intended to make worshipers out of rebels; to restore the place of worship which our first parents knew when they were created! MWTMay25

Lord, today I want to give You first place in my life all over again. It's all about You, Lord. You deserve all my worship.

In the Hands of God

And he is not served by human hands, as if he needed anything.
Rather, he himself gives everyone life and breath
and everything else.
—ACTS 17:25

Love is the principle of good will. The angels sang, "Good will toward men" (Luke 2:14). Love always wills the good of its object and never wills any harm to its object. If you love somebody, really love him, you'll want to be good to him and to do good to him. You'll never want any harm to come to him if you can help it. That's why John says, "There is no fear in love; but perfect love casteth out fear" (1 John 4:18). If I know a man loves me, I'm not afraid of him. If I'm not sure he does, I may be a bit cagey around him. Love casts out fear, for when we know we are loved, we are not afraid. Whoever has God's perfect love, fear is gone out of the universe for him . . .

I'm in the hands of God. And I appeal, not to delegates or any other human, but to the most high God. God is my friend through Jesus Christ, and He wants me to prosper. Therefore, I'm not afraid; I put myself in His hands without fear. Love casts out fear. Love is the principle of good will, and God wants to be our friend. AOGII199,201

Lord, You don't need me, yet You love me and choose me to be Your child. I don't deserve it, but I accept and thank You for Your gracious gift of life and love. Amen.

Toward the Mark

Forgetting what is behind and straining toward what is ahead,
I press on toward the goal to win the prize for which God has
called me heavenward in Christ Jesus.
—PHILIPPIANS 3:13–14

It is one of the devil's oldest tricks to discourage Christian believers by causing them to look back at what they once were. It is indeed the enemy of our souls who makes us forget that we are never at the end of God's love.

No one will make progress with God until the eyes are lifted to the faithfulness of God and we stop looking at ourselves!

Our instructions in the New Testament all add up to the necessity of looking forward in faith—and not spending our time looking back or just looking within.

Brethren, our Lord is more than able to take care of our past. He pardons instantly and forgives completely, and his blood makes us worthy!

The goodness of God is infinitely more wonderful than we will ever be able to comprehend. If the "root of the matter" is in you and you are born again, God is prepared to start with you where you are!

MWTOctober4

Thank You, Lord, that we can never reach the end of Your love for us. Your love, like all Your attributes, is never-ending.

Divine Transcendence

Yours, LORD, is the greatness and the power and the glory
and the majesty and the splendor, for everything in heaven and
earth is yours. Yours, LORD, is the kingdom; you are exalted
as head over all.

—1 CHRONICLES 29:11

The term divine transcendence may sound like something that takes a lot of learning, or at least a lot of profound thinking to understand, but it doesn't. Transcend simply means to go above, to rise above, to be above. Of course, it's very difficult to think of God as transcendent and also as immanent or omnipresent at the same time. It is difficult to understand how He can be here with us, in us, pervading all things, but at the same time transcending all things. It looks like a contradiction, but as with many other apparent contradictions, it's not at all contradictory; the two thoughts are entirely in accord with each other.

God is always nearer than you may imagine Him to be. God is so near that your thoughts are not as near as God; your breath is not as near as God; your very soul is not as near to you as God is. And yet, because He is God, His uncreated Being is so far above us that no thought can conceive it nor words express it. . . .

There is a vast gulf between the great I AM and all created things. God's uncreated quality of life causes Him to be transcendent, to rise high above all creatures. AOGII034, 037

---

*Lord, how awesome that You can be above all and yet so close.
I am Your humble servant; may I act according to Your will
today. Amen.*

God Is Far Above

"For my thoughts are not your thoughts, neither are your ways
my ways," declares the Lord. "As the heavens are higher than
the earth, so are my ways higher than your ways
and my thoughts than your thoughts."
—ISAIAH 55:8–9

I want to make it very clear that when I say "far above," I do not mean geographically or astronomically removed. It's an analogy. Because we are human beings and live in this world, we learn to speak by analogy. . . .

So when we say that God is far above, we're using an analogy. We're thinking about a star that's way above, way out yonder in space—but that isn't what we really mean when we think about the transcendent God.

If you miss this point, you might as well stop reading, because this is critical to understanding what follows. When we say that God's transcendence is "farness above," we are not thinking about astronomical distances or physical magnitude. God never thinks about the size of anything, because God contains everything. He never thinks about distance, because God is everywhere. He doesn't have to go from one place to another, so distance doesn't mean anything to Him. We humans use these expressions to help us to think—they're analogies and illustrations. AOGII034-035

Lord, even our human expressions of Your greatness amaze me.
How much more wonderful must You be in all Your infinite
glory! Amen.

That Cross!

Come to me, all you who are weary and burdened, and I will give you rest. Take my yoke upon you and learn from me, for I am gentle and humble in heart, and you will find rest for your souls.
—MATTHEW 11:28–29

Saint Theresa, that dear woman of God, said that the closer we are to God, the more conscious we are of how bad we are. Oh, the paradox, the mystery, the wonder of knowing that God, that transcendent One who is so high above all others that there is a gulf fixed that no one can cross, condescends to come and dwell among us. The God who is on the other side of that vast gap one day came and condensed Himself into the womb of the virgin, was born and walked among us. The baby that tramped around on the floor of Joseph's carpenter shop, that got in the way and played with the shavings, was the great God so infinitely lifted up and so transcendent that the archangels gazed upon Him. There He was! . . .

A great gulf lies between me and the transcendent God, who is so high I cannot think of Him, so lofty that I cannot speak of Him, before whom I must fall down in trembling fear and adoration. I can't climb up to Him; I can't soar in any man-made vehicle to Him. I can't pray my way up to Him. There is only one way: "Near, near thee, my son, is that old wayside cross." And the cross bridges the gulf that separates God from man. That cross! AOGII048-049

Thank You, Father, for the miracle of the cross, the marvelous bridge that allows me to have fellowship with You. Amen.

The Eternity of God

For this is what the high and exalted One says—he who lives
forever, whose name is holy: "I live in a high and holy place,
but also with the one who is contrite and lowly in spirit, to revive
the spirit of the lowly and to revive the heart of the contrite."
—ISAIAH 57:15

If I thought that the word "eternal" as referring to God meant only "lasting until the end of the age," I'd just fold my Bible up and go home and wait for the end. If I had a God that only lasted so long, that didn't have eternity in His heart, I couldn't possibly find it worthwhile to preach. . . .

The Old Testament Hebrew has exhausted itself—wrung its language as you wring a towel, to get the last drop of meaning out of it—to say that God is forever and ever endlessly, unto perpetuity, world without end. The New Testament Greek has done the same. There aren't any other words in the Greek language that can be used to mean "unto perpetuity, having no end, going on and on and on and on endlessly and forever." . . .

Eternal, everlasting, forever, unto perpetuity, world without end— all of those words mean just what they say. When God talks about Himself, that's what He means—the High and Lofty One who exists eternally, forever, unto perpetuity, world without end. AOGII053-055

*Lord, I bow today before the high and lofty One who far surpasses
my comprehension. Holy is the Lord! Amen.*

There You Have God

LORD, you have been our dwelling place throughout all
generations. Before the mountains were born or you brought
forth the whole world, from everlasting to everlasting
you are God.
—PSALM 90:1–2

Shake your head to get all the wheels going and try to stretch your mind all you can, then think, if you can, about the past. Think your hometown out of existence. Think back to when there wasn't anything here but some Indians. Then go back and think all those Indians away, back to before the Indians got here. Go back before that and think away the North American continent. And then think away all this earth of ours. And then let's go back and think that there are no planets and no stars dotting the clear night sky; they have all vanished away and there is no Milky Way, no anything.

Go to the throne of God and think away the angels, the archangels, the seraphim and the cherubim that sing and worship before the throne of God. Think them all away until there is no creation: not an angel waves its wing, not a bird flies in the sky—there's no sky to fly in. Not a tree grows on a mountain, there is no mountain for a tree to grow on. But God lives and loves alone. The Ancient of Days, world without end, to the vanishing point back as far as the human mind can go—there you have God. AOGII055-056

*Lord, before the foundation of the world, You knew me and chose
me to be Your child. I praise You today. Amen.*

God Was, That's All!

Your throne was established long ago; you are from all eternity.
—PSALM 93:2

God never began to be. I want you to kick that word "began" around a little bit in your mind and think about it. "In the beginning God created the heaven and the earth" (Gen. 1:1), but God Himself never began to be! "Began" is a word that doesn't affect God at all. There are many concepts and ideas that don't touch God at all, such as the concept of beginning or creation, when God spoke and things began to be. "In the beginning God created"—but before the beginning, there wasn't any "beginning"; there wasn't any "before"! The old theologians used to say that eternity is a circle. Round and round the circle we go, but back before there was any circle, God was!

God didn't begin to be—God was. God didn't start out from somewhere—God just is. . . .

But there never was a time when God was not! No one said, "Let God be"! Otherwise, the one who said "Let God be" would have to be God. And the one about whom He said "Let him be" wouldn't be God at all, but a secondary "god" who wouldn't be worth our trouble. God, back there in the beginning, created. God was, that's all! AOGII057-058

Lord, You are beyond my comprehension and worthy of my praise.
Thou art from everlasting, the great I AM. Amen.

An Everlasting Now

But you remain the same, and your years will never end.
—PSALM 102:27

Time cannot apply to God. C.S. Lewis gave us an illustration which I'd like to pass on to you. If you can, think of eternity, of infinitude, as a pure white sheet of paper extending infinitely in all directions. Then think about a man taking a pencil and drawing a line, one inch long, on that infinitely extended sheet of paper. And that little line is time. It begins and it moves an inch and ends. It begins on the paper and it ends on the paper. So time began in God and will end in God. And it doesn't affect God at all. God dwells in an everlasting now. . . .

You and I are creatures of time and change. It is in "now" and "was" and "will be" and "yesterday" and "today" and "tomorrow" that we live. That's why we get nervous breakdowns, because we're always just one jump ahead of the clock. We get up in the morning, look at the clock and let out a gasp of dismay. We rush for the bathroom, brush our teeth, tear downstairs for breakfast, eat a half-cooked egg and rush out to catch the commuter bus. That's time, you see—time is after us! But God Almighty sits in His eternal now. And all the time that ever was is only a tiny mark upon the infinitely extended bosom of eternity. AOGII058

No beginning, no ending, no time limitations, no start, no finish.
I am so small, Lord, and yet You care for me. Thank You, Loving
Father. Amen.

God Is Here; God Is Now

Teach us to number our days, that we may gain a heart of wisdom.
—PSALM 90:12

It is a wonderful thought that God has already lived all of our tomorrows. God has no yesterdays and no tomorrows. The Scriptures say, "Jesus Christ the same yesterday, and to day, and for ever" (Heb. 13:8), but it's not His yesterday—it's yours and mine. Jesus Christ the Lord is the One who came out of Bethlehem, out of Judea, whose goings forth have been even from everlasting. He can't have yesterdays and tomorrows, because yesterday is time and tomorrow is time, but God surrounds it all and God has already lived tomorrow. The great God who was present at the beginning when He said, "Let there be" and there was, is also now present at the end, when the worlds are on fire and all creation has dissolved and gone back into chaos—and only God and His redeemed saints remain. Remember that God has already lived our tomorrows. . . .

The Scripture says in Psalm 90:12 that because God is eternal, we must learn "to number our days, that we may apply our hearts unto wisdom." God is in our today because God was in our yesterday and will be in our tomorrow. God is! And because God is, then God is here and God is now. God dwells in an everlasting and eternal now.

AOGII059-060

Lord, You are eternal, but I am of now. Teach me to number my time-oriented days, so I might use them wisely. Amen.

Omnipotent and Almighty

Then I heard what sounded like a great multitude, like the roar of
rushing waters and like loud peals of thunder, shouting: "Halle-
lujah! For our Lord God Almighty reigns."
—REVELATION 19:6

I suppose the first thing to do would be to define omnipotence. It
comes, of course, from omni, meaning "all," and potent, meaning
"able to do and to have power." And so omnipotent means "able to
do all and to have all power." It means having all the potency there is.

Then we come to a second word, Almighty. Now, that means
exactly the same thing as omnipotent. Almighty means "having an
infinite and absolute plenitude of power." When you use the words infinite and absolute, you can only be talking about one person—God.

There is only one infinite Being, because infinite means without
limit. And it is impossible that there should be two beings in the
universe without limit. So if there is only one, you are referring to
God. Even philosophy and human reason, as little as I think of them,
have to admit this. . . .

God has power and whatever God has is without limit; therefore,
God is omnipotent. God is absolute and whatever touches God or
whatever God touches is absolute; therefore, God's power is infinite.
God is Almighty. AOGII072, 074

*What assurance to know I rest in the arms of an all-powerful
God. Alleluia, for the Lord God omnipotent reigns! Amen.*

The Source of All Power

Sovereign LORD, you have begun to show to your servant your greatness and your strong hand. For what god is there in heaven or on earth who can do the deeds and mighty works you do?
—DEUTERONOMY 3:24

God is the source of all the power there is. There isn't any power anywhere that doesn't have God as its source, whether it be the power of the intellect, of the spirit, of the soul, of dynamite, of the storm, or of magnetic attraction. Wherever there is any power at all, God is the author of it. And the source of anything has to be greater than that which flows out of it.

If you pour a quart of milk out of a can, that can has to be equal to or greater than a quart. The can has to be as big as or bigger than that which comes out of it. The can may contain several gallons, though you may pour out only a quart. The source has to be as big or bigger than that which comes out of it. So if all the power there is came from God—all the power—therefore, God's power must be equal to or greater than all the power there is. AOGII074-075

Lord, why do we worry and fear so much when we are the dear children of the One who has such power? Strengthen me today with the promise of Your power. Amen.

He'll Hold You Up

For no word from God will ever fail.
—LUKE 1:37

I cannot for the life of me see any reason in the world why anyone should be fearful and timid, saying, "I'm afraid I can't make it; I'm afraid God can't keep me." God can keep the stars in their courses and the planets in their orbits; God can keep all His vast display of might everywhere throughout His universe. Surely God can keep you!

It's like a fly perched on a seat in an airplane, moaning and trembling for fear that the plane can't carry its weight. That plane weighs several tons and it has several tons of people and baggage on it. That fly is so light that it's impossible, outside of a laboratory, to even weigh the little guy. And yet we can imagine him sitting there, flapping his little wings and saying, "I'm just afraid this plane won't hold me up!"

The great God Almighty stretches forth His broad wings and moves upon the wind. God will hold you up. He'll keep you if you turn yourself over to Him! He'll hold you when nothing else can; nothing will be able to destroy you. AOGII076

Lord, I'm reminded of the words of Psalm 3:5: "I laid me down and slept; I awaked; for the LORD sustained me." I'll rest calmly in Your power today. Amen.

Too Hard for God?

I am the LORD, the God of all mankind. Is anything too hard
for me?
—JEREMIAH 32:27

What does it mean to us, that God Almighty has all the power there is? It means that since God has the ability always to do anything He wills to do, then nothing is harder or easier with God. "Hard" and "easy" can't apply to God because God has all the power there is. Hard or easy applies to me. . . .

God, who has all the power there is, can make a sun and a star and a galaxy as easily as He can lift a robin off a nest. God can do anything as easily as He can do anything else.

This truth applies specifically to the area of our unbelief. We hesitate to ask God to do "hard" things because we figure that God can't do them. But if they are "easy" things, we ask God to do them. If we have a headache we say, "Oh God, heal my headache." But if we have a heart condition, we don't ask the Lord about that, because that's "too hard" for the Lord! What a shame! Nothing is hard for God— nothing whatsoever. Nothing! In all God's wisdom and power He is able to do anything as easily as He is able to do anything else. AOGII084

---

*Lord, no matter where You lead me today or what circumstances
come my way, I rest in the knowledge that there is no such thing
as "hard" or "easy" with You. Amen.*

I Change Not

I the Lord do not change. So you, the descendants of Jacob,
are not destroyed.
—MALACHI 3:6

To announce that you're going to speak on the immutability of God is almost like putting up a sign saying, "There'll be no service here tonight!" Nobody wants to hear anybody talk about it, I suppose. But when it's explained, you'll find you've struck gold and diamonds, milk and honey.

Now the word immutable, of course, is the negative of mutable. And mutable is from the Latin, meaning "subject to change." Mutation is a word we often use to mean "a change in form, nature or substance." Immutability, then, means "not subject to change." . . .

Now there is in God no mutation possible. As it says in James, "with whom is no variableness, neither shadow of turning" (1:17)—there is no variation due to change. And there is also that verse in Malachi: "I am the LORD, I change not" (3:6). . . .

Incidentally, He's the only One in the universe that can say that. And He did say it! He simply says that He never changes, that there is no change possible in God. God never differs from Himself. If you get ahold of this, it can be to you an anchor in the storm, a hiding place in danger. There is no possibility of changing in God. And God never differs from Himself. AOGII089-091

Thank You, Father, that despite my ever-changing world You are ever constant, my anchor in the storm. Amen.

Arms Wide Open

This brother of yours was dead and is alive again; he was lost and is found.
—LUKE 15:32

Those of every race and color around the world that have come back all come back in Christ. And they've all come back in the person of that prodigal.

Do you know what they found the Father to be like? They found He hadn't changed at all, in spite of the insults, wrongs and his neighbors pitying him, saying, "Oh, isn't it terrible the way that boy treated his poor old dad?" His father was humiliated and shamed and sorry and grieved and heartbroken, but when the boy came back, he hadn't changed at all.

Jesus was saying to us, "You went away in Adam, but you're coming back in Christ. And when you come back you'll find the Father hasn't changed. He's the same Father that He was when you all went out, every man to his own way. But when you come back in Jesus Christ you'll find Him exactly the same as you left Him—unchanged." And the Father ran and threw His arms around him and welcomed him and put a robe and a ring on him and said, "This my son was dead, and is alive again" (15:24). This is the grace of God. Isn't it worth believing in, preaching, teaching, singing about while the world stands?
AOG114–115

There is a wonderful stability in this truth, Lord, that You welcome sinners into Your arms. Thank You for Your mercy and grace. Amen.

Eternally Unchanging

Because God wanted to make the unchanging nature of his
purpose very clear to the heirs of what was promised, he con-
firmed it with an oath. God did this so that, by two unchangeable
things in which it is impossible for God to lie, we who have fled to
take hold of the hope set before us may be greatly encouraged.
—HEBREWS 6:17–18

The perfect and the absolute and the infinite God cannot become
anything else but what He is. . . .

If you remember that, it will help you in the hour of trial. It will
help you at the time of death, in the resurrection, and in the world
to come to know that all that God ever was, God still is. All that God
was and is, God ever will be. His nature and attributes are eternally
unchanging. I have preached about the uncreated selfhood of God;
I'll never have to change or edit it in any way. I go back over some
of my old sermons and articles, and I wonder why I wrote them like
that. I could improve them now. But I can't improve on the statement that God is always the same—He is self-sufficient, self-existent,
eternal, omnipresent, and immutable. There would be no reason to
change that because God changes not. His nature, His attributes, are
eternally unchanging. AOGII096, 099

---

*Thank You, Lord, for the strong consolation and hope that
is based upon the immutability of Your counsel and the
unchangeableness of Your nature. Amen.*

He Knows Everything

Nothing in all creation is hidden from God's sight. Everything
is uncovered and laid bare before the eyes of him to whom we
must give account.
—HEBREWS 4:13

God's understanding is limitless . . . His knowledge is perfect, and . . . there isn't a creature anywhere in the universe that isn't plainly visible to His sight. Nothing is shut before the eyes of God. That is what is called divine omniscience, one of the attributes of God. An attribute, as I have said before, is something which God has declared to be true about Himself.

God has declared by divine revelation that He is omniscient, that He knows everything. The human mind staggers under this truth when we consider how much there is to know and how little we know. . . .

When I received one of the honorary degrees that have been bestowed on me, I said, "The only thing that is learned about me is this pair of glasses." If a man has his hair slicked back and a pair of learned-looking glasses, they call him a doctor. We don't know very much, really, and when we consider the great God who knows all there is to know with perfection of knowledge, we stagger under that. The weight of the truth is too much for our minds. AOGII105-106

*I stagger and am challenged, but I take comfort in knowing that
You know all things. I rest in Your perfect knowledge today. Amen.*

God Already Knows!

You have searched me, LORD, and you know me. . . .
You discern my going out and my lying down;
you are familiar with all my ways.
—PSALM 139:1, 3

In the same way, God, in one effortless act, knows instantly (not a little at a time, but instantly and perfectly) all things that can be known. That's why I say that God cannot learn. As I said before, if we realized that God couldn't learn, we could shorten our prayers quite a bit and step up their power. There is no reason to tell God things that He knew before you were born!

God knows the end from the beginning, and He knew it long before it happened. Long before your parents met, God knew what you would be doing at this very moment. Before your grandparents met, before England was a nation, or the Roman Empire dissolved, or the Roman Empire was formed, God knew all about us. He knew everything about us—every hair on our head, our weight, our name, our past. And He knew it before we were born.

He knew it before Adam was. And when Adam walked in the garden with God, God knew all about Adam, all about Eve, all about their sons, all about the human race. God never gets astonished, astounded, or surprised because He already knows. You can walk down the street, turn the corner, and get the surprise of your life. But God never turned the corner and got surprised, for the simple reason that God was already around that corner before He turned it. God already knew before He found out! God knows all things. AOGII113-114

*Lord, I'm thankful that with You there are no surprises, nothing
You don't know ahead of time. Thank You. Amen.*

What a Great Consolation!

What more can David say to you? For you know your servant,
Sovereign LORD.
—2 SAMUEL 7:20

It is a great consolation to me that God knows instantly, effort-lessly, and perfectly all matter and all matters . . . all causes and all relations, all effects and all desires, all mysteries and all enigmas, all things unknown and hidden. There are no mysteries to God. . . .

I'm not worried about these satellites they're shooting around the earth. I'm not worried about Kruschev [former leader of the Soviet Union] or any of the rest of those fellows over there with names you can't pronounce. Because God's running His world, and He knows all about it. He knows where these men will die, He knows where they will be buried, and He knows when they'll be buried. God knows all hidden things, "dwelling in the light which no man can approach unto" (1 Tim. 6:16).

And He also knows His people. You who have fled for refuge to Him, Jesus Christ the Lord, He knows you, and you're never an or-phan. A Christian is never lost, though he may think he is. The Lord knows where he is. The Lord knows all about him. He knows about his health and knows about his business. Isn't it a consolation to you that our Father knows it all? AOGIII 16-117

Yes, Father, it is a huge consolation to me that You know all there is to know. I rest in that comfort today. Amen.

God Knows

Cast all your anxiety on him because he cares for you.
—1 PETER 5:7

It's nice to sit down and talk things over with God. The Psalms are full of that, as well as the history of the saints. It's good to talk to God, even though we are talking to God about things He already knows. But this idea of giving God a lecture, I never did believe very much in it. . . .

If there was anything God could learn, it would mean that God didn't know it before. If He didn't know it before, then He didn't know everything. And if He didn't know everything, He wouldn't be perfect, and if He isn't perfect then He isn't God. The God who can learn anything is not God. God already knows all that can be learned, all there is to know, and He knows it instantly and perfectly and without strain or self-consciousness. He knows it all. That's what Paul meant in Romans 11:33–36:

O the depth of the riches both of the wisdom and knowledge of God! how unsearchable are his judgments, and his ways past finding out! For who hath known the mind of the Lord? or who hath been his counselor? Or who hath first given to him, and it shall be recompensed unto him again? For of him, and through him, and to him, are all things: to whom be glory for ever. Amen. AOGII123-124

Lord, as David said, "such knowledge is too wonderful for me" (Ps. 139:6). Thank You for Your intimate knowledge and Your infinite care. Amen.

Flawless Precision

With all wisdom and understanding, he made known to us
the mystery of his will according to his good pleasure,
which he purposed in Christ.
—EPHESIANS 1:8–9

What is wisdom? It is the skill to achieve the most perfect ends by the most perfect means. Both the means and the ends have to be worthy of God. Wisdom is the ability to see the end from the beginning, to see everything in proper relation and in full focus. It is to judge in view of final and ultimate ends and to work toward those ends with flawless precision.

God Almighty must be flawlessly precise. God doesn't bumble. The British used to say of themselves, "We muddled through," meaning they got through somehow, playing it by ear, hoping for the best and taking advantage of situations. They've done it well for the last thousand years. That's the way we have to do it, but God never works that way. If God worked that way, it would prove that God didn't know any more than we did about things. But God works with flawless precision because God sees the end from the beginning, and He never needs to back up. AOGII130

Thank You, Lord, that You don't have to muddle through and hope for the best. Thank You for the flawless precision with which You work. Amen.

The Mysterious Ways of the Omniscient One

Yes, Father, for this is what you were pleased to do.
—MATTHEW 11:26

A determination to know what cannot be known always works harm to the Christian heart.

Ignorance in matters on our human level is never to be excused if there has been opportunity to correct it. But there are matters which are obviously "too high for us." These we should meet in trusting faith and say as Jesus said, "Even so, Father: for so it seemed good in thy sight." . . .

Human curiosity and pride often combine to drive us to try to understand acts of God which are plainly outside the field of human understanding. We dislike to admit that we do not know what is going on, so we torture our minds trying to fathom the mysterious ways of the Omniscient One. It's hard to conceive of a more fruitless task. . . .

Under such circumstances the Christian thing to do is to say, "That thou mightest be justified when thou speakest, and be clear when thou judgest. . . . Even so, Father: for so it seemed good in thy sight" (Ps. 51:4; Matt. 11:26). A blind confidence which trusts without seeing is far dearer to God than any fancied knowledge that can explain everything. . . .

To the adoring heart, the best and most satisfying explanation for anything always will be, "It seemed good in thy sight." NCA057-058

Lord, whatever comes my way today, I'll accept it gratefully, for I'll know it is good in Your eyes. Amen.

Wisdom and Goodness

By wisdom the LORD laid the earth's foundations,
by understanding he set the heavens in place.
—PROVERBS 3:19

It tells us in Proverbs 3:19 and Jeremiah 10:12 that the Lord founded the earth, established and stretched out the heavens by wisdom, understanding, and discretion. Those are two of many verses in the Bible that tell us about the wisdom of God. . . .

It is necessary to our humanity that we grant God two things at least: wisdom and goodness. The God who sits on high, who made the heaven and the earth, has got to be wise, or else you and I cannot be sure of anything. He's got to be good, or earth would be a hell and heaven a hell, and hell a heaven. We have to grant goodness and wisdom to God, or we have no place to go, no rock to stand on, no way to do any thinking or reasoning or believing. We must believe in the goodness and in the wisdom of God, or we betray that in us which differentiates us from the beasts—the image of God Himself.

So we begin with the assumption—not a guess, not a hope, but a knowledge—that God is wise. AOGII124-125

Lord, I do believe and will place my confidence in the fact that You are both infinitely wise and infinitely good. What need I fear? Amen.

God's Wisdom or Yours

We all, like sheep, have gone astray, each of us has turned
to our own way.
—ISAIAH 53:6

A ll that you and I have lived for, hoped for, and dreamed over in our heart of hearts—life, safety, happiness, heaven, immortality, the presence of God—hinges on whether you're going to accept the ultimate wisdom of the triune God, as revealed in the Scriptures and in His providential working in mankind. Or are you going to go your own way?

The most perfect definition of sin that I know of is given by Isaiah in 53:6: "All we like sheep have gone astray; we have turned every one to his own way." Turning to our own way is the essence of sin. I turn to my way because I think it is wiser than God's way. . . .

This is the crux of our life. This is the difference between revival and a dead church. This is the difference between a Spirit-filled life and a self-filled life. Who's running it? Who's the boss? Whose wisdom is prevailing—the wisdom of God or the wisdom of man?

AOGII135-136

---

*Lord, how foolish I am when I trust in my own limited knowledge
instead of Your infinite wisdom. Take over and be the Boss
today. Amen.*

Let Me Run This Thing!

To God belong wisdom and power; counsel and understanding
are his.

—JOB 12:13

Once I got on a flight out of New York and as we started off, it was terribly windy. But when we were in that turbulence, I didn't jump up and run into the cockpit and say to the pilots, "Now listen, boys, let me take over." Do you know where we'd have been if I'd have taken over? We'd have been nose down in Times Square. I didn't take over; I let the pilots have the controls.

I don't mind a little turbulence when we're landing or taking off, but when we're flying up there at 17,000 feet and the "fasten your seat belt" sign comes on, I say to myself, "Uh-oh—what are we in for now?" But I have always kept my head, and I've never gone forward to the cockpit and said, "Now, you two fellows get out of here"—never.

And yet we're doing that to God all the time. We go to church and we pray to give our heart to the Lord; we join the church and get baptized. But then things get turbulent and we run and say, "Lord, let me run this thing!" That's why we're so messed up in our Christian lives. We're not ready to let God run our world for us—to run our family, our business, our home, our job, our everything. AOGII137-138

Lord, no matter how turbulent my life may get, I commit here and now to letting You keep the controls. Amen.

Anything He Wills to Do

Acknowledge and take to heart this day that the LORD is God
in heaven above and on the earth below. There is no other.
—DEUTERONOMY 4:39

To say that God is sovereign is to say that He is supreme over all things, that there is no one above Him, that He is absolute Lord over creation. It is to say that His Lordship over creation means that there is nothing out of His control, nothing that God hasn't foreseen and planned. . . .

God's sovereignty logically implies His absolute freedom to do all that He wills to do. God's sovereignty does not mean that He can do anything, but it means He can do anything that He wills to do. The sovereignty of God and the will of God are bound up together. The sovereignty of God does not mean that God can lie, for God does not will to lie. God is truth and therefore God cannot lie, for He wills not to lie. God cannot break a promise, because to break a promise would be to violate His nature, and God does not will to violate His nature.

Therefore it is silly to say that God can do anything. But it is scriptural to say that God can do anything He wills to do. God is absolutely free—no one can compel Him, no one can hinder Him, no one can stop Him. God has freedom to do as He pleases—always, everywhere, and forever. AOGII144-145

God in heaven above and on the earth beneath, I wilingly give
You my life; take it and sovereignly do whatever You will to do
with it. Amen.

Authority and Power

All the peoples of the earth are regarded as nothing. He does as he pleases with the powers of heaven and the peoples of the earth. No one can hold back his hand.
—DANIEL 4:35

The sovereignty of God involves all authority and all power. I think you can see instantly that God could never be sovereign without the power to bring about His will or the authority to exercise His power. Kings, presidents, and others who rule over men must have the authority to govern and the power to make good on that authority. A ruler cannot stand up and say, "Do this, please; if you feel like doing it, do it." He says, "Do it," and then has an army and a police force behind him. He has authority to command and power to carry out his commands. And God has to have both of these.

I can't conceive of a God who has power and no authority. Samson was a man who had power but no authority, and didn't know what to do with it. There are men who have authority but no power. Authority without the power to carry out that authority is a joke. Power without authority puts a man where he can't do anything. But God Almighty, to be sovereign, must have authority and power. AOGII146

Lord, though the forces of evil often seem to have control of this chaotic world, I will rest in Your authority and power. My hope is in You. Amen.

Free Will Versus Sovereignty

But if serving the LORD seems undesirable to you, then choose
for yourselves this day whom you will serve. . . . But as for me
and my household, we will serve the LORD.
—JOSHUA 24:15

The matter of man's free will versus God's sovereignty can be explained in this way: God's sovereignty means that He is in control of everything, that He planned everything from the beginning. Man's free will means that he can, anytime he wants, make most any choice he pleases (within his human limitations, of course). Man's free will can apparently defy the purposes of God and will against the will of God. Now how do we resolve this seeming contradiction? . . .

Here is what I see: God Almighty is sovereign, free to do as He pleases. Among the things He is pleased to do is give me freedom to do what I please. And when I do what I please, I am fulfilling the will of God, not controverting it, for God in His sovereignty has sovereignly given me freedom to make a free choice.

Even if the choice I make is not the one God would have made for me, His sovereignty is fulfilled in my making the choice. And I can make the choice because the great sovereign God, who is completely free, said to me, "In my sovereign freedom I bestow a little bit of freedom on you. Now 'choose you this day whom ye will serve' (Josh. 24:15)." AOGII149-150

*May I use my free will wisely, Lord, and choose wisely whom I will
serve. May I be in complete submission to Your will. Amen.*

No Accidents with God

Which of all these does not know that the hand of the LORD
has done this? In his hand is the life of every creature
and the breath of all mankind.

—JOB 12:9–10

There are also no accidents in God's eyes, because God's wisdom prevents an accident. You may be driving down the highway at forty miles an hour. A tire blows and you turn over in the ditch. Somebody didn't make that tire quite right, and it didn't hang together. But God Almighty's wisdom never has a blowout. God Almighty knows what He's doing; He's utterly wise and there can be no accident. . . .

Who can countermand an order given by the great God Almighty? When the Sovereign God says it shall be this way, it's that way and nobody can change it!

Some may wonder if God might fail because of weakness. But the omnipotent God couldn't be weak, because God has all the power there is. H-bombs, cobalt bombs, A-bombs, and all the rest of them—they are nothing! They are the marbles God plays with. God, in His infinite strength, wisdom, authority, and power, is having His way in the whirlwind and the storm. That's what sovereignty means. AOGIII171-172

Because with You there are no unforeseen circumstances,
Lord, I'll leave my prayer time in complete peace. Because
with You there are no accidents, I'll meet this day with bold
confidence. Amen.

We Can Afford to Be Calm

That is why I am suffering as I am. Yet this is no cause for shame, because I know whom I have believed, and am convinced that he is able to guard what I have entrusted to him until that day.
—2 TIMOTHY 1:12

For the warmth of his heart the Christian has the love of God which is "shed abroad" by the Holy Ghost, while from his vantage point in the "heavenly places," he is able to look down calmly upon the excited happenings of men. In his flesh he may be a part of the human scene, but in his spirit he is far above it all and is never at any time too much moved by what he sees.

From the Word of God he learns the direction things are going and is thus able in God to see the end from the beginning and call the things that are not as though they were.

The life of the Christian is bound up in the sovereignty of God, i.e., His full ability to carry out His plans to their triumphant conclusion. Since he is a part of God's eternal purpose, he knows he must win at last, and he can afford to be calm even when the battle seems to be temporarily going against him.

The world has no such "blissful center" upon which to rest and is therefore constantly shifting about, greatly elated today, terribly cast down tomorrow and wildly excited the next day. TET041-042

Lord, thank You for the assurance that You are in control. In turbulent times, in uncertain days, and in difficult circumstances, I will rest in You. Amen.

His Eternal Purpose

The LORD is my shepherd, I lack nothing. He makes me lie down
in green pastures, he leads me beside quiet waters.
—PSALM 23:1–2

God's sovereignty means that if there's anybody in this wide
world of sinful men that should be restful and peaceful in an
hour like this, it should be Christians. We should not be under the
burden of apprehension and worry because we are the children of a
God who is always free to do as He pleases. There is not one rope or
chain or hindrance upon Him because He is absolutely sovereign.

God is free to carry out His eternal purposes to their conclusions.
I have believed this since I first became a Christian. I had good
teachers who taught me this, and I have believed it with increasing
joy ever since. God does not play by ear, or doodle, or follow whatever happens to come into His mind, or let one idea suggest another.
God works according to the plans which He purposed in Christ Jesus
before Adam walked in the garden, before the sun, moon, and stars
were made. God, who has lived all our tomorrows and carries time in
His bosom, is carrying out His eternal purposes. AOGII145

*Forgive me for my worry, Father. I know I can be at peace when
I have such a calm Shepherd, a sovereign God working out His
eternal purpose in my life. Amen.*

God Our Servant?

By myself I have sworn, my mouth has uttered in all integrity
a word that will not be revoked: Before me every knee will bow;
by me every tongue will swear.
—ISAIAH 45:23

I can empathize with those troubled beings who lie awake at night worrying about the possible destruction of the race through some evil, misguided use of the world's store of nuclear weapons. The tragedy is that they have lost all sense of the sovereignty of God! I, too, would not sleep well if I could not trust moment by moment in God's sovereignty and omnipotence and in His grace, mercy and faithfulness. . . .

Revelation describes the age-ending heavenly and earthly events when our Lord and Savior is universally acknowledged to be King of kings and Lord of lords. All will acclaim Him victor. God's Revelation leaves us with no doubt about that.

In our present period of time, however, there is little recognition of God's sovereignty or of His plan for His redeemed people. Go into the marketplace, into our educational institutions and—yes—even into our popular religious circles, and you will find a growing tendency to make mankind large and to make God small. Human society is now taking it for granted that if God indeed exists, He has become our servant, meekly waiting upon us for our will. JIV014-016

Lord, I long for the day when every knee will bow and every tongue will swear allegiance to You. Come, take the throne You so rightly deserve. Amen.

True to Himself

I will sing of the LORD's great love forever; with my mouth I will
make your faithfulness known through all generations.
—PSALM 89:1

Faithfulness is that in God which guarantees that He will never
be or act inconsistent with Himself. You can put that down as an
axiom. It is good for you now and good for you when you're dying. It
will be good to remember as you rise from the dead and good for all
the eons and millenniums to come. God will never cease to be what
He is and who He is. Everything God says or does must be in accord
with His faithfulness. He will always be true to Himself, to His works
and to His creation. . . .

Now that may sound a little dry, but if you get that inside of you
and build on it, you'll be glad you know it the next time you're in
a tough circumstance. You can live on froth and bubbles and little
wisps of badly understood theology—until the pressure is on. And
when the pressure is on, you'll want to know what kind of God
you're serving.

This is the kind of God you're serving: All that God says or does
must accord with all of His attributes, including His attribute of
faithfulness. Every thought that God thinks, every word that God
speaks, every act of God must accord with His faithfulness, wisdom,
goodness, justice, holiness, love, truth, and all His other attributes.

AOGII164-165

*The next time I'm in tough circumstances, Lord, I will trust Your
faithfulness, for I know that's the kind of God I serve! Amen.*

You Can Count on That!

If we are faithless, he remains faithful, for he cannot disown himself.
—2 TIMOTHY 2:13

God says in the Psalms that "He hath remembered his covenant for ever, the word which he commanded to a thousand generations" (Ps. 105:8). And our Lord said, "Till heaven and earth pass, one jot or one tittle shall in no wise pass from the law, till all be fulfilled" (Matt. 5:18). You can count on that.

That is the fact before us: God is faithful! He will remain faithful because He cannot change. He is perfectly faithful because God is never partly anything. God is perfectly all that He is and never partly what He is. You can be sure that God will always be faithful. This faithful God, who never broke a promise and never violated a covenant, who never said one thing and meant another, who never overlooked anything or forgot anything, is the Father of our Lord Jesus and the God of the gospel. This is the God we adore and the God we preach. AOGII169-170

Oh, Lord, You are indeed perfectly faithful because that is what You are. Thank You, Father, for the kind of God You are. Amen.

Faithful to Condemn

But because of your stubbornness and your unrepentant heart,
you are storing up wrath against yourself for the day of God's
wrath, when his righteous judgment will be revealed.

—ROMANS 2:5

Let us now look at God's faithfulness in its application. As it applies to sinners, if you are lost and you know it, God has declared that He will banish from His presence all who love sin and reject His Son. God has promised that; He has declared that; He has warned and threatened, and it will be so. Let no one trust a desperate hope, for it is based on the belief that God threatens but doesn't fulfill. No, God waits that He may be gracious! And He will sometimes postpone in order to give us another thirty days, another sixty days, to make up our minds. But just as sure as the mills of God grind, the souls of men fall into them and are ground exceedingly small. God moves slowly and is very patient, but God has promised that He will banish from His presence all who love sin, who reject His Son and refuse to believe.

That is the message for the sinner who won't come, who loves his sin. AOGII170

---

*Lord, help me do my part to warn unrepentant sinners that "it is
a fearful thing to fall into the hands of the living God" (Heb. 10:31)
and that our sentence has been postponed only because we have
a merciful God. Amen.*

Faithful to Forgive

If we confess our sins, he is faithful and just and will forgive us our sins and purify us from all unrighteousness.

—1 JOHN 1:9

Frances Havergal said that she came to a spot where she believed that the Lord meant exactly what He said. When He said, "If we confess our sins, he is faithful and just to forgive us our sins, and to cleanse us from all unrighteousness" (1 John 1:9), she found out that the Lord meant exactly what He said.

Why don't you start reading your Bible with the thought that God meant exactly what He said there? . . .

When you read your Bible, instead of wondering about it, say to yourself, "God wrote this and God is faithful; God cannot lie." For example, read 1 John 1:7:

> But if we walk in the light, as he is in the light, we have fellow-ship one with another, and the blood of Jesus Christ his Son cleanseth us from all sin.

That's a heartening and wonderful truth, if you are a Christian who may have sinned. AOGII172-173

Thank You, Lord, that what You have spoken in Your Word, You truly meant—especially about Your much-needed forgiveness of our sin! Amen.

Faithful to the Tempted

No temptation has overtaken you except what is common
to mankind. And God is faithful; he will not let you be tempted
beyond what you can bear. But when you are tempted, he will
also provide a way out so that you can endure it.
—1 CORINTHIANS 10:13

God is also faithful to the tempted. First Corinthians 10:13 tells us,

> There hath no temptation taken you but such as is common to
> man: but God is faithful, who will not suffer you to be tempted
> above that ye are able; but will with the temptation also make
> a way to escape, that ye may be able to bear it.

The faithfulness of God is operating to deliver us also from the
temptations that bother us.

Some poor, suffering Christians say, "I feel all boxed in, as if there
was a wall all around me." Someone has pointed out that when you
can't escape to the right, the left, forward, or backward, you can always go up. God's faithfulness is the way out because it's the way up.
You can be sure of that. Your temptation is common to everybody. If
you're on the borderline of the victorious life and you say, "Under the
circumstances in which I live, I just can't make it," remember God
says your temptation is common to all. AOGII174-175

Lord, this promise is a major source of encouragement to me.
Thank You for this reminder of Your faithfulness. Amen.

Faithful to the Discouraged

The one who calls you is faithful, and he will do it.
—1 THESSALONIANS 5:24

Then there's the discouraged person. "Faithful is he that calleth you, who also will do it" (1 Thess. 5:24). You may have been serving God quite a while, but instead of getting better, you feel you're getting worse. You know what's happening to you? You're getting to know yourself better! There was a time when you didn't know who you were, and you thought you were pretty fine. Then, by the good grace of God, He showed you yourself—and it was shocking and disappointing to you. But don't be discouraged, because He is faithful that calls you, and He will also do it. God will finish the job. . . .

God sometimes makes us wait. He made the disciples wait in Jerusalem for the Holy Spirit (Acts 1:4), and He may make you wait. But remember, God is faithful who called you, and He also will do it. This is our faithful God. I recommend to you that you withdraw your hope from a changing, treacherous, and false world and put your trust in Jesus Christ. He is faithful, who also will do it. AOGII178-179

God, continue to accomplish that work You began in my life. Even when I feel discouraged, I will rest in the promise of Your faithfulness. Amen.

God's Eccentricity

Greater love has no one than this: to lay down one's life
for one's friends.
—JOHN 15:13

Now, what is our great encouragement in view of all that we know about ourselves? It is the fact that God loves us without measure, and He is so keenly interested in our spiritual growth and progress that He stands by in faithfulness to teach and instruct and discipline us as His dear children!

I once wrote something about how God loves us and how dear we are to Him. I wasn't sure I should put it down on paper, but God knew what I meant. I said, "The only eccentricity that I can discover in the heart of God is that a God such as He is should love sinners such as we are!" God has that strange eccentricity but it still does not answer our wondering question, "Why did God love us?" . . .

You can put all of your confidence in God. He is not angry with you, His dear child! He is not waiting to pounce on you in judgment— He knows that we are dust, and He is loving and patient toward us.

If it were true that the Lord would put the Christian on the shelf every time he failed and blundered and did something wrong, I would have been a piece of statuary by this time! I know God, and He isn't that kind of God. ITB125-126

Thank You, Father, that in Your eccentricity You loved me enough to lay down Your life for me, to forgive my failures and call me Your child. Amen.

Comprehending the Incomprehensible

Whoever does not love does not know God, because God is love.
—1 JOHN 4:8

The love of God is the hardest of all His attributes to speak about. You may not understand God's love for us. I don't know that I do myself. We are trying to comprehend the incomprehensible. It is like trying to take the ocean in your arms, or embrace the atmosphere, or rise to the stars. No one can do it, so I suppose I must do the best I can and trust the Holy Spirit to make up for human lack. . . .

When it says, "God is love," it means that love is an essential attribute of God's being. It means that in God is the summation of all love, so that all love comes from God. And it means that God's love, we might say, conditions all of His other attributes, so that God can do nothing except He does it in love. . . .

What we mean when we say, "God is love," is what we mean when we say of a man, "He is kindness itself." We don't mean that kindness and the man are equated and identical, but we mean the man is so kind that kindness is all over him and conditions everything he does. So when we say, "God is love," we mean that God's love is such that it permeates His essential being and conditions all that He does. Nothing God ever does, or ever did, or ever will do, is done separate from the love of God. AOGII182-183

Loving Father, I can't comprehend Your love, but I revel in it. I fall to my knees in worship. Amen.

God So Loved the World

This is love: not that we loved God, but that he loved us and sent
his Son as an atoning sacrifice for our sins.
—1 JOHN 4:10

God is love, so His loving is not something He may do or not do
at His will. Loving us is not an intermittent act or series of acts
which God does in between other acts. His love flows steadily out
upon the whole human race in an unbroken and continuous fullness. There is not a time, not a fraction of time, when God's love is
not active toward us. It is as constant as the being of God, for it is the
being of God in unforced, normal expression. . . .

We are often tempted to wonder how God could love us, but honest as this feeling is, it is nevertheless the result of a wrong way of
looking at things. God does not love us because we are hard or easy to
love; He loves us because He is God, not because we are good or bad
or more attractive or less so. God's love is not drawn out of Him by its
object; it flows out from God in a steady stream because He is love.

"God so loved the world," not because the world was lovable but
because God is love. Christ did not die for us that God might love us;
He died for us because God already loved us from everlasting. Love
is not the result of redemption; it is the cause of it. NCA107-108

---

*Father, I'm so glad You didn't look for something lovable within
me before deciding to redeem me. While I was yet a sinner,
You loved me and chose me. You gave me the gift of life.
I praise You. Amen.*

Love Casts Out Fear

There is no fear in love. But perfect love drives out fear.
—1 JOHN 4:18

L ove always wills the good of its object and never wills any harm to its object. If you love somebody, really love him, you'll want to be good to him and to do good to him. You'll never want any harm to come to him if you can help it. If I know a man loves me, I'm not afraid of him. If I'm not sure he does, I may be a bit cagey around him. Love casts out fear, for when we know we are loved, we are not afraid. Whoever has God's perfect love, fear is gone out of the universe for him.

All real fear goes when we know that God loves us, because fear comes when we're in the hands of someone who does not will our good. A little boy lost in a department store will stand in a paroxysm of hysterical fear; people's faces are strange, even those who want to be kind. The child is afraid that he may be in the hands of somebody who wills him harm. But when he sees the familiar face of his mother, he runs sobbing to her and climbs into her arms. He's never afraid in the hands of his mother, because experience has taught him that Mother wills his good. Perfect loves casts out his fear. When the mother is not there, fear fills the little child's heart, but Mother's kind, smiling, eager face drives out fear. AOGII184-185

Lord, help me to really know Your love for me, that any fear I may have will disappear. Thank You for Your peace which surpasses comprehension. Amen.

Divine Nearness

Surely your goodness and love will follow me all the days of my life, and I will dwell in the house of the LORD forever.

—PSALM 23:6

I believe that most Christians do suffer from a sense of divine remoteness. They know God is with them, and they're sure they're God's children. They can take you to their marked New Testament and prove to you seriously and soberly that they're justified and regenerated, that they belong to God, that heaven is going to be their home, and that Christ is their Advocate above. They've got the theology; they know all this in their head, but they're suffering from a sense of remoteness.

To know something in your head is one thing; to feel it in your heart is another. And I think most Christians are trying to be happy without having a sense of the Presence. It's like trying to have a bright day without having the sun. . . .

The yearning to be near to God and have God come nearer to us is universal among born-again Christians. And yet we think of God as coming from across distance to us, when the Bible and Christian theology, all the way back to David, declare that God is already here—now. God doesn't dwell in space, and therefore God doesn't have to come like a ray of light from some remote place. AOG142-144

Almighty God, forgive me for my lack of yearning to be near You, and increase my desire to dwell in Your presence. Amen.

The Greatness of God's Love

But God demonstrates his own love for us in this: While we were
still sinners, Christ died for us.
—ROMANS 5:8

If I were to try to talk about the greatness of love. I would only run in
circles, because I can't speak of that which cannot be spoken of. But
to break it down a little, this love of God is an attribute of God, which
means it is eternal, immutable, and infinite. It never began to be and it
can never end; it can never change and there is no boundary to it. . . .

Every time God thinks about you, He thinks about you lovingly.
Even if He must chastise you, or allow hardships to come to you, it
is love that allows it to come and love that sends it. And we never
should be afraid of love, because love casts out fear. . . .

The best preservative in the world is the love of God. Some people
believe in the security of the saints from theological grounds. They
take it from a text somewhere. I believe in the security of the saints
because God is love, and God always keeps that which He loves. We
always keep what we love—always. . . .

He loves us so that no creature—neither seraphim nor cherubim
nor archangel nor principality nor power nor all of them added together in all the vast universe of God—can ever hope to know how
overpassingly great is the love of God, and how tenderly, how sweetly,
and how much He loves us. AOGII194-195, 198

Lord, I can't even comprehend the immensity of Your love for me.
May I be aware of all the expressions of Your love that I encounter
as I go about my day. Amen.

The Creator of All

The heavens declare the glory of God; the skies proclaim
the work of his hands.

—PSALM 19:1

Reading my Bible, I am greatly impressed by the manner in which godly men of old revealed in their writings an intense love for every natural beauty around them. They saw nature as the handiwork of an all-powerful and all-glorious Creator!

The Old Testament is a marvelous rhapsody on the creation. Start with Moses, and when you get beyond the Levitical order, you will find him soaring in his acute consciousness of the presence of God in all creation.

Go to the book of Job. In the closing section you will be amazed at the sublimity of the language describing the world around us. Then go to the Psalms, with David literally dancing with ecstatic delight as he gazes out upon the wonders of God's world. Go to Isaiah, where imagery is neither fanciful nor flighty but a presentation of the wonders of creation.

In our generation, how rarely we get into a situation where we can feel the impulses of nature communicated to us. We seldom have time to lift our eyes to look at God's heaven—except when we are wondering if we should wear our boots! MWTJULY10

---

*Dear heavenly Father, You have created a beautiful world.
Continue to reveal Your power and presence through Your majestic
creation to those who doubt Your existence. Amen.*

Infinite God

But will God really dwell on earth? The heavens, even the
highest heaven, cannot contain you. How much less this temple
I have built!

—1 KINGS 8:27

We can always measure things. We know how big the sun is, how big the moon is, how much the earth weighs, how much the sun and other heavenly bodies weigh. We know approximately how much water is in the ocean. It seems boundless to us, but we know how deep it is and we can measure it, so it really isn't boundless at all. There is nothing boundless but God and nothing infinite but God. God is self-existent and absolute; everything else is contingent and relative. There is nothing very big and nothing very wise and nothing very wonderful. It's all relatively so. It is only God who knows no degrees. . . .

God doesn't extend into space; God contains space. C. S. Lewis said that if you could think of a sheet of paper infinitely extended in all directions, and if you took a pencil and made a line one inch long on it, that would be time. When you started to push your pencil, it was the beginning of time, and when you lifted it off the paper, it was the end of time. And all around, infinitely extended in all directions, is God. That's a good illustration. AOG005

Holy Father, You are infinite, incapable of being contained or comprehended. I submit myself to You, knowing that nothing and no one compares to You. Amen.

God's Hidden Wisdom

The secret things belong to the LORD our God, but the things revealed belong to us and to our children forever, that we may follow all the words of this law.
—DEUTERONOMY 29:29

Notice that when God did His most awful, majestic works, He always did them in the darkness. . . . When God incarnated His Son, bringing Him into the world as a man, He did not send Him down out of heaven, shining like a meteor to startle the world. He formed Him in the sweet darkness of the virgin's womb, unseen by mortal eye. . . . It was as if God were saying, "In My infinite wisdom, I am incarnating My eternal Word in the form of a Man, and no one will see My mystery." And they never did!

And when He was nailed on the cross, hanging there twisting and writhing in death for you and me, darkness settled down on the earth, like a cloud upon Him—as though God were saying, "You can't see Him; I won't even let you see Him die. I'm doing my wonders of the atonement in the darkness." And when the atonement was done and He said, "It is finished" (John 19:30), God lifted the night, and they took Him down and put Him away in the tomb.

And when they came to see Him rise, He was already risen. They came a long while before day, when it was still dark, but He was not there; He was risen! Every great thing that God has done, He has done in the silence and the darkness because His wisdom is such that no man could understand it anyhow. AOGII142-143

Father, Your ways and Your understanding are far above mine. I thank You for what You have revealed to me in Your Word and through Your Son, Jesus Christ. I trust that You are good, and by faith I submit myself to You when I do not understand. Amen.

The Greatness of God's Love

Give thanks to the LORD, for he is good; his love endures forever.
—1 CHRONICLES 16:34

Talking about the love of God is like going around the globe, visiting every country in the world, then spending five minutes telling your friends about it. You can't do it! The love of God is so great that even preachers such as Spurgeon and Chrysostom cannot hope to rise in the oratory of the pulpit to do it justice.

Julian of Norwich explained it this way:

> For our soul is so specially loved of Him that is highest, that it overpasseth the knowing of all creatures: that is to say, there is no creature that is made that may [fully] know how much and how sweetly and how tenderly our Maker loveth us. And therefore we may with grace and His help stand in spiritual beholding, with everlasting marvel of this high, overpassing, inestimable Love that Almighty God hath to us of His Goodness.

Then she adds this little sentence, "And therefore we may ask of our Lover with reverence all that we will." He loves us so that no creature—neither seraphim nor cherubim nor archangel nor principality nor power nor all of them added together in all the vast universe of God—can ever hope to know how overpassingly great is the love of God, and how tenderly, how sweetly, and how much He loves us. AOGII214

Father, I believe that You love me with an everlasting love. Give me the ability not only to sense Your love and receive, but also to extend it to everyone I encounter. Amen.

JULY

Our Keeper

The LORD watches over you—the LORD is your shade
at your right hand.
—PSALM 121:5

People aren't going to lose anything they love if they can help it. A mother may lose her baby by death, but she won't do it if she can help it. A man may lose a property or his car or his job, but he won't if he can help it. And so God Almighty is in a position never to lose anything, because He's able not to lose it. He keeps it because He loves it, and He loves it because He made it—or did He make it because He loves it?—I don't know.

I heard an Episcopalian rector preach a sermon on immortality. He gave one of the finest arguments for immortality that I've ever heard. "The Bible says that Abraham was a friend of God," said the rector. . . . "Well, God Almighty is able to keep His friend. So that's why we know that Abraham will rise again from the dead, because he is God's friend, and God isn't going to allow His friend to lie around and rot forever. He's going to bring him out of the grave again. And that's why I believe in immortality. I believe that God made us and God loves what He made and is keeping what He loves." . . .

I want you to think of God the Keeper, if you're a real Christian. If you're not a real Christian, if you've not been born anew and washed in the blood of the Lamb, this doesn't apply to you, and there isn't any use in my trying to make it apply. But if you're a true Christian, this applies to you. AOG027-028

Father, thank You for watching over me and keeping me. I trust
that You will preserve my life and bring me into Your kingdom, for
you are all-powerful and ever faithful. Amen.

Seeking God

If from there you seek the LORD your God, you will find him if you
seek him with all your heart and with all your soul.
—DEUTERONOMY 4:29

Most of us, when we pray, we bring our grocery list and say,
"Lord, we'd like this and this and this." We act as if we were
running to the corner store to get something. . . .

Now God does give us what we want—He's a good God. God's
goodness is one of His attributes. But I hope that we'll not imagine
that God exists simply to answer the prayers of people. A businessman wants to get a contract, so he goes to God and says, "God, give
me." A student wants to get a good grade, so she goes to God and
says, "Give me." A young man wants the girl to say yes, so he gets
on his knees and says, "Father, give her to me." We just use God as a
kind of source of getting what we want.

Our Heavenly Father is very, very kind, and He tells us that we
are to ask. Whatever we ask in the name of His Son, He'll give us,
if it's within the confines of His will. And His will is as broad as the
whole world. Still, we must think of God as the Holy One, not just as
the One from whom we can get things. God is not a glorified Santa
Claus, who gives us everything we want then fades out and lets us
run our own way. He gives, but in giving He gives us Himself, too.
And the best gift God ever gives us is Himself. He gives answers to
prayer, but after we've used up the answer or don't need it anymore,
we still have God. AOGII024-025

---

*Father, forgive for the ways in which I have sought Your gifts
and not You Yourself. Help me to understand that You are all
I need. Amen.*

Abba!

. . . our Father in heaven . . .
—MATTHEW 6:9

We need to remember, of course, that when we think of that vast mysterium tremendium, that mysterious wonder that fills this universe, and all the other big words that philosophers use to describe God Almighty, He is the same God who called Himself "I Am That I Am" (Ex. 3:14). And His Son taught us to call Him "Our Father which art in heaven" (Luke 11:2). A king sits on a throne, inhabits a palace, wears a crown and a robe, and they call him "your majesty." But when his little children see him, they run to him and yell, "Daddy!"

I remember when the present Queen Elizabeth was growing up. I've followed her life since she was a wee little tot. One time when she was walking about the palace with her dignified but kindly old grandfather, George V, the old king left the door open. Little Elizabeth turned to him and said, "Grandpa, go close that door." And the great king of England went and closed the door at the voice of a little girl! He couldn't pull any of that "your majesty" business on little Elizabeth. She was just his granddaughter. And so, no matter what awful terms the philosophers want to apply to the power that rules this universe, you and I can say, "Our Father which art in heaven, hallowed be Thy name" (Luke 11:2). AOGII085

Father in heaven, hallowed be Your name. I thank You that You have adopted me as Your child and made me an heir with Your only begotten Son, Jesus Christ. Help me to understand more deeply Your fatherly love. Amen.

Our Concept of God

No one is like you, LORD; you are great.
—JEREMIAH 10:6

Christianity rises like an eagle and flies over the top of all the mountain peaks of all the religions of the world, chiefly because of her lofty concept of God, given to us in divine revelation and by the coming of the Son of God to take human flesh and dwell among us. Christianity, the great church, has for centuries lived on the character of God. She's preached God, she's prayed to God, she's declared God, she's honored God, she's elevated God, she's witnessed to God—the triune God.

But in recent times, there has been a loss suffered. We've suffered the loss of that high concept of God, and the concept of God handled by the average gospel church now is so low as to be unworthy of God and a disgrace to the church. It is by neglect, degenerate error, and spiritual blindness that some are saying God is their "pardner" or "the man upstairs." One Christian college put out a booklet called "Christ Is My Quarterback"—He always calls the right play. And a certain businessman was quoted as saying, "God's a good fellow and I like Him." . . .

If we can restore again knowledge of God to men, we can help in some small way to bring about a reformation that will restore God again to men. AOGII006-007, 012

God Almighty, forgive me for holding a lowly concept of You. I know that You are far greater than I could ever imagine, so give me humility to acknowledge that I will never fully understand You, and may I ever live in awe of who You are. Amen.

Trusting God's Revelation

I keep asking that the God of our Lord Jesus Christ, the glorious
Father, may give you the Spirit of wisdom and revelation, so that
you may know him better.
—EPHESIANS 1:17

It is vitally important that we think soundly about God. Since He is the foundation of all our religious beliefs, it follows that if we err in our ideas of God, we will go astray on everything else.

The false gods of mankind have been and are many—almost as many as the worshipers themselves. It would require a good-size book just to list the gods that have received a name and been worshiped at sometime, somewhere in the world. For sheer depravity the obscene phallic gods of the ancients were probably the lowest. Near to them and not far up on the scale came the scarab, the serpent, the bull and a whole menagerie of birds, four-footed beasts and creeping things. Paul says plainly that such degraded worship sprang from vain imaginations and darkened hearts resulting from the rejection of the knowledge of God. . . .

The Scriptures are the only trustworthy revelation of God, and we depart from them at our own peril. Nature tells us something about Him but not enough to save us from drawing erroneous conclusions about Him. What we can learn from nature must be completed and corrected by the Scriptures if we would escape wrong and unworthy concepts of God. TWP013-015

*Lord, give Your church and its leaders a spirit of wisdom and
revelation, that we might indeed have an adequate appreciation
of who You are. Amen.*

A God of Glory

No one is like you, Lord; you are great, and your name is mighty
in power.
—JEREMIAH 10:6

This tragic and frightening decline in the spiritual state of the
churches has come about as a result of our forgetting what kind
of God God is.

We have lost the vision of the Majesty on high. I have been reading in the book of Ezekiel over the last weeks, reading slowly and
rereading, and I've just come to that terrible, frightening, awful passage where the Shekinah, the shining presence of God, lifts up from
between the wings of the cherubim, goes to the altar, lifts up from
the altar, goes to the door, and there is the sound of the whirring of
wings (Ezek. 10:4–5). And then the presence of God goes from the
door to the outer court (10:18–19) and from the outer court to the
mountain (11:23) and from the mountain into the glory.

And it has never been back, except as it was incarnated in Jesus
Christ when He walked among us. But the Shekinah glory that had
followed Israel about all those years, that shone over the camp, was
gone. God couldn't take it any longer, so He pulled out His Majesty,
His Shekinah glory, and left the temple. And I wonder how many
gospel churches, by their frivolousness, shallowness, coarseness, and
worldliness have grieved the Holy Ghost until He's withdrawn in
hurt silence. We must see God again; we must feel God again; we
must know God again; we must hear God again. Nothing less than
this will save us. AOGII012-014

---

*Everlasting God, forgive Your church for failing to see how great
you truly are. We cannot comprehend You in Your fullness, yet fill
our hearts with wonder for who You are. Amen.*

The Sweet Mystery of the Godhead

Oh, the depth of the riches of the wisdom and knowledge of God! How unsearchable his judgments, and his paths beyond tracing out!
—ROMANS 11:33

Christian theology teaches that God in His essential nature is both inscrutable and ineffable. By simple definition this means that He is incapable of being searched into or understood, and that He cannot tell forth or utter what He is.

This inability lies not in God but in the limitations of our creature-hood: "Why inquirest thou after my name, for it is secret?"

Only God knows God in any final meaning of the word know: "Even so the things of God knoweth no man, but the Spirit of God."

God in His essential being is unique in the only sense that word will bear. That is, there is nothing like Him in the universe. What He is cannot be conceived by the mind because He is "altogether other" than anything with which we have had experience before. The mind has no material with which to start. No man has ever entertained a thought that can be said to describe God in any but the vaguest and most imperfect sense. Where God is known at all it must be otherwise than by our creature-reason.

In a famed treatise on the Trinity written in the third century, Novatian said, "Every possible statement that can be made about God expresses some possession or virtue of God, rather than God Himself. The conception of God as He is can only be grasped in one way—by thinking of Him as a Being whose attributes and greatness are beyond our powers of understanding, or even of thought." POM101-103

Lord, You are great and greatly to be praised. May Your church bask in the mystery of who You are. Amen.

Undivided Trinity

Jesus called out with a loud voice, "Father, into your hands
I commit my spirit." When he had said this, he breathed his last.
—LUKE 23:46

Even when Christ Jesus died on that unholy, fly-infested cross
for mankind, He never divided the Godhead. As the old theologians pointed out, you cannot divide the substance. Not all of Nero's
swords could ever cut down through the substance of the Godhead
to cut off the Father from the Son.

It was Mary's son who cried out, "Why have you forsaken Me?"
(see Mark 15:34). It was the human body which God had given Him.
It was the sacrifice that cried, the lamb about to die. It was the human
Jesus. It was the Son of Man who cried.

Believe it that the ancient and timeless Deity was never separated;
He was still in the bosom of the Father when He cried, "Into thy
hands I commend my spirit" (Luke 23:46).

So the cross did not divide the Godhead—nothing can ever do
that. One forever, indivisible, the substance undivided, three persons
unconfounded. CES015-016

*Lord, may I unhesitatingly believe what I can't begin to
comprehend. You are an awesome mystery. Amen.*

He Is All

. . . one God and Father of all, who is over all and through all and in all.

—EPHESIANS 4:6

An old archbishop once said, "God is over all things, under all things, outside all things; within, but not enclosed, without, but not excluded; above, but not raised up, below, but not depressed; wholly above presiding, wholly beneath sustaining; wholly without embracing, and wholly within filling." . . .

When I say God, I mean the triune God. Someone once accused me of talking about God all the time, while others talk about Jesus all the time. Well, I didn't answer him. I never answer a critic; I am afraid to. I know how sharp my tongue is, so I keep my mouth shut. But I know this: when I say God, I mean Jesus and the Father and the Holy Spirit. So when I talk about God, I do not split up the Godhead. You cannot divide the Godhead, brother. The old Creed said that "We are not to confound the persons nor divide the substance." And God cannot be anywhere partly present.

Wherever God is, God is all there, because you cannot divide the substance that is God. So that where the Father is, there also is the Son and the Holy Spirit. And where the Son is, there is the Father and the Holy Spirit. And where the Holy Spirit is, there is the Father and the Son. So the blessed Trinity is here—He is all here, not partly but all here. God doesn't send representatives; God Himself is here. And if that is not good news to you, you need to be born again. SAT037, 041-042

My Lord, give Your church the eyes to see and experience You more fully, that we be continually transformed in our whole beings and proclaim Your glory throughout the world. Amen.

The Godhead Never Works Separately

Jesus replied, "Anyone who loves me will obey my teaching.
My Father will love them, and we will come to them and make
our home with them."
—JOHN 14:23

What we have in the Christian doctrine of the Holy Spirit is Deity present among us. He is not God's messenger only; He is God. He is God in contact with His creatures, doing in them and among them a saving and renewing work.

The Persons of the Godhead never work separately. We dare not think of them in such a way as to "divide the substance." Every act of God is done by all three Persons. God is never anywhere present in one Person without the other two. He cannot divide Himself.

Where the Spirit is, there also is the Father and the Son. "We will come unto him, and make our abode with him" (John 14:23). For the accomplishment of some specific work one Person may for the time be more prominent than the others are, but never is He alone. God is altogether present wherever He is present at all. POM077

Almighty God, I cannot completely comprehend how You work,
but I trust that Your word is true, and that You alone work in
perfect unity. Help me to understand more deeply Your ways, that
I may glorify You and proclaim Your goodness to all those
I encounter. Amen.

Effected by the Trinity

How much more, then, will the blood of Christ, who through
the eternal Spirit offered himself unblemished to God, cleanse
our consciences from acts that lead to death, so that we may
serve the living God!
—HEBREWS 9:14

The Bible makes it plain that the redemption of our lost race was effected on our behalf by the eternal Trinity—God the Father, God the Son, and God the Holy Spirit.

We cannot overestimate the full significance of that statement in terms of our redemption and God's atoning work.

There likewise is no ground for a thoughtful, thankful believer to deny that his or her salvation was wrought by the same eternal Trinity—Father, Son, and Holy Spirit. This is the whole emphasis of Hebrews 9:14. . . .

Hebrews 9:14 informs us that Christ, who is God the Son, through the divine Spirit, offered Himself to God, the heavenly Father. Thus we have in the act of redemption the involvement of the Trinity, the Godhead.

Keep in mind that the persons of the Godhead cannot fulfill their ministries separately. We may think of them separately, but they can never be separated. The early Church fathers recognized this wholeness of God's person. They said we must not divide the substance of the Trinity, though we recognize the three persons. JMI106-108

*Lord God, forgive the church for the ways in which we have
imagined that You—Father, Son, and Spirit—have not been united
in the work of redemption. Help us to see more clearly how You
have accomplished our salvation, that we may be ever grateful
for what You have done. Amen.*

God Delights in Himself

And a voice from heaven said, "This is my Son, whom I love;
with him I am well pleased."
—MATTHEW 3:17

God takes pleasure in Himself and rejoices in His own perfection. I've prayed and thought and searched and read the Word too long to ever take that back. God takes pleasure in Himself and He rejoices in His own perfection. The divine Trinity is glad in Himself! God delights in His works.

When God created the heaven and the earth and all things that are upon the earth, He kept saying, "It was good" (Genesis 1:4, 10, 12, 18, 21, 25). Then when God created man in His own image, He looked and said, "It was very good" (1:31). God rejoiced in His works. He was glad in what He had done. . . .

It is the same with this awesome, eternal, invisible, infinite, all-wise, omniscient God, the God of our fathers, the God and Father of our Lord Jesus Christ, and the God we call "our Father which art in heaven." He is boundless and infinite; He can't be weighed or measured; you can't apply distance or time or space to Him, for He made it all and contains it all in His own heart. While He rises above it all, at the same time this God is a friendly, congenial God, and He delights in Himself. The Father delights in the Son: "This is my beloved Son, in whom I am well pleased" (Matt. 3:17). The Son delighted in the Father: "I thank thee, O Father, Lord of heaven and earth" (Matt. 11:25). And certainly the Holy Ghost delights in the Father and the Son. AOG008-009

*Triune God, knowing that You take everlasting joy in Yourself,
grant that I would cease looking to created things for my satisfaction and that I would delight solely in You. Amen.*

The Trinity Works Together

In the beginning was the Word, and the Word was with God,
and the Word was God. He was with God in the beginning.
—JOHN 1:1–2

Critics often have declared that the Bible contradicts itself in matters relating to the Trinity. For example, Genesis speaks of God's creating the heavens and the earth. The New Testament declares that the Word—God the Son—created all things. Still other references speak of the Holy Spirit's work in creation. These are not contradictions. Father, Son, and Spirit worked together in the miracles of creation, just as they worked together in the planning and effecting of human redemption. The Father, Son, and Holy Spirit are consubstantial . . . one in substance and cannot be separated.

When Jesus was to launch His earthly ministry, He went to John at the Jordan River to be baptized. The record speaks of the Trinity's involvement. As Jesus stood on the bank of the river following His baptism, the Holy Spirit descended as a dove upon Him, and the voice of God the Father was heard from heaven saying, "This is my beloved Son, in whom I am well pleased" (Matt. 3:17). JMI106

Almighty God, what a wonder it is that You are united in all Your purposes and ways. Grant that the church would be united and so reflect Your glory. Amen.

No Parts in God

Hear, O Israel: The LORD our God, the LORD is one.
—DEUTERONOMY 6:4

The Jews always believed in the unitary God. "Hear, O Israel: The LORD our God is one LORD" (Deut. 6:4). Now Israel was not only saying that there is only one God. The Jews taught the unitary being of God, and the Church teaches (so far as the Church teaches anything now—you can go to church a lifetime and not get much theology) that the being of God is unitary. "There is one Lord" doesn't mean merely that there is only one God; it means that God is one.

God has no parts anymore than a diamond has parts. God is all one God, and everything that God does harmonizes with everything else that God does perfectly because there are no parts to get out of joint and no attributes to face each other and fight it out. All God's attributes are one, and together. AOG064-065

I can't comprehend You entirely, God, but I thank You for what You have revealed. Help me to learn all I can about You through an understanding of Your attributes. Amen.

Ever Near

But as for me, it is good to be near God. I have made the
Sovereign LORD my refuge; I will tell of all your deeds.
—PSALM 73:28

S cripture does indeed confirm that the Trinity will fill our hearts.
"No man hath seen God at any time. If we love one another, God
dwelleth in us, and his love is perfected in us. Hereby know we that
we dwell in him, and he in us, because he hath given us of his Spirit"
(1 John 4:12–13). There you have the Father and the Spirit. "And we
have seen and do testify that the Father sent the Son to be the Savior
of the world. Whosoever shall confess that Jesus is the Son of God,
God dwelleth in him, and he in God" (4:14–15). There you have the
Father and the Son, or the Trinity.

"Neither pray I for these alone, but for them also which shall believe on me through their word; that they all may be one; as thou,
Father, art in me, and I in thee, that they also may be one in us: that
the world may believe that thou hast sent me" (John 17:20–21). Do
you believe on Jesus Christ through the word of the apostles? If you
do, then Jesus said distinctly here, "I'm praying for you that you all
may be one as the Father is in me and I in him, that you may be one
in us. I in you and the Father in me." AOG002-003

*Triune God, forgive me for the times when I have not rightly
recognized Your presence in my life. Grant not only that You will
fill my heart, but also that I would remain in You. Amen.*

God's Kind of Love

Whoever has my commands and keeps them is the one who
loves me. The one who loves me will be loved by my Father,
and I too will love them and show myself to them.
—JOHN 14:21

God, being Himself God, an uncreated being, deriving from no one, owing nothing to anybody, must necessarily be the fountain of all the love there is! That is why I say that as our God, He must love Himself forever with pure and perfect love.

This kind of love, God's love, holy and blameless—this is the love which the three Persons of the Godhead feel and hold for one another. The Father to the Son; the Son to the Father; the Father and Son to the Spirit; the Spirit to the Father and Son—the divine Trinity in perfect and blameless and proper love; loving one another with a holy, poured out devotion! The Trinity's three fountains, eternal, infinite, pouring without measure into each other from the bottomless, boundless, shoreless sea of perfect love and bliss. . . .

God being who and what He is, is Himself the only being that He can love directly. Everything else and everyone else that God loves, He loves for His own sake. EFE012-013

*Lord God, so often I fail to see how deep, long, broad, and wide
Your love is. Give me eyes to see and a heart to receive Your love
for me. Amen.*

Equal in Glory and Honor

I have given them the glory that you gave me, that they may
be one as we are one.
—JOHN 17:22

Everything that is true of God is true of the three Persons of the Trinity. Did you know that there was a time when the idea of Jesus being God—being truly God—was believed by one branch of the church, but not by another?

A man named Arius came along and began to teach that Jesus was a good man, a superior man, but He wasn't God. And the leaders of the church met together, a council, they called it. They studied the issue, and they gave us the Athanasian Creed. Here's what they arrived at, and I'll never get over thanking God for these wonderful, learned, godly men. They said, "We worship one God in Trinity, and Trinity in Unity."

I am a unitarian in that I believe in the unity of God. I am a trinitarian in that I believe in the trinity of God. And they're not contrary one to the other.

We worship one God in Trinity, and Trinity in Unity;

Neither confounding the persons nor dividing the substance.

For there is one person of the Father, another of the Son, and another of the Holy Spirit.

But the Godhead of the Father, of the Son, and of the Holy Spirit is all one, the glory equal, the majesty coeternal. AOGII019-021

Lord, keep me from holding false notions about who You are and project my own notions upon You. May sound doctrine guard my heart and excite my mind to love You. Amen.

Infinite Love Poured Out

Praise the LORD. Give thanks to the LORD, for he is good;
his love endures forever.
—PSALM 106:1

We are surely aware that as human beings we can never know all of the Godhead. If we were capable of knowing all of the Godhead perfectly, we would be equal to the Godhead.

The early fathers in the church, in illustrating the trinity, pointed out that God the eternal Father is an infinite God, and that He is love. The very nature of love is to give itself, but the Father could not give His love fully to anyone not fully equal to Himself. Thus we have the revelation of the Son, Who is equal to the Father, and of the eternal Father pouring out His love into the Son, Who could contain it, because the Son is equal with the Father!

Further, those ancient wise men reasoned, if the Father were to pour out His love on the Son, a medium of communication equal both to the Father and to the Son would be required, and this was the Holy Ghost!

So we have their concept of the Trinity—the ancient Father in the fullness of His love pouring Himself through the Holy Ghost, Who is in being equal to Him, into the Son, Who is in being equal to the Spirit and to the Father!

Thus, all that man can know of God and His love in this life is revealed in Jesus Christ. EWTMARCH25

Lord, You are the God of love, and I worship you. So fill me
with Your love that it overflows like a waterfall to all those
I encounter, that they may glimpse who You are and that You
may be glorified. Amen.

God Loves Himself

As the Father has loved me, so have I loved you.
—JOHN 15:9

God loves Himself—the Father loves the Son, the Son loves the Father, and the Son and the Father love the Holy Spirit. They understood this in the olden times, when men were thinkers instead of imitators and they thought within the confines of the Bible.

Incidentally, in discussing God's attributes, I am not trying to think my way up to God. You can't think your way up to God any more than you can climb a ladder to the moon. You can't think your way into the kingdom of heaven—you go in by faith. But after you're in, you can think about the kingdom of heaven. You can't think your way to England, but after you get there, you can think about England.

So God loves Himself. And He loves Himself because He is the God who originated love. He is the I AM of love, the essence of all holiness, and the fountain of all self-conscious light.

The words "I" and "I am" always refer to the self. I knew a dear old brother—God bless him, he's in heaven now and he'll wear a crown so big that it'll come down over my shoulders, I'm sure—he'd been a missionary to China and he didn't believe much in saying "I." He knew that "I" meant self, and a fallen self is a sinful thing, so he would always say "one." And he'd say things like, "When one was in China one said this, and one did this." He meant himself—he was afraid to say "I." I suppose if he'd been writing Psalm 23, he'd make it read like this: "The Lord is one's Shepherd, one shall not want." AOGII026-027

Lord God, help me to understand more deeply the depths of Your love, for Yourself, the world, and me. May all the fruits of Your Spirit, especially love, fill my heart increasingly. Amen.

The Glory of the Trinity

For there are three that testify: the Spirit, the water and the blood; and the three are in agreement. We accept human testimony, but God's testimony is greater because it is the testimony of God, which he has given about his Son.

—1 JOHN 5:7–9

I have often wondered why the rabbis and saints and hymnists of those olden times did not come to the knowledge of the Trinity just from the seraphim's praise, "Holy, holy, holy." I am a Trinitarian—I believe in one God, the Father Almighty, maker of heaven and earth. I believe in one Lord Jesus Christ, Son of the Father, begotten of Him before all ages. I believe in the Holy Spirit, the Lord and giver of life, who with the Father and Son together is worshiped and glorified.

This is a very moving scene—the seraphim worshiping God. The more I read my Bible, the more I believe in the triune God.

In Isaiah's vision the seraphim were chanting their praises to the Trinity 800 years before Mary cried with joy and her Baby wailed in Bethlehem's manger, when the second person of the Trinity, the eternal Son, came to earth to dwell among us. The key words then and the keynote still of our worship must be, "Holy, holy, holy!" WHT066

Lord, You are truly majestic, the holy One. Grant that I may understand more deeply how awesome You are, and give the church a greater sense of Your glory. Amen.

The Trinity Will Fill Our Hearts

No one has ever seen God; but if we love one another, God lives in us and his love is made complete in us.

—1 JOHN 4:12

I want to quote what [Julian of Norwich] said about the Trinity: "Suddenly the Trinity filled my heart with joy. And I understood that so it shall be in heaven without end." This is a step up from the utilitarian heaven that most people want to go to, where they'll have everything right—a split-level home, two cars and a fountain, a swimming pool, and golden streets. Lady Julian saw that heaven will be heaven because the Trinity will fill our hearts with "joy without end," for the Trinity is God and God is the Trinity. The Trinity is our Maker and Keeper, and the Trinity is our everlasting love and everlasting joy and bliss. . . .

I wouldn't quote anybody unless there were Scripture to confirm it, and Scripture does indeed confirm that the Trinity will fill our hearts. "No man hath seen God at any time. If we love one another, God dwelleth in us, and his love is perfected in us. Hereby know we that we dwell in him, and he in us, because he hath given us of his Spirit" (1 John 4:12–13). There you have the Father and the Spirit. "And we have seen and do testify that the Father sent the Son to be the Saviour of the world. Whosoever shall confess that Jesus is the Son of God, God dwelleth in him, and he in God" (4:14–15). There you have the Father and the Son, or the Trinity. AOG002-003

Triune God, I can't comprehend how You, the infinite and holy God, fill my heart, but I thank You for residing in me. Help me to sense Your presence at every moment of the day, that I may praise and glorify You. Amen.

Our Enthusiastic God

The joy of the LORD is your strength.
—NEHEMIAH 8:10

God is boundlessly enthusiastic. I'm glad somebody is, because I don't find very many Christians who are. If they are, they're not enthusiastic about the things that matter. If they're going to a movie, they can get all steamed up about that. If they're going on a moonlight cruise, they get all worked up over that. But if you just say, "Look, look, behold God, behold God!" you can't get much enthusiasm.

God is enthusiastic. He's enthusiastic for Himself in the Persons in the Godhead. The Persons of the Godhead are infinitely delighted with each other. The Father is infinitely delighted with the Son, and the Son is infinitely delighted with the other two Persons of the Godhead. He is delighted with His whole creation, and especially with men made in His image. Unbelief comes and throws a cloud over us and shuts out the light of God, and we don't believe that God is delighted, infinitely delighted with us.

And here's a little prayer that was made by Lady Julian:

O God, of Thy goodness give me Thyself, for Thou art enough for me, and I may ask nothing that is less and find any full honors to Thee. God give me Thyself! AOG031-032

Almighty God, too often Your church is unenthusiastic about You and what You have done. Revive our hearts so that we may rejoice in You and show the world how incredible You truly are. Amen.

God Is the Deeper Life

Now this is eternal life: that they know you, the only true God,
and Jesus Christ, whom you have sent.
—JOHN 17:3

The deeper life has . . . been called the "victorious life," but I do not like that term. It appears to me that it focuses attention exclusively upon one feature of the Christian life, that of personal victory over sin, when actually this is just one aspect of the deeper life—an important one, to be sure, but only one.

That life in the Spirit that is denoted by the term "deeper life" is far wider and richer than mere victory over sin, however vital that victory may be. It also includes the thought of the indwelling of Christ, acute God-consciousness, rapturous worship, separation from the world, the joyous surrender of everything to God, internal union with the Trinity, the practice of the presence of God, the communion of saints, and prayer without ceasing. TWP120

Lord God, forgive me for the times when I have sought meaning and victory outside You. You alone satisfy my heart and give me what I need. You are my portion forever, my reward. Amen.

Real Faith

However, to the one who does not work but trusts God who
justifies the ungodly, their faith is credited as righteousness.
—ROMANS 4:5

Faith is of two kinds: nominal and real. But there is another kind of faith: it is faith that depends upon the character of God. You will remember that the Scripture does not say, "Abraham believed the text, and it was counted unto him for righteousness." It says, "Abraham believed God" (Rom. 4:3). It was not what Abraham believed, it was who Abraham believed that counted. Abraham believed God, and the man of true faith believes God and his faith rests on the character of God. The man who has real faith rather than nominal faith has found a right answer to the question, "What is God like?" There is no question more important. The man of true faith has found an answer to that question by revelation and illumination.

The difficulty with the church now—even the Bible-believing church—is that we stop with revelation. But revelation is not enough. Revelation is God's given Word. It's an objective thing, not subjective; it's external, not internal. It is God's revelation of truth. A man may believe that and believe it soundly and hold it to be truth. And yet he will have only an objective revelation of truth that has been objectively revealed. AOG018-019

Almighty God, may I not simply believe truths about You,
but grant me faith in You. For only in believing You am I counted
righteous. And only in knowing You are the desires of my heart
satisfied. Amen.

Repentance of Unlikeness

If my people, who are called by my name, will humble themselves and pray and seek my face and turn from their wicked
ways, then I will hear from heaven, and I will forgive their sin
and will heal their land.

—2 CHRONICLES 7:14

Have you any tears for your unlikeness? Have you any tears for that distance between you and God that you know isn't there and yet feel is there? You're not diminishing in any way the things God has already done in your life. You're grateful and thankful for every blessing, for justification, for the good grace of God on your life. But you can't escape that sense of remoteness, and many a day is a heavy one because God seems far from you. You know He isn't but you feel He is. He can't show His face. You've allowed self-indulgence, harshness, a vengeful spirit, luke-warmness, pride, and worldliness to put a cloud over the face of God.

I think that repentance is called for. We need to repent of unlikeness; of unholiness in the presence of the holy; of self-indulgence in the presence of the selfless Christ; of harshness in the presence of the kind Christ; of hardness in the presence of the forgiving Christ; of luke-warmness in the presence of the zealous Christ, burning like a fiery flame; of worldliness and earthliness in the presence of the heavenly Christ. AOG 154-155

Holy Father, I repent for not wanting to be more like You, for not seeking holiness with my whole being. Grant by Your Spirit that I would be conformed to the image of Your Son. Amen.

Irresistible Love of God

But God demonstrates his own love for us in this: While we were
still sinners, Christ died for us.
—ROMANS 5:8

God is not revolted by our wretchedness. He has no despite of anything that He has made, nor does He disdain the service in the simplest office that to our body belongs. The Lord will be your Nurse, your Caretaker, your Helper, and He's not revolted by anything about you. He wills that you joy along with Him. The everlasting marvel and the high, overpassing love of God, the irresistible love of God, out of His goodness sees us perfect even though we are not perfect. And He wants us to be glad in Him.

He takes no pleasure in human tears. He came and wept that He might stop up forever the fountain of human tears. He came and bereaved His mother that He might heal all bereavement. He came and lost everything that He might heal the wounds that we have from losing things. And He wants us to take pleasure in Him. Let us put away our doubts and trust Him. AOG054–055

Thank You, holy Father, that You want me to be glad as You are glad. Heal my wounds today and cleanse me of my sin, that I may delight in You and become more like Your Son. Amen.

The Justice of God

I said to myself, "God will bring into judgment both the righteous
and the wicked, for there will be a time for every activity,
a time to judge every deed."
—ECCLESIASTES 3:17

If you know God, you know He is absolutely and perfectly just.
But we have to define this term first. What do we mean by justice?

In looking this up very carefully in the Scriptures, I find that justice is indistinguishable from righteousness in the Old Testament. It's the same root word with variations according to the part of speech used. It means uprightness or rectitude. To say that God is just or that the justice of God is a fact is to say that there is uprightness and rectitude in God. Psalm 89:14 says, "Justice and judgment are the habitation of thy throne." Psalm 97:2 says, "Righteousness and judgment are the habitation of his throne." Justice and righteousness are indistinguishable from each other. . . .

Justice is not something that God has. Justice is something that God is. A grammarian might say it should be phrased, "Just is something that God is." But I say, "No, justice is something that God is." God is love and just as God is love, God is justice. AOG 060-061

---

*Lord God, You are the just and merciful Judge. Help me to trust
that You will right all wrongs in the world, and help me to live my
life in a manner that is pleasing to You. Amen.*

God, The Holy Spirit

Don't you know that you yourselves are God's temple
and that God's Spirit dwells in your midst?
—1 CORINTHIANS 3:16

Our blunder (or shall we frankly say our sin?) has been to neglect the doctrine of the Spirit to a point where we virtually deny Him His place in the Godhead. This denial has not been by open doctrinal statement, for we have clung closely enough to the biblical position wherever our credal pronouncements are concerned. Our formal creed is sound; the breakdown is in our working creed.

This is not a trifling distinction. A doctrine has practical value only as far as it is prominent in our thoughts and makes a difference in our lives. By this test the doctrine of the Holy Spirit as held by evangelical Christians today has almost no practical value at all. In most Christian churches the Spirit is quite entirely overlooked. Whether He is present or absent makes no real difference to anyone. Brief reference is made to Him in the doxology and the benediction. Further than that He might as well not exist. So completely do we ignore Him that it is only by courtesy that we can be called Trinitarian. The Christian doctrine of the Trinity boldly declares the equality of the Three Persons and the right of the Holy Spirit to be worshiped and glorified. Anything less than this is something less than Trinitarianism. POM060-061

Father, help me to be conscious of the Holy Spirit within me today. I yield my temple to Him, that He might indeed make a difference in my life. Amen.

God Is Merciful

He is good; his love endures forever.

2 CHRONICLES 5:13

God is merciful. As I said about the other attributes of the Deity, mercy is not something God has but something God is. If mercy was something God had, conceivably God might mislay it or use it up. It might become less or more. But since it is something that God is, then we must remember that it is uncreated. The mercy of God did not come into being. The mercy of God always was in being, for mercy is what God is, and God is eternal. And God is infinite.

There has been a lot of careless teaching that implies that the Old Testament is a book of severity and law, and the New Testament is a book of tenderness and grace. But do you know that while both the Old Testament and the New Testament declare the mercy of God, the word mercy appears in the Old Testament over four times more often than in the New? That's a bit hard to believe, but it's true.

This popular idea is a great error because the God of the Old Testament and the God of the New is one God. He did not change. He is the same God and, being the same God and not changing, He must therefore necessarily be the same in the Old as He is in the New. He is immutable, and because He is perfect, He cannot be added to. God's mercy was just as great in the Old Testament as it was and is in the New. AOG077-078

Father, thank You for showing me, a sinner, Your mercy. May I be ever receptive to You and never take Your mercy for granted. Amen.

Actively Compassionate

The LORD is gracious and compassionate, slow to anger and rich
in love. The LORD is good to all; he has compassion on all
he has made.

PSALM 145:8–9

When God actively exercised compassion on these people, He
did four things: He heard their groanings; He remembered
His covenant; He looked upon their sufferings and pitied them; and
He immediately came down to help them. The same thing is true in
the New Testament, where it is said of our Lord Jesus that when He
saw the multitude, He "was moved with compassion toward them,
because they were as sheep not having a shepherd" (Mark 6:34). He
said to the disciples, "Give ye them to eat" (6:37). That is being actively compassionate.

A great many people are very merciful in their beds, in their lovely
living rooms, in their new cars. They have compassion (a noun), but
they never "compassionate" (a verb). They read something in the
newspaper about somebody suffering and say, "Aw, isn't that terrible!
That poor family was burned out and they're out on the street with
no place to go," and then they turn the radio on and listen to some
program. They're very compassionate—for a minute and a half—but
they don't "compassionate"; that is, they don't do anything about it.
But God's compassion leads Him to actively "compassionate." He did
it by sending Moses down to deliver the children of Israel. AOG 080–081

*Almighty God, thank you for your compassion, and for being
compassionate toward me, for looking upon me in my pitiful state
and saving me. Amen.*

Eternal Mercy

Be merciful, just as your Father is merciful.
LUKE 6:36

One fact about the mercy of God is that it never began to be. I've heard of men who were hard-hearted or careless, but they began to get stirred up and mercy blossomed forth. It never was so of God. God never lay in lethargy without His compassion. God's mercy is simply what God is—uncreated and eternal. It never began to be; it always was. Heaven and earth were yet unmade and the stars were yet unformed and all that space men are talking about now was only a thought in the mind of God. God was as merciful as He is now. And not only did it never begin to be, but the mercy of God also has never been any more than it is now.

God has mercy enough to enfold the whole universe in His heart, and nothing anybody ever did could diminish the mercy of God. A man can walk out from under and away from the mercy of God as Israel did and as Adam and Eve did for a time, as the nations of the world have done, and as Sodom and Gomorrah did. We can make the mercy of God inoperative toward us by our conduct, since we are free moral agents. But that doesn't change or diminish the power of the Word of God nor the mercy of God. And it doesn't alter the quality of it. AOG 080, 083

Lord, thank you for extending your uncreated and unending mercy toward me. Grant that I may be merciful as you are merciful, so that you may be glorified and sinners are drawn near to you. Amen.

AUGUST

Harmony of Attributes

But because of his great love for us, God, who is rich in mercy,
made us alive with Christ even when we were dead in
transgressions—it is by grace you have been saved.
EPHESIANS 2:4–5

God always feels this overwhelming plentitude of goodness and He feels it in harmony with all His other attributes. There's no frustration in God. Everything that God is He is in complete harmony, and there is never any frustration in Him. . . .

A lot of people have talked about the goodness of God and then gotten sentimental about it and said, "God is too good to punish anybody," and so they have ruled out hell. But the man who has an adequate conception of God will not only believe in the love of God, but also in the holiness of God. He will not only believe in the mercy of God, but also in the justice of God. And when you see the everlasting God in His holy, perfect union, when you see the One God acting in judgment, you know that the man who chooses evil must never dwell in the presence of this holy God.

But a lot of people have gone too far and have written books and poetry that gets everybody believing that God is so kind and loving and gentle. God is so kind that infinity won't measure it. And God is so loving that He is immeasurably loving. But God is also holy and just. AOG107

Almighty God, forgive me for the ways in which I have made You in my own image by embracing certain truths about You but not others. May I ever recognize You for who You are. Amen.

Near to You Now

This is how we know that we live in him and he in us: He has
given us of his Spirit.

—1 JOHN 4:13

When Jonah refused to obey God and broke off and alienated his heart, he got in a ship to get away from the presence of God. He thought he could get away from God. How foolish of him to think he could get away from God! Then there was Peter, who knelt down and said, "Depart from me; for I am a sinful man, O Lord" (Luke 5:8).

It is the heart that puts distance between us and God. We must not think of God as being far away, for the reason that God does not dwell in space and "the heaven of heavens cannot contain Him" (2 Chron. 2:6), but He contains the heaven of heavens. And therefore God is near to you now—nearer to you than you are to yourself.

And yet the sinner is far from God. He isn't far from God—and yet he is. God is not far away like a Roman god up on a holy mountain. God is far away in His holy unlikeness to everything sinful. He's far away in the sense of alienation and enmity. The natural man cannot please God (see Rom. 8:8), for God and man are alienated. This is the terrible law of the world: alienation. AOG126-127

---

*Almighty God, forgive me for the sin that separates me from You.
Remove it so that I may grow closer to you. Amen.*

Reconciling the Gulf

But now in Christ Jesus you who once were far away have been
brought near by the blood of Christ.
—EPHESIANS 2:13

Human nature is so dissimilar to God's nature that it creates a
remote, everlasting, unbridgeable gulf. The Ethiopian cannot
change his skin nor the leopard his spots (see Jer. 13:23)—in other words, the person born in sin can't get out of it. God will never
change, and man can't change himself. How then can God and the
human race ever come together?

The dissimilarity can be reconciled only by One who is both God
and man. The man cannot educate himself into a likeness of God, and
he cannot cultivate himself into a likeness of God. . . . Man can't right
himself. Religions have tried it, philosophies have tried it, school
systems have tried it, the police try it. We try everywhere to bring a
similarity that God will recognize so that instead of our having that
sense of infinite remoteness, we can say with Jacob, "Surely the LORD
is in this place" (Gen. 28:16). But we can't get it. How can it be done?

It says in 2 Corinthians 5:19 that "God was in Christ, reconciling."
God's love in Christ was reconciling. AOG 129-130

Father, thank You for unspeakable love You have shown me in
Christ, for reconciling me to Yourself through Him. Empower me
by your Spirit to proclaim the gospel of reconciliation to others
that they too may be united to You. Amen.

A Fixture in God's Mind

The LORD sustains them on their sickbed and restores them
from their bed of illness.
—PSALM 41:3

It says in Hebrews 2:6, quoting from Psalm 8:4, "What is man, that thou art mindful of him?" The Greek word for mindful means "fixture in the mind." We're a fixture in God's mind. And the only wonderful, strange eccentricity of the great free God is that He allows Himself to be emotionally identified with me, so whatever hurts me, hurts Him. Whenever I'm in pain, God is in pain; whenever I suffer, He suffers. Scripture says, "The LORD . . . wilt make all [our beds in our] sickness" (Ps. 41:3). God sits beside us and grieves when we grieve.

Love also feels pleasure in its object. God is happy in His love. When people love each other, they're very happy. . . .

A young mother is always happy over her baby. I've never seen one that wasn't. Sometimes a mother may get a little angry when the child gets big enough to push things over, but for the most part, love is a pleasurable thing. And God is happy in His love toward all that He has made. AOGII189-190

How amazing that You would take delight in loving me! Thank You, Father, for understanding me so well and for Your unfailing love. Amen.

Source of Everything

For it is by grace you have been saved, through faith—and this is not from yourselves, it is the gift of God—not by works, so that no one can boast.

—EPHESIANS 2:8–9

Nobody ever got anything from God on the grounds that he deserved it. Having fallen, man deserves only punishment and death. So if God answers prayer it's because God is good. From His goodness, His lovingkindness, His good-natured benevolence, God does it! That's the source of everything. These are the only ground upon which anybody has ever been saved since the beginning of the world. . . .

And it was all out of God's goodness. We say sometimes, "The justice of God requires Him to do so and so." Never use that language—even if you hear me using it! There is never anything that requires God to do anything. God does what He does because of what He is, and there is not something standing outside of Him requiring Him to do something. He does what He does out of His own heart. All the attributes of God are simply facets of one God in three persons.

AOG047, 050

Thank you, merciful Father, for acting toward me with such grace that You have given me that which I did not deserve. You are awesome and mighty! Amen.

The Holy One

Come near to God and he will come near to you. Wash your hands, you sinners, and purify your hearts, you double-minded.
—JAMES 4:8

This Holy One confronts the sinner, who thinks he is going to decide when he'll serve Christ. He is going to push God around. He is going to decide whether to accept Jesus or not, receive Him or not, obey Him or not. He is going to go proudly down the aisle with his chest out. . . .

If we came to God dirty, but trembling and shocked and awe-struck in His presence, if we knelt at His feet and cried with Isaiah, "I am undone; because I am a man of unclean lips" (Isa. 6:5), then I could understand. But we skip into His awful presence. We're dirty, but we have a book called Seven Steps to Salvation that gives us seven verses to get us out of our problems. And each year we have more Christians, more people going to church, more church buildings, more money—and less spirituality and less holiness. We're forgetting "holiness, without which no man shall see the Lord."

I tell you this: I want God to be what God is: the impeccably holy, unapproachable Holy Thing, the All-Holy One. I want Him to be and remain THE HOLY. I want His heaven to be holy and His throne to be holy. I don't want Him to change or modify His requirements. Even if it shuts me out, I want something holy left in the universe.

AOG169, 171-172

Almighty God, forgive me for not seeing you as You truly are—awesome and holy. Give me eyes to see You and ears to hear You, that I may know You as You are truly are. Amen.

Reverence of Majesty

LORD, you are my God; I will exalt you and praise your name,
for in perfect faithfulness you have done wonderful things,
things planned long ago.
—ISAIAH 25:1

My conviction has been growing for years that we must recapture the concept of the perfections of God. We must see again how awful [awe-full] God is, how beautiful and how perfect. And we must begin to preach it, sing it, write about it, promote it, talk it, tell it, and pray it until we have recaptured the concept of majesty, until the awareness of the divine is back in our religion again, until we have regained the ability and desire to retire within our own hearts and worship God in the silence of our own spirits.

I have tried to turn people from the externals to the internals of religion. I have tried to take away the clouds and show God in His glory. I have stood almost alone in preaching this, and it has been a strange thing. It is rare to hear a man preach anything about God the Holy One. People like to hear about it, and they invite me here and there to preach on it. But why don't we get hold of this idea? I don't know why, but I'm not discouraged. AOG181-182

Almighty God, grant that I may see again how awful, beautiful, and perfect You are, that I may recapture the concept of your majesty and proclaim it to those I encounter. Amen.

Unqualified Perfection

He is the Rock, his works are perfect, and all his ways are just.
A faithful God who does no wrong, upright and just is he.
—DEUTERONOMY 32:4

Sometimes when we speak of perfection we use the word excellence. Did you ever stop to think what that word means? It means "being in a state of excelling," which implies a comparison to something or somebody. Excellence in a musician means that he is a better musician than the other musicians. If he has a high degree of excellence, we could say he has perfection in his field. He doesn't, but we could use the word.

But when you come to God, He says, "To whom then will ye liken me, or shall I be equal?" (Isa. 40:25). You don't compare God. We say that God is incomparable, and by that we mean that God stands alone as God, that nothing can be compared with Him. Isaiah was very strong here, and he wrote some very beautiful and eloquent language, telling us that we must not compare God with anything or anybody—anything in heaven above or on the earth beneath. . . .

When we apply perfection to God, we mean that He has unqualified fullness and completeness of whatever He has. He has unqualified plenitude of power. He also has unqualified fullness of wisdom. He has unqualified knowledge. He has unqualified holiness. AOG184-186

Holy Father, there is none like You. No one can compare with You. May I be ever satisfied knowing that You are perfect in all Your ways. Amen.

God Has Power

One thing God has spoken, two things I have heard:
"Power belongs to you, God."
—PSALM 62:11

The man Paul, one of the greatest intellects that the world ever knew, said this: "For the invisible things of him [God] from the creation of the world are clearly seen, being understood by the things that are made, even his eternal power and Godhead" (Rom. 1:20). You look up at the starry heavens above and see the eternal power of God there. God's power and Godhead are found there. . . .

God has power, and whatever God has is without limit; therefore, God is omnipotent. God is absolute, and whatever touches God or whatever God touches is absolute; therefore, God's power is infinite; God is Almighty. . . .

God delegates power to His creation, but He never relinquishes anything of His essential perfection. God gives power, but He doesn't give it away. When God gives power to an archangel, He still retains that power. When God the Father gives power to the Son, He keeps that power. When God pours power upon a man, He still keeps that power. God can't give anything of Himself away. God can't relinquish any of His power, because if He did, He would be less powerful than He was before. And if He were less powerful than He was before, He would not be perfect, for perfection means that He has all power. God can't "give away" His power. AOGII077-079

Father, You are almighty, and I look to you today for all that I need. Thank you for the power You give me to seek and know you, and to make you known. May I never look outside You for anything I need. Amen.

God Is Not Made

The LORD is exalted over all the nations, his glory above the heavens. Who is like the LORD our God, the One who sits enthroned on high, who stoops down to look on the heavens and the earth?
—PSALM 113:4–6

Now an attribute of God is not that of which God is composed. The very fact that God is God indicates that God isn't "composed" at all. You and I are composed. We're composed of body, soul, mind, spirit, imagination, thought, and memory. We're a composition, because there was Someone there to compose us. God took clay and His own breath, and as an artist brings the paints to the canvas, God brought all of His genius to the matter and spirit out of which man is made and He composed man. And so the attributes of man are the component parts; they compose the man.

But when we talk about the attributes of God, we have no such idea in mind at all because He said, "I Am That I Am." Anything that is composed has to have been composed by someone, and the composer is greater than the composition. If God the Father Almighty had been composed, somebody greater than God would have had to be out there to "make" God. But God is not made! Therefore, we cannot say that the attributes of God are the parts of which God is made, because God is not "made" of parts. AOGII16

God Almighty, forgive me for holding a lowly concept of You. You are far greater than I could ever imagine. Give me humility to acknowledge that I will never fully understand You, and may I ever live in awe of who You are. Amen.

Imperfect Knowledge

As you do not know the path of the wind, or how the body is formed in a mother's womb, so you cannot understand the work of God, the Maker of all things.

—ECCLESIASTES 11:5

The human mind must kneel before the great God Almighty. What God is can never quite be grasped by the mind; it can only be revealed by the Holy Spirit. If the Holy Spirit does not reveal what I am trying to tell you about God, then you only know about God. . . . .

There are some things the intellect can know about God. And even though we can't know, except by the Holy Spirit, about God, yet the mind is never better employed than when it is seeking to know this great God Almighty.

And if even the imperfect knowledge that you and I can have of our Father which art in heaven raises us to such rapture, and satisfies so deeply the roots of our being, then what must it be in that day when we look on His face! What will it be in the day when we no longer depend upon our minds, but when, with pioneer eyes of our souls, we look without mediation upon the face of God Himself! Wonderful! AOGII017-019

God Almighty, You are awesome, exceedingly greater than I could ever imagine. May Your Spirit reveal to me just how great You are, that I may worship and adore you with my whole being. Amen.

God So Loved

For God so loved the world that he gave his one and only
Son, that whoever believes in him shall not perish but have
eternal life.
—JOHN 3:16

If we were to judge John 3:16 on the basis of its value to the human race, we would have to say that it is probably the most precious cluster of words ever assembled by the mind of an intelligent man; a twenty-five-word compendium in which is contained the eternal Christian evangel, the message of genuine good news! . . .

We learn in school that diamonds are made from native carbon which has been placed under tremendous pressure which in time brings about the process of crystallization.

If we will just let our imaginations soar a bit, we can properly say that the Holy Ghost has taken the redemptive evangel and has placed it under the emotional pressure of the triune God, so unbelievably strong and powerful that it has been crystallized into this shining diamond of truth.

Using our imaginations again, I believe that if we could place this John 3:16 text on one side of some vast eternal scale held in space by some holy one to measure its value to mankind, it would prove to be more precious than all of the books that have ever been written by men. CES083-084

I worship You today, Lord, for the truth of John 3:16, a precious nugget that expresses Your saving grace. Amen.

The Vast Darkness of Emptiness

For although they knew God, they neither glorified him as God
nor gave thanks to him, but their thinking became futile
and their foolish hearts were darkened.
—ROMANS 1:21

God originally created man in His own image so that man could know companionship with God in a unique sense and to a degree which is impossible for any other creature to experience.

Because of his sin, man lost this knowledge, this daily partnership with God. In the first chapter of Romans, Paul gives us a vivid picture of men and women whom God gave over to a reprobate mind because they did not wish to retain God in their knowledge, their foolish hearts being darkened.

This is the biblical portrait of man. He has that great potential of knowing God as no other creature can, but he is lost; and without God in his knowledge, his conduct is unworthy of his high origin and his being despairs in its encompassing emptiness. . . .

There is no question about man's sin—therefore, there is no question about his being lost. A man is lost if he is not converted—overwhelmed in the vast darkness of emptiness. He was created to know God, but he chose the gutter. ITB018-019

---

*What a tragic picture of mankind today, Lord. My heart cries out
for those around me to be freed from their bondage to sin and to
come to know You, the One who is life eternal. Amen.*

God Calling

*Suppose one of you has a hundred sheep and loses one of them.
Doesn't he leave the ninety-nine in the open country and go after
the lost sheep until he finds it?*
—LUKE 15:4

Although the human mind stubbornly resists and resents the suggestion that it is a sick, fallen planet upon which we ride, everything within our consciousness, our innermost spirit, confirms that the voice of God is sounding in this world—the voice of God calling, seeking, beckoning to lost men and women! . . .

Sacred revelation declares plainly that the inhabitants of the earth are lost. They are lost by a mighty calamitous visitation of woe which came upon them somewhere in that distant past and is still upon them.

But it also reveals a glorious fact—that this lost race has not been given up!

There is a divine voice that continues to call. It is the voice of the Creator, God, and it is entreating them. Just as the shepherd went everywhere searching for his sheep, just as the woman in the parable went everywhere searching for her coin, so there is a divine search with many variations of the voice that entreats us, calling us back.

EFE003, 008

---

*Lord, we would all be lost but for Your seeking and calling,
in Your inestimable grace. I worship You today for that gracious
calling. Amen.*

Lost but Not Abandoned

But the angel said to them, "Do not be afraid. I bring you good
news that will cause great joy for all the people."
—LUKE 2:10

The announcement of the birth of Christ came as a sunburst of joy to a world where grief and pain are known to all and joy comes rarely and never tarries long.

The joy the angel brought to the awestruck shepherds was not to be a disembodied wisp of religious emotion, swelling and ebbing like the sound of an aeolian harp in the rising and falling of the wind. Rather it was and is a state of lasting gladness resulting from tidings that there was born in the city of David a Savior which is Christ the Lord. It was an overflowing sense of well-being that had every right to be there. . . .

Man is lost but not abandoned. The coming of Christ to the world tells us both of these things.

Had men not been lost, no Savior would have been required. Had they been abandoned, no Savior would have come. But He came, and it is now established that God has a concern for men. Though we have sinned away every shred of merit, still He has not forsaken us. "For the Son of man is come to seek and to save that which was lost" (Luke 19:10). SOS149, 151

---

*This is indeed a message of great joy! Thank You, Lord, that while
we were eternally lost in our sin, You did not leave us there. Amen.*

The Work of God in Redemption

I will set out and go back to my father and say to him: Father,
I have sinned against heaven and against you.
—LUKE 15:18

God formed us for His pleasure, and so formed us that we, as well as He, can, in divine communion, enjoy the sweet and mysterious mingling of kindred personalities. He meant us to see Him and live with Him and draw our life from His smile. But we have been guilty of the "foul revolt" of which Milton speaks when describing the rebellion of Satan and his hosts. We have broken with God. We have ceased to obey Him or love Him and in guilt and fear have fled as far as possible from His presence. . . .

The whole work of God in redemption is to undo the tragic effects of that foul revolt and to bring us back again into right and eternal relationship with Himself. This requires that our sins be disposed of satisfactorily, that a full reconciliation be effected and the way opened for us to return again into conscious communion with God and to live again in the Presence as before. Then by His prevenient working within us He moves us to return. This first comes to our notice when our restless hearts feel a yearning for the presence of God and we say within ourselves, "I will arise and go to my Father." That is the first step, and as the Chinese sage Lao-Tze has said, "The journey of a thousand miles begins with a first step." POG032-033

Lord, we all know people who have yet to take that first step back
to You. May I today be an instrument the Holy Spirit can use
to draw others to You. Amen.

On Our Knees

It is written: "'As surely as I live,' says the Lord, 'every knee will bow before me; every tongue will acknowledge God.'"
—ROMANS 14:11

We must come to God reverently, on our knees. You always see God when you're on your knees. You never see God when you're standing boldly on your feet, in full confidence that you'll amount to something. God is unimaginable, inconceivable; you cannot get into your head what God is like, or visualize God's being. The rule is, if you can think it, God isn't like that. . . .

We are driven to the use of negative statements when speaking about God. When we speak of the self-existence of God, we say God has no origin. When we speak of God's eternity, we say God has no beginning. When we speak of the immutability of God, we say God has no change. When we speak of the infinity of God, we say that God has no limits. When we speak of the omniscience of God, we say that God has no teachers and cannot learn. All these are negative statements. . . . I cannot know with my head, but I can have it revealed to my spirit by the Holy Spirit. AOGII117-119

Lord, I come You on my knees today, knowing that you are the supreme being to whom none can compare. I cannot fully grasp Your majesty, yet give me the ability to know and love you more. Amen.

God Must Be First

This, then, is how you should pray: "Our Father in heaven,
hallowed be your name."
—MATTHEW 6:9

The flaw in current evangelism lies in its humanistic approach It is frankly fascinated by the great, noisy, aggressive world with its big names, its hero worship, its wealth and its garish pageantry. To the millions of disappointed persons who have always yearned for worldly glory but never attained to it, the modern evangel offers a quick and easy shortcut to their heart's desire. Peace of mind, happiness, prosperity, social acceptance, publicity, success in sports, business, the entertainment field, and perchance to sit occasionally at the same banquet table with a celebrity—all this on earth and heaven at last. Certainly no insurance company can offer half as much. . . .

Always and always God must be first. The angels, approaching from above, chanted, "Glory to God in the highest, and on earth peace, good will toward men" (Luke 2:14). This puts the glory of God and the blessing of mankind in their proper order, as do also the opening words of the prayer, "Our Father which art in heaven, Hallowed by thy name." Before any petitions are allowed, the name of God must be hallowed. God's glory is and must forever remain the Christian's true point of departure. Anything that begins anywhere else, whatever it is, is certainly not New Testament Christianity. BAM022-023

*Lord, help me remember to keep things in the proper order,
to glorify You first above all else. Amen.*

The Transcendent One

He sits enthroned above the circle of the earth.
—ISAIAH 40:22

I point you to God the Transcendent One! And then I point you to the cross. But you will never know the meaning nor the value of the cross until God the Holy Ghost has done something within you to break you down and destroy your pride, humble your stubbornness, change your mind about your own goodness, blast away your defenses, and take away your weapons. He will do what the Quakers call "meek" you—He will cause you to come down, to become meek.

What about you? You may be saved, or half-saved, or badly and poorly saved. Perhaps you knew God wanted you but you wandered away; you compromised with your business or your school and now God seems so far away from you.

And He is far away, in one sense, but in another He is as near as your heartbeat, for the cross has bridged the gulf. Let the blood of Jesus cleanse us from all sin. He who is God the Transcendent One says, "Come unto me, all ye that labour and are heavy laden, and I will give you rest. Take my yoke upon you, and learn of me; for I am meek and lowly in heart: and ye shall find rest unto your souls" (Matt. 11:28–29). AOG054-055

Almighty God, I bow myself before You today and trusting that You have bridged the gulf between me and You by the Cross of Christ. Amen.

What Then Shall We Do?

For we know that our old self was crucified with him so that
the body ruled by sin might be done away with, that we should
no longer be slaves to sin.

—ROMANS 6:6

Seeing who God is and who we are, a right relationship between God and us is of vital importance. That God should be glorified in us is so critically important that it stands in lonely grandeur, a moral imperative more compelling than any other which the human heart can acknowledge. To bring ourselves into a place where God will be eternally pleased with us should be the first responsible act of every man.

Knowing our sin and moral ignorance, the impossibility of effecting such a happy relationship becomes instantly evident. Since we cannot go to God, what then shall we do? The answer is found in the Christian witness: it is that God came to us in the Incarnation. "Who is Jesus?" asks the world, and the church answers, "Jesus is God come to us." He is come to seek us, to woo us, to win us to God again. And to do this, He needed to die for us redemptively. He must in some manner undo our sins, destroy our record of sins committed, and break the power of sins entrenched within us. All this, says the Christian witness, He did upon the cross perfectly, effectually and for good. GTM039-040

---

*Thank You, Lord, that You came to us. May I always remember
to give You all glory, for You chose me. Amen.*

He Is That Majesty on High

He was afraid and said, "How awesome is this place! This is
none other than the house of God; this is the gate of heaven."
—GENESIS 28:17

God has indeed lent to every man the power to lock his heart and
stalk away darkly into his self-chosen night, as He has lent to
every man the ability to respond to His overtures of grace, but while
the "no" choice may be ours, the "yes" choice is always God's. . . .

How deeply do men err who conceive of God as subject to our
human will or as standing respectfully to wait upon our human pleasure. Though He in condescending love may seem to place Himself
at our disposal, yet never for the least division of a moment does He
abdicate His throne or void His right as Lord of man and nature. He
is that Majesty on high. To Him all angels cry aloud, the heavens and
all the powers therein: to Him cherubim and seraphim continually
do cry, "Holy, Holy, Holy, Lord God of Sabaoth, heaven and earth are
full of the majesty of thy glory." He is the Fear of Isaac and the Dread
of Jacob, and before Him prophet and patriarch and saint have knelt
in breathless awe and adoration. POM039-041

---

*Lord, help me recapture some of that dread and awe and
admiration with which You were viewed in the Old Testament. I've
become too familiar, and I've distorted and cheapened the picture
in the process. Amen.*

God Is Transcendent

As the heavens are higher than the earth, so are my ways higher
than your ways and my thoughts than your thoughts.
—ISAIAH 55:9

A great gulf lies between me and the transcendent God, who is
so high I cannot think of Him, so lofty that I cannot speak of
Him, before whom I must fall down in trembling fear and adoration.
I can't climb up to Him; I can't soar in any man-made vehicle to Him.
I can't pray my way up to Him. There is only one way: "Near, near
thee, my son, is that old wayside cross." And the cross bridges the
gulf that separates God from man. That cross!

God is transcendent. You'll never find Him on your own. Muslims
can search for Him for a thousand years and not find Him. Hindus
can cut themselves and lie on beds of glass and walk through fire and
not find Him. Protestants can join churches and lodges and all other
things and not find Him. Philosophers can rise on rung after rung of
thought and not find Him. Poets can soar away on imagination and
not find Him.

Musicians can compose heavenly music. When listening to Bach's
Christmas oratorio, I think to myself that such music never was on
earth. And yet we can listen to that and enjoy it until it breaks our
heart and not find Him—never, never find Him! . . . So I offer you
the cross. AOGII053-054

---

*Father, thank You for the cross. Thank You for sending Your Son
to reveal Yourself to us and reconcile us to You. Amen.*

God Has No Beginning

"I am the Alpha and the Omega," says the Lord God, "who is,
and who was, and who is to come, the Almighty."
—REVELATION 1:8

God is not dependent upon His world, upon kings and presidents, upon businessmen and preachers, upon boards and deacons. God is not dependent upon anything. We have thought our way back until there's no history—back to God Himself, God the Eternal One.

God never began to be. I want you to kick that word began around a little bit in your mind and think about it. "In the beginning God created the heaven and the earth" (Gen. 1:1), but God Himself never began to be! "Began" is a word that doesn't affect God at all. There are many concepts and ideas that don't touch God at all, such as the concept of beginning or creation, when God spoke and things began to be. "In the beginning God created"—but before the beginning, there wasn't any "beginning"; there wasn't any "before"! The old theologians used to say that eternity is a circle. Round and round the circle we go, but back before there was any circle, God was! . . .

But there never was a time when God was not! No one said, "Let God be"! Otherwise, the one who said "Let God be" would have to be God. And the one about whom He said "Let him be" wouldn't be God at all, but a secondary "god" who wouldn't be worth our trouble. God, back there in the beginning, created. God was, that's all!

AOGII061-062

---

*I worship You today, Lord, as the great Creator, the uncaused
Cause behind my very existence. Amen.*

No Problem to God

For it is by grace you have been saved, through faith—and this is
not from yourselves, it is the gift of God—not by works, so that
no one can boast.
—EPHESIANS 2:8–9

O ur theology is too much colored by our secret self-admiration.
We picture God as draining . . . draining the last ounce of His
strength to save us. This gives us a highly enjoyable feeling that we
are capable of mighty world-shaking deeds so terrible that even God
respects our power to do evil. The lurid overcoloring of pulpit rhetoric has worked to destroy the truth of God's sovereignty and to greatly
overstate man's prowess as a sinning rebel.

A man may sin to the limit of his ability and still be no great problem to the Deity. "But where sin abounded, grace did much more
abound" (Rom. 5:20).

God is infinite and man is finite, which is to say that every man's
sin, however terrific it may seem to him, must have a limit, while
God's grace can have none. Always God must be out ahead, or He
would not be God.

Let us put our pride under our feet and admit frankly that our sins
are not big nor mighty nor noble. There is nothing romantic about
sin. It is a sordid and shameful thing practiced by moral cads so weak
that they take advantage of God's kindness to defy Him and so cow-
ardly that they run whining to Him for help when trouble comes.

TET055-056

---

*Lord, keep before me always the exceeding ugliness of my sin
that I may not take pride in it. Thank You that Your grace is so
much bigger than my sin. Amen.*

God Acts Like God

But the tax collector stood at a distance. He would not even look
up to heaven, but beat his breast and said, 'God, have mercy
on me, a sinner.'

—LUKE 18:13

Always, always, always God acts like God. Aren't you glad you
aren't going to sneak into heaven through a cellar window? . . .

Aren't you glad that you're not going to get into heaven by God's
oversight? God is so busy with His world that you sneak in. You're
there a thousand years before God sees you!

Aren't you glad that you're not going to get in just by being a
member of a church? God says, "Well, that's a pretty good church.
Let's let him in." . . .

All of this cheap talk about St. Peter giving us an exam to see if
we're all right—it's all nonsense! The Great God Almighty, always
one with Himself, looks upon a moral situation and He either sees
death or life. And all of God is on the side of death or life. If there is
an iniquitous, unequal, unatoned, uncleansed, unprotected sinner in
his sin, there's only one answer—all of God says, "Death and hell."
And all of heaven can't pull that man up.

But if he beats his breast and says, "God be merciful to me a sinner" (Luke 18:13), and takes the benefits of the infinite agony of God
on a cross, God looks on that moral situation and says, "Life!" And
all of hell can't drag that man down. Oh, the wonder and the mystery
and the glory of the being of God! AOG073-074

*Thank You, Lord, for Your consistent grace, which does not
allow us to slip through the cracks but has mercy on us and
saves us. Amen.*

No Compromise with Sin

God was reconciling the world to himself in Christ, not counting
people's sins against them. And he has committed to us the
message of reconciliation.

—2 CORINTHIANS 5:19

But how can God say to the sinner, "I'll move over halfway"? Can He say, "You're blind, so I'll move over and be half blind, and you'll move over and be half blind . . . "? And thus by God coming halfway and compromising Himself, could He and man be reconciled? To do that God would have to void His Godhead and cease to be God.

I'd rather go to hell than go to a heaven presided over by a god who would compromise with sin, and I believe every true man and woman would feel the same. We want God to be the holy God that He is. The prodigal son and his father did not meet halfway to the far country. The boy came clear back where he belonged. And so the sinner in his repentance comes all the way back to God, and God doesn't move from His holy position of infinite holiness, righteousness and loveliness, world without end.

God never compromises and comes halfway down. God stays the God that He is. This is the God we adore—our faithful, unchangeable Friend whose love is as great as His power and knows neither limit nor end. We don't want God to compromise. We don't want God to wink at our iniquity. We want God to do something about it.

AOG130-131

Thank You, Father, that You never compromise but instead
provide a way for me to come to You through Your Son. What a
plan! Amen.

Deity Indwelling Men!

The world cannot accept [the Spirit of Truth], because it neither sees him nor knows him. But you know him, for he lives with you and will be in you.

—JOHN 14:17

Here is the whole final message of the New Testament: Through the atonement in Jesus' blood, sinful men may now become one with God. Deity indwelling men! That is Christianity in its fullest effectuation, and even those greater glories of the world to come will be in essence but a greater and more perfect experience of the soul's union with God.

Deity indwelling men! That, I say, is Christianity, and no man has experienced rightly the power of Christian belief until he has known this for himself as a living reality. Everything else is preliminary to this. Incarnation, atonement, justification, regeneration—what are these but acts of God preparatory to the work of invading and the act of indwelling the redeemed human soul? Man, who moved out of the heart of God by sin, now moves back into the heart of God by redemption. God, who moved out of the heart of man because of sin, now enters again His ancient dwelling to drive out His enemies and once more make the place of His feet glorious. POM100-101

Thank You, Father, for that divine indwelling and all its implications. Thank You that fellowship, union, and power are all mine when the Holy Spirit is within me. Amen.

God Has No Past or Future

Before the mountains were born or you brought forth the whole world, from everlasting to everlasting you are God.

PSALM 90:2

God has no past! Now I want you to hear that. And I want you to shake your head hard here, because this is an idea that the old church fathers knew, but that we, their children, don't seem to care much about. God has no past. You have a past; it isn't really very long, although you may wish it wasn't so long. But God has no past and no future. Why doesn't God have a past or a future? Because past and future are creature words, and they have to do with time. They have to do with the flowing motion of time. But God is not riding on the bosom of time. Time is a little mark across the bosom of eternity. And God sits above time, dwelling in eternity: "from everlasting to everlasting, Thou art God." . . .

He can't have yesterdays and tomorrows, because yesterday is time and tomorrow is time, but God surrounds it all and God has already lived tomorrow. The great God who was present at the beginning when He said, "Let there be" and there was, is also now present at the end, when the worlds are on fire and all creation has dissolved and gone back into chaos—and only God and His redeemed saints remain. Remember that God has already lived our tomorrows.

AOGII063-064

Holy Father, You are infinite, incapable of being contained or comprehended. I submit myself to You, knowing that nothing and no one compares to You. Amen.

Saved by Grace

For it is by grace you have been saved, through faith—and this is
not from yourselves, it is the gift of God—not by works, so that
no one can boast.
—EPHESIANS 2:8–9

Nobody has ever been saved, from the day that Abel offered his
bloody lamb on a homemade altar, down to the latest convert
made today, except out of the goodness of God. Because of God's
grace, His mercy, His lovingkindness, His goodness and gracious-
ness, His cordiality and approachability, He kindly saved people.
We've taken the word "grace" and made a technical term out of it.

The people in the Old Testament were not saved by keeping anything, because we deserved hell, and if God had acted according
to justice alone, He simply would have pulled the stopper out and
flushed us all down to hell and been done with it. But God out of His
lovingkindness graciously forgave those who would come according
to the conditions God laid down. Everybody is saved by grace. Abel
was saved by grace. Noah was saved by grace—"Noah found grace
in the eyes of the LORD" (Gen. 6:8). So was Moses and all the rest
down to the coming of Jesus and His dying on the cross. All were saved
by grace out of the goodness of God. And everybody's been saved by
grace out of the goodness of God ever since. AOG047-048

---

*Lord, thank You for Your wonderful grace, which saved me from
the judgment I deserved. May I remember that it is a gift extended
to me out of Your lovingkindness. Amen.*

Behold the Marvels of God

In a loud voice they were saying: "Worthy is the Lamb, who was
slain, to receive power and wealth and wisdom and strength
and honor and glory and praise!"
—REVELATION 5:12

If a doctor saves a man who has only a runny nose, he wouldn't
write a book about it. He didn't do much. The fellow would get
well anyhow. But the doctor who takes a man with a brain tumor,
puts him asleep and, with great care, prayer, and skill, brings that
man back to life—he has done something.

He "saved a wretch like me." He "turned all our blame into endless
worship." I believe the Bible teaches—our Lord hinted at it and Paul
developed it further—that the day will come when they will gather
around us from everywhere, and say, "Behold the marvels of God."
You read in the book of Acts (4:14) of seeing the man that was healed
standing among them, and they could say nothing. And seeing that
wicked sinner standing there, we can only say, "Worthy is the Lamb
that was slain" (Rev. 5:12). And worthy is the goodness of God that
out of His infinite kindness, His unchanging, perfect lovingkindness,
He made amends for us, "full, fair and many," turning all our sin into
endless worship. AOG052

---

*Great God, You are indeed worthy to receive praise and honor and
glory and blessing, because You brought about the marvelous
work of redemption. I'll worship You for all eternity, beginning
even now. Amen.*

Friendship with God

I no longer call you servants, because a servant does not know his master's business. Instead, I have called you friends, for everything that I learned from my Father I have made known to you.

—JOHN 15:15

The idea of the divine-human friendship originated with God. Had not God said first, "Ye are my friends" (John 15:14), it would be inexcusably brash for any man to say, "I am a friend of God." But since He claims us for His friends, it is an act of unbelief to ignore or deny the relationship. . . .

The more perfect our friendship with God becomes, the simpler will our lives be. Those formalities that are so necessary to keep a casual friendship alive may be dispensed with when true friends sit in each other's presence. True friends trust each other.

There is a great difference between having "company" and having a friend in the house. The friend we can treat as a member of the family, but company must be entertained.

God is not satisfied until there exists between Him and His people a relaxed informality that requires no artificial stimulation. The true friend of God may sit in His presence for long periods in silence. Complete trust needs no words of assurance. Such words have long ago been spoken, and the adoring heart can safely be still before God.

TIC145, 147-148

I am honored, Father, to be called Your friend. May I never treat our friendship lightly. Amen.

SEPTEMBER

Only a Few Things Matter

What good is it for someone to gain the whole world,
yet forfeit their soul?
—MARK 8:36

It has been suggested here before that life, for all its apparent complexities, is at bottom very simple indeed if we could only realize it. Thank God, only a few things matter. The rest are incidental and unimportant. . . .

What really matters after all? My personal relation to God matters. That takes priority over everything else. A man may be born in a sanitary hospital, receive his education in progressive schools, ride in an air-conditioned car, sleep on a foam rubber mattress, wear synthetic clothing, eat vitamin-enriched food, read by fluorescent lights, speak across 12,000 miles of empty space to a friend on the other side of the world, lose his anxieties by taking tranquilizing pills, die without pain by the aid of some new drug, and be laid to rest in a memorial park as lovely as a country garden; yet what will all this profit him if he must later rise to face in judgment a God who knows him not and whom he does not know? To come at last before the bar of eternal justice with no one to plead his cause and to be banished forever from the presence of the great Judge—is that man any better off than if he had died a naked savage in the hinterlands of Borneo?

BAM088, 090

Lord, we have so much, yet that "much" so often gets in the way of our finding the only thing that matters. Keep me uncluttered and focused on eternity, I pray. Amen.

Death Sorts Us Out

Let both grow together until the harvest. At that time I will tell
the harvesters: First collect the weeds and tie them in bundles
to be burned; then gather the wheat and bring it into my barn.
—MATTHEW 13:30

Right now we live in a . . . mixed-up world. Some people get the
headlines who, if the truth were known, should be getting a
striped suit in a prison somewhere.

There are other worthy persons who are completely ignored in
this world, and, if the truth were known, they would be on the front
covers of the news magazines next week.

God is not mixed up, though. . . . He has His own process for
sorting things out. Many a person receiving the praise and plaudits
of the world today will be sorted out when God's time comes. He
does not sort them out down here in our time. He did not even sort
them when His twelve disciples were with Him. Peter was a coward
and Judas was a lover of money and a betrayer, but not until the last
minute did He even mention it. But when Judas died, he was sorted
out. He died and went to his own place.

Death sorts us out, and if we go to heaven, it is because we have a
nature that belongs there. It is not hard for the sovereign God to sort
out all the natures that belong in heaven and take them there. EFE103

*Thank You, Father, for the surety I have of heaven through the
blood of Jesus Christ, which is mine regardless of my position
in the eyes of the world. Amen.*

Simply God

Every good and perfect gift is from above, coming down from
the Father of the heavenly lights, who does not change like
shifting shadows.
—JAMES 1:17

God, being the eternal, holy God, cannot change. He will not go
from better to worse. You cannot think of God being any less
holy than He is now, any less righteous than He is now. God must
remain infinitely holy, fixed, forever unchanging in holiness. . . .

You and I, however, can. Thank God we can! "[H]e that is holy, let
him be holy still," it says in Revelation 22:11. And I believe that since
we are creatures and capable of mutation upward toward the image of
God, we will become holier and wiser and better while the ages roll.
But remember that in becoming holier and better and wiser, we will
only be moving toward the perfect likeness of God, who is already
all-wise and good and holy. God cannot become any better than He is.

These words that you and I use—holier, wiser, better—we use
about ourselves. A man is a good man; another man is a better man.
But you cannot say "better" about God because God is already the
apex, the fountain, the top. There are no degrees in God. There are
degrees in angels, I suppose. There are certainly degrees in people
too. But there are no degrees in God.

That is why you cannot apply such words as "greater" to God. God
is not "greater." God is great. "Greater" is a word applied to creatures
who are trying to be like God. But you cannot say that God is greater,
because that would put God in a position where He was in competi-
tion with someone else who was great. God is simply God. AOGII100-101

*There is a wonderful stability in this truth, Lord. Thank You for
Your unchangeable perfection. Amen.*

Lord or Judge

Whoever serves me must follow me; and where I am, my servant also will be. My Father will honor the one who serves me.
—JOHN 12:26

Every man holds his future in his hand. Not the dominant world leader only, but the inarticulate man lost in anonymity is a "man of destiny." He decides which way his soul shall go. He chooses, and destiny waits on the nod of his head. He decides, and hell enlarges herself, or heaven prepares another mansion. So much of Himself has God given to men. . . .

"If any man will . . . let him . . . follow me," Christ says, and some will rise and go after Him, but others give no heed to His voice (see Matt. 16:24, Luke 9:23). So the gulf opens between man and man, between those who will and those who will not. Silently, terribly, the work goes on, as each one decides whether he will hear or ignore the voice of invitation. He will not put Himself again on trial; He will not argue, but the morning of the judgment will confirm what men in the twilight have decided. . . .

Christ will be Lord, or He will be Judge. Every man must decide whether he will take Him as Lord now or face Him as Judge then.

SOS040-042

Lord, give me a sensitivity to those around me who have not yet accepted Christ. It may be my words that could help them come to know You as Lord and keep them from facing You as judge. Amen.

We Need God

And my God will meet all your needs according to the riches
of his glory in Christ Jesus.
—PHILIPPIANS 4:19

Remember that God is to you a necessity. I preach the gospel of Jesus Christ and say, "Come unto me, all ye that labour and are heavy laden, and I will give you rest" (Matt. 11:28), quoting the lovely words of Jesus that warmed my heart when I was a boy and helped bring me to Him. When I quote those words and when I quote the words of the gospel that "whosoever believeth in him should not perish, but have everlasting life" (John 3:16), I'm doing you a tremendous favor—because you need God!

We are slaves to time; we find our immortality in God and nowhere else. We sing, "O God, our help in ages past"—what ages past? God's ages past? No, God lives in now. Our ages past—the brief race of men. "Our hope for years to come"—and your hope and my hope for years to come. And may this God "be Thou our guide while life shall last and our eternal home." I need somebody to guide me. I can't go it alone. I'm too small and weak and stupid and vulnerable. . . . Immortality and eternity you'll only find in God—and you'll only find God through Jesus Christ the Lord. AOGII070

Almighty God, I am ever dependent upon You for life and salvation. Keep me humble that I may love You, serve You, and magnify Your great name. Amen.

Truth Divorced from Life

How can a young person stay on the path of purity? By living according to your word. . . . I have hidden your word in my heart that I might not sin against you.
—PSALM 119:9, 11

There is scarcely anything so dull and meaningless as Bible doctrine taught for its own sake. Truth divorced from life is not truth in its biblical sense, but something else and something less. Theology is a set of facts concerning God, man, and the world. These facts may be and often are set forth as values in themselves, and there lies the snare both for the teacher and for the hearer. . . .

The Bible, however, is more than a volume of hitherto unknown facts about God, man, and the universe. It is a book of exhortation based upon those facts. By far the greater portion of the book is devoted to an urgent effort to persuade people to alter their ways and bring their lives into harmony with the will of God. . . .

No man is better for knowing that God in the beginning created the heavens and the earth. The devil knows that, and so did Ahab and Judas Iscariot. No man is better for knowing that God so loved the world of men that He gave His only begotten Son to die for their redemption. In hell there are millions who know that. Theological truth is useless until it is obeyed. The purpose behind all doctrine is to secure moral action. OGM025-026

Lord, help me move beyond knowing You and Your Word only academically. Lead me to obedience, to submission, and to proper moral action. Amen.

Divine Indwelling

And in him you too are being built together to become a dwelling
in which God lives by his Spirit.
—EPHESIANS 2:22

The doctrine of the divine indwelling is one of the most important in the New Testament, and its meaning for the individual
Christian is precious beyond all description. To neglect it is to suffer
serious loss. The Apostle Paul prayed for the Ephesian Christians
that Christ might dwell in their hearts by faith. Surely it takes faith
of a more than average vitality to grasp the full implications of this
great truth. . . .

Without question, the teaching of the New Testament is that the
very God Himself inhabits the nature of His true children. How this
can be I do not know, but neither do I know how my soul inhabits my
body. Paul called this wonder of the indwelling God a rich mystery:
"Christ in you, the hope of glory" (Col. 1:27). And if the doctrine involved a contradiction or even an impossibility, we must still believe
what the mouth of the Lord has spoken. "Yea, let God be true, but
every man a liar" (Rom. 3:4). . . .

And what kind of habitation pleases God? What must our natures
be like before He can feel at home within us? He asks nothing but
a pure heart and a single mind. He asks no rich paneling, no rugs
from the Orient, no art treasures from afar. He desires but sincerity,
transparency, humility, and love. He will see to the rest. TIC041-042, 044

---

*Lord, give me the purity, integrity, and focus to be the kind
of vessel You would desire. Amen.*

Elbethel

There he built an altar, and he called the place El Bethel,
because it was there that God revealed himself to him when
he was fleeing from his brother.

—GENESIS 35:7

Jacob, after his memorable experience in the wilderness, where he saw a ladder set up on the earth and saw God standing above it, called the place of his encounter Beth-el, which means "the house of God," beth being house and el, God.

Many years later, after he had suffered and sinned and repented and discovered the worthlessness of all earthly things, had been conquered and blessed by God at Peniel, and had seen the face of God in an hour of spiritual agony, he renamed the place Elbethel, which means "the God of the house of God." Historically the place was always known as Bethel, but in Jacob's worshiping heart it would forever be El Bethel.

The change is significant. Jacob had shifted his emphasis from the house to the One whom he met there. God Himself now took the center of his interest. He had at last been converted from a place to God Himself. A blessed conversion.

Many Christians never get beyond Beth-el. God is in their thoughts, but He is not first. OGM133-134

*Oh, Lord, take me past Beth-el and mere knowledge of You
to a deepening experience of Elbethel, that I may be aware
of Your actual presence in my life. Amen.*

Meet God First

Then, because so many people were coming and going that they did not even have a chance to eat, he said to them, "Come with me by yourselves to a quiet place and get some rest."
—MARK 6:31

The whole Bible and all past history unite to teach that battles are always won before the armies take the field. The critical moment for any army is not the day it engages the foe in actual combat; it is the day before or the month before or the year before. . . .

It did not take Moses long to lead the children of Israel out through the Red Sea to deliverance and freedom, but his fittedness to lead them out was the result of years of hard discipline. It took David only a few minutes to dispose of Goliath, but he had beaten the giant long before in the person of the lion and the bear. Christ stood silent in the presence of Pilate, and for our sake went calmly out to die. He could endure the anguish of the cross because He had suffered the pains of Gethsemane the night before; there was a direct relationship between the two experiences. One served as a preparation for the other. . . .

Preparation is vital. . . . We can seek God today and get prepared to meet temptation tomorrow, but if we meet the enemy without first having met God, the outcome is not conjectural. The issue is already decided. We can only lose. NCA084-086

Lord, I am going to meet the enemy not only tomorrow, but even today. Prepare my heart as I come apart to meet with You first, before I go to meet the day. Amen.

Get Alone with God

God is our refuge and strength, an ever-present help in trouble.
—PSALM 46:1

I delight in the inward knowledge that Jesus Christ, the Son of God and our coming Lord, will be sufficient for every situation which is yet to come to pass. We will never panic along with this present world system as long as we are fortified with our knowledge of who Jesus Christ really is.

The Word of God is the foundation of our peace and rest. Even in these dangerous and dramatic hours: "God is our refuge and strength, a very present help in trouble" (Ps. 46:1). . . .

Notice that this is the kingly strength and dominion of our Lord—not the United Nations! . . .

"Be still, and know that I am God: I will be exalted among the heathen, I will be exalted in the earth. The LORD of hosts is with us" (46:10–11). Fear not, little flock—it is the Father's good pleasure to give you the kingdom.

And the gates of hell cannot prevail against it! WPJ093-095

---

*Lord, help me to be still as I meet alone with You today. Grant me
a very real sense of Your strong presence, of the refuge I have
in You. Amen.*

Come with Courage

Let us then approach God's throne of grace with confidence,
so that we may receive mercy and find grace to help us in our
time of need.
—HEBREWS 4:16

In a world like ours, courage is an indispensable virtue. The coward may snivel in his corner, but the brave man takes the prize. And in the kingdom of God, courage is as necessary as it is in the world.

When entering the prayer chamber, we must come filled with faith and armed with courage. Nowhere else in the whole field of religious thought and activity is courage so necessary as in prayer. The successful prayer must be one without condition. We must believe that God is love and that, being love, He cannot harm us but must ever do us good. Then we must throw ourselves before Him and pray with boldness for whatever we know our good and His glory require, and the cost is no object! Whatever He in His love and wisdom would assess against us, we will accept with delight because it pleases Him. Prayers like that cannot go unanswered. The character and reputation of God guarantee their fulfillment.

We should always keep in mind the infinite lovingkindness of God. No one need fear to put his life in His hands. His yoke is easy; His burden is light. WTA048

I come boldly, Father, because I have been given access to You through the blood of Jesus. I come with courage because I have been given all the promises of a gracious God. Amen.

What Really Matters?

Why, you do not even know what will happen tomorrow. What is your life? You are a mist that appears for a little while and then vanishes.

—JAMES 4:14

What does matter after all? . . . . What are the axiomatic truths upon which all human life may rest with confidence? Fortunately they are not many. Here are the chief ones:

1. Only God is great. . . .
2. Only God is wise. . . .
3. Apart from God nothing matters. We think that health matters, that freedom matters, or knowledge or art or civilization. And but for one insistent word they would matter indeed. That word is eternity.

Grant that men possess perpetual being, and the preciousness of every earthly treasure is gone instantly. God is to our eternal being what our heart is to our body. The lungs, the liver, the kidneys have value as they relate to the heart. Let the heart stop, and the rest of the organs promptly collapse. Apart from God, what is money, fame, education, civilization? Exactly nothing at all, for men leave all these things behind them and one by one go to eternity. Let God hide His face, and nothing thereafter is worth the effort.

4. Only what we do in God will remain to us at last. . . .

MDP128-129

Slow me down, Lord, and help me focus on the few things that really matter in light of eternity. Amen.

Only God Matters

And the scripture was fulfilled that says, "Abraham believed God, and it was credited to him as righteousness," and he was called God's friend.

—JAMES 2:23

Ultimately Abraham discovered that only God matters. He discovered in that revelation the greatest concept in the world. . . .

It is as if Abraham laid hold of God's favor and promise with rejoicing, saying to himself, "When I have God, I need nothing more!"

Abraham was completely satisfied with God's friendship. He becomes to us a faithful example in his willingness to put God first. With Abraham, only God mattered. . . .

In Abraham's encounter with God, he learned why he was here upon earth. He was to glorify God in all things and to continually worship. . . .

Abraham heard from God. Abraham met with God. Abraham listened to God. Abraham responded to God. He knew the meaning of an altar of worship and praise. Our altar of devotion and worship within our hearts should be as real.

These truths concerning Abraham and his wholehearted response to God cause me to wonder. How can we bring our lukewarm Christians into a realization that nothing in the world is as important to them as God's love and God's will? MMG027, 029-030

Lord, teach me today what Abraham learned over the course of a lifetime—that only God matters. Amen.

Be Exalted, O God

Be exalted, O God, above the heavens; let your glory be over
all the earth.

—PSALM 57:5

This was written by David when fleeing from Saul and surrounded by his foes. In that brilliant way he had of describing things, David said that he found himself among lions, men whose teeth were spears and arrows and whose tongues were as sharp swords. He was surrounded by them and they had the authority of King Saul back of them, and David had nobody but God. So David, being taught in the ways of the Spirit, did something that we probably wouldn't have thought of doing. David immediately put God between him and his enemies.

David knew that he must have the victory, but he knew if he was to have anything like permanent victory he couldn't ask God to exalt him. So he didn't say, "Oh God, I am Your king, to be successor to Saul, the sinning king. Now God, I want You to come to my rescue and crush these enemies under my feet." He knew better than that. So, he prayed . . . "Be thou exalted, O God, above the heavens; let thy glory be above all the earth" (Ps. 57:5). He was saying, "Whatever happens to me, God, be exalted. Whatever these men with sharp teeth and claws and spears and arrows do to me, God, let Your glory be over all the earth. My heart is fixed on this, O God, and I will sing praise because I want You to be exalted above the heavens and Your glory over all the earth." SAT134

Lord, it is my prayer today that You are exalted in all circumstances. Whatever I may face today, Lord, I exalt You. Amen.

For His Glory Alone

He said to me, "You are my servant, Israel, in whom I will display my splendor."
—ISAIAH 49:3

The glory of God is the health of the universe; the essential soundness of things requires that He be honored among created intelligences.

Where God is honored fully is heaven, and it is heaven for that reason. Where He is honored not at all is hell, and for that cause it is hell. Among men we see a mixture of honor and dishonor. Basically this is the cause of earth's tragic, confused history.

God has not finished with His saints till He has brought them to a place where they honor Him on earth as He is honored in heaven.

God gives away His full purpose in redeeming man when He says, "Thou art my servant, O Israel, in whom I will be glorified" (Isa. 49:3).

If we can convince God that we are sold out to His high honor, the problem of unanswered prayer is solved. God will withhold nothing from that man who is determined to live to His glory alone. . . .

God has said, "them that honour me I will honour" (1 Sam. 2:30). He can honor us only when He knows His glory is safe in our hands.

TET019-020

Lord, may I honor You today on earth as You are honored in heaven. Be glorified in and through me today. Amen.

Sure Tests

I am the LORD; that is my name! I will not yield my glory
to another or my praise to idols.
—ISAIAH 42:8

One vital test of all religious experience is how it affects our relation to God, our concept of God, and our attitude toward Him.

God, being who He is, must always be the supreme arbiter of all things religious. The universe came into existence as a medium through which the Creator might show forth His perfections to all moral and intellectual beings: "I am the LORD: that is my name: and my glory will I not give to another" (Isa. 42:8). "Thou art worthy, O Lord, to receive glory and honour and power: for thou hast created all things, and for thy pleasure they are and were created" (Rev. 4:11).

The health and balance of the universe require that in all things God should be magnified. "Great is the LORD, and greatly to be praised; and his greatness is unsearchable" (Ps. 145:3). God acts only for His glory, and whatever comes from Him must be to His own high honor. Any doctrine, any experience that serves to magnify Him is likely to be inspired by Him. Conversely, anything that veils His glory or makes Him appear less wonderful is sure to be of the flesh or the devil. MDP134-135

Lord, may I clearly see Your glory today. May I not be fooled by any experience or thought that does not magnify You, and may You be pleased with my worship this day. Amen.

Not What I Want to Be

Being confident of this, that he who began a good work in you
will carry it on to completion until the day of Christ Jesus.
—PHILIPPIANS 1:6

There comes a time when the true believer must take his stand on the oath and covenant of God and refuse to be shaken. He must lift high his happy affirmation, not in arrogance, but in faith and in deep humility. Perhaps his declaration of independence will go something like this:

I am not yet perfect, but I thank God and my Lord Jesus Christ that I am done with the past and I do now trust in my Savior for full deliverance from all sins. I cannot pray like Daniel, but I shall never cease to praise God that He inclines His ear to me. I am not as wise as Solomon, but I glory in this, that "I know whom I have believed, and am persuaded that he is able to keep that which I have committed unto him against that day" (2 Tim. 1:12). I have not the gifts of Moses or Isaiah or John, but I'll be everlastingly grateful that I have been given the moral perception to understand and appreciate such men as these. I am not what I want to be, but thanks be to God that I do want to be better than I am; and I am sure that "he which hath begun a good work in [me] will perform it until the day of Jesus Christ" (Phil. 1:6).

Here I stand. I can do nothing else, so help me God. SIZ104-105

Lord, do the work that must be done in Your power, by Your Holy Spirit, to bring Your work to completion in my life. Amen.

Be Ye Holy!

But just as he who called you is holy, so be holy in all you do;
for it is written: "Be holy, because I am holy."
—1 PETER 1:15–16

You cannot study the Bible diligently and earnestly without being struck by an obvious fact—the whole matter of personal holiness is highly important to God!

Neither do you have to give long study to the attitudes of modern Christian believers to discern that by and large we consider the expression of true Christian holiness to be just a matter of personal option. . . .

Personally, I am of the opinion that we who claim to be apostolic Christians do not have the privilege of ignoring such apostolic injunctions. I do not mean that a pastor can forbid or that a church can compel. I only mean that morally we dare not ignore this commandment, "Be ye holy." . . .

Brethren, we are still under the holy authority of the apostolic command. Men of God have reminded us in the Word that God does ask us and expect us to be holy men and women of God, because we are the children of God, who is holy. The doctrine of holiness may have been badly and often wounded—but the provision of God by His pure and gentle and loving Spirit is still the positive answer for those who hunger and thirst for a life and spirit well-pleasing to God.

ICH061-062, 068

---

*Lord, may I no longer see the pursuit of holiness as optional.
Rather, may I strive to fulfill Your expectations for my life. Amen.*

Trustworthy and Able

Being fully persuaded that God had power to do
what he had promised.
—ROMANS 4:21

I must confess that in my ministry I keep repeating some of the things I know about God and His faithful promises. Why do I insist that all Christians should know for themselves the kind of God they love and serve? It is because all the promises of God rest completely upon His character.

Why do I insist that all Christians should search the Scriptures and learn as much as they can about this God who is dealing with them? It is because their faith will only spring up naturally and joyfully as they find that our God is trustworthy and fully able to perform every promise He has made. . . .

God's eternal blessings do not depend on how you feel today. If my eternal hope rested on how I felt physically, I might as well begin packing for a move to some other region! Even if I do not feel heavenly, my feelings in no way change my heavenly hope and prospect.

I dare not relate even a fraction of my faith and hope to my emotions of the moment and to how I feel today. My eternal hope depends on God's well-being—on whether God Himself is able to make good on His promises. And about that there is no doubt. JMI081-083

Lord, forgive me for my faltering faith. Remind me constantly that my hope rests on Your good character, in which I have confidence. Amen.

Faith's Foundation

Now faith is confidence in what we hope for and assurance
about what we do not see.
—HEBREWS 11:1

If our faith is to have a firm foundation we must be convinced beyond any possible doubt that God is altogether worthy of our trust. . . .

As long as we question the wisdom of any of God's ways, our faith is still tentative and uncertain. While we are able to understand, we are not quite believing. Faith enters when there is no supporting evidence to corroborate God's word of promise and we must put our confidence blindly in the character of the One who made the promise. . . .

Remember that faith is not a noble quality found only in superior men. It is not a virtue attainable by a limited few. It is not the ability to persuade ourselves that black is white or that something we desire will come to pass if we only wish hard enough. Faith is simply the bringing of our minds into accord with the truth. It is adjusting our expectations to the promises of God in complete assurance that the God of the whole earth cannot lie. . . .

A promise is only as good as the one who made it, but it is as good, and from this knowledge springs our assurance. By cultivating the knowledge of God, we at the same time cultivate our faith.

TIC021-022, 024

---

*Lord, as I come to know You more fully, I have every reason
to place implicit trust in You and Your promises. Thank You for
the firm foundation of my faith. Amen.*

Faith Rests on Character

In the hope of eternal life, which God, who does not lie,
promised before the beginning of time.
—TITUS 1:2

I have heard ministers say that if the people in their congregations would memorize more Bible promises, they would immediately have more faith. Yes and no.

Study the Scriptures, and you will find that we are not going to have more faith by counting the promises of God. Faith does not rest upon promises. Faith rests upon character. Faith must rest in confidence upon the One who makes the promises.

Faith says, "God is God! He is the holy God who cannot lie. He is the God who is infinitely honest—He has never cheated anyone. He is the God who is faithful and true!"

Yes, we must be concerned with the person and character of God and not just with His promises. Through promises we learn what God has willed to us, we learn what we may claim as our heritage, we learn how we should pray. But faith itself must rest upon the character of our God.

When I think of the angels in heaven who veil their faces before the holy God who is totally truthful, I wonder why every preacher does not begin preaching about God—who He is, His attributes, His perfection, His being, and why we love Him and why we should trust Him! JAF006-007

Lord, make Your good and holy character always visible to me so that I may know You more and trust You completely. Amen.

Let God Be True

Let God be true, and every human being a liar. As it is written:
"So that you may be proved right when you speak and prevail
when you judge."
—ROMANS 3:4

True faith rests upon the character of God and asks no further proof than the moral perfections of the One who cannot lie. It is enough that God said it, and if the statement should contradict every one of the five senses and all the conclusions of logic as well, still the believer continues to believe. "Let God be true, but every man a liar" (Rom. 3:4), is the language of true faith. Heaven approves such faith because it rises above mere proofs and rests in the bosom of God. . . .

Faith as the Bible knows it is confidence in God and His Son Jesus Christ, it is the response of the soul to the divine character as revealed in the Scriptures, and even this response is impossible apart from the prior inworking of the Holy Spirit. Faith is a gift of God to a penitent soul and has nothing whatsoever to do with the senses or the data they afford. Faith is a miracle. It is the ability God gives to trust His Son, and anything that does not result in action in accord with the will of God is not faith but something else short of it. MDP029-030

*Lord, bestow Your gift of faith on my soul, and let it be enough
for me that You have said it. Amen.*

What Faith Depends On

*Yet he did not waver through unbelief regarding the promise
of God, but was strengthened in his faith and gave glory to God,
being fully persuaded that God had power to do what
he had promised.*
—ROMANS 4:20–21

We have confidence and boldness in God because He is God. We have learned enough about His character to know that we can lean upon Him fully.

You may have been told that if you will memorize more Bible verses you will have more faith. I have been memorizing the Scriptures ever since I was converted, but my faith does not rest on God's promises. My faith rests upon God's character. Faith must rest in confidence upon the One who made the promises. It was written of Abraham that "He staggered not at the promise of God through unbelief; but was strong in faith, giving glory to God; and being fully persuaded that, what he had promised, he was able also to perform" (Rom. 4:20–21). The glory went to God, not to the promise or to Abraham's faith.

So, what is the promise for? A promise is given to me so that I may know intelligently what God has planned for me, what God will give me, and so what to claim. Those are the promises and they are intelligent directions. They rest upon the character and ability of the One who made them. FBR042-043

---

*Heavenly Father, I praise You for the promises You have given
me, but even more I praise You for Your unchanging character.
You are the object of my faith! Amen.*

No More Doubts

God is faithful, who has called you into fellowship with his Son,
Jesus Christ our Lord.
—1 CORINTHIANS 1:9

Are we going to trust God? Are we going to commit our entire future to Him? What more assurance do we need than the character of God Himself? It is God's own eternal Person and His faithful character that tell us our salvation is secured through the blood of Jesus Christ, our Savior. It is because God is who He is that we can trust Him and be assured that His covenant will never change.

How rewarding it is to be able to make a proclamation like this! Our forgiveness, our hope for salvation, our confidence in the life to come rest upon God's unchanging love and faithfulness. . . .

Because holiness is God's being, He cannot lie. Because He is God, He cannot violate the holy nature of His being. God does not will to lie. He does not will to cheat. He does not will to deceive. He does not will to be false to His own dear people.

Or to put it positively, in the very perfection of His character, God wills to be true to His children. Because He is perfect and because He is holy, His believing children are safe. Confidently knowing that the Lord God omnipotent reigns, and knowing that He is able to do all that He wills to do, I have no more doubts. I am safely held in the arms of the all-powerful God. JMI087-089

---

*Thank You, Father, that You are faithful to Your promises.
I'll trust you and have no doubts today. Amen.*

The Devotional Mood

Keep this Book of the Law always on your lips; meditate on it day
and night, so that you may be careful to do everything written
in it. Then you will be prosperous and successful.
—JOSHUA 1:8

Maintenance of the devotional mood is indispensable to success in the Christian life.

Holiness and power are not qualities that can be once received
and thereafter forgotten as one might wind a clock or take a vitamin
pill. The world is too much with us, not to mention the flesh and the
devil, and every advance in the spiritual life must be made against
the determined resistance of this trinity of evil. Gains made must be
consolidated and held with a resolution equal to that of an army in
the field.

To establish our hearts in the devotional mood we must abide in
Christ, walk in the Spirit, pray without ceasing, and meditate on the
Word of God day and night. Of course this implies separation from
the world, renunciation of the flesh, and obedience to the will of God
as we are able to understand it.

And what is the devotional mood? It is nothing else than constant awareness of God's enfolding presence, the holding of inward
conversations with Christ and private worship of God in spirit and
in truth. SOS129

*Lord, keep me constantly aware of Your presence as I meditate
on Your Word. I abide in You today. Amen.*

Distractions

But when you pray, go into your room, close the door and pray to your Father, who is unseen. Then your Father, who sees what is done in secret, will reward you.

—MATTHEW 6:6

Among the enemies to devotion none is so harmful as distractions. Whatever excites the curiosity, scatters the thoughts, disquiets the heart, absorbs the interests, or shifts our life focus from the kingdom of God within us to the world around us—that is a distraction and the world is full of them. Our science-based civilization has given us many benefits, but it has multiplied our distractions and so taken away far more than it has given. . . .

The remedy for distractions is the same now as it was in earlier and simpler times, viz., prayer, meditation, and the cultivation of the inner life. The psalmist said, "Be still, and know" (Ps. 46:10), and Christ told us to enter into our closet, shut the door, and pray unto the Father. It still works. . . .

Distractions must be conquered, or they will conquer us. So let us cultivate simplicity; let us want fewer things; let us walk in the Spirit; let us fill our minds with the Word of God and our hearts with praise. In that way we can live in peace even in such a distraught world as this. "Peace I leave with you, my peace I give unto you" (John 14:27). SOS130-132

Lord, it is difficult to find that "closet" where I can commune with You in unhurried, uncluttered quiet. Calm me now as I seek that peaceful meditation. Amen.

Vacate the Throne Room of Your Heart

And he is the head of the body, the church; he is the beginning
and the firstborn from among the dead, so that in everything he
might have the supremacy.
—COLOSSIANS 1:18

Fénelon teaches that to make our deeds acceptable to God, it is not necessary that we change our occupation (if it is honest), but only that we begin to do for Christ's sake what we had formerly been doing for our own. To some of us this will seem too tame and ordinary. We want to do great things for God, to hazard our lives in dramatic acts of devotion that will attract the attention of fellow Christians and perhaps of the larger world outside. Visions of Huss at the stake, Luther at the Diet of Worms, or Livingstone in the heart of Africa flit before our minds as we think on spiritual things. Plain, workaday Christians like us—how can we rise to such heroic heights? With our families to support, with our lot cast in the dull routine of the commonplace, with no one threatening us with imprisonment or death: how can we live lives acceptable to God? What can we do to satisfy the heart of our Father in heaven?

"The answer is nigh thee, even in thy mouth" (Rom. 10:8). Vacate the throne room of your heart and enthrone Jesus there. Make Him your all in all, and try yourself to become less and less. Dedicate your entire life to His honor alone, and shift the motives of your life from self to God. Let the reason back of your daily conduct be Christ and His glory, not yourself, nor your family, nor your country, nor your church. In all things let Him have the preeminence. BAM069-070

It is my prayer, Lord, that in all things Christ might have preeminence so I can do great things for You. Amen.

For Thy Sake

For whoever wants to save their life will lose it, but whoever
loses their life for me will save it.
—LUKE 9:24

A Christian poet of a bygone generation wrote a rather long hymn around a single idea: You can, by three little words, turn every common act of your life into an offering acceptable to God. The words are "For Thy sake." . . .

All this seems too simple to be true, but Scripture and experience agree to declare that it is indeed the way to sanctify the ordinary. "For Thy sake" will rescue the little, empty things from vanity and give them eternal meaning. The lowly paths of routine living will by these words be elevated to the level of a bright highway. The humdrum of our daily lives will take on the quality of a worship service and the thousand irksome duties we must perform will become offerings and sacrifices acceptable to God by Christ Jesus.

To God there are no small offerings if they are made in the name of His Son. Conversely, nothing appears great to Him that is given for any other reason than for Jesus' sake. If we cannot die for Christ, we can live for Him, and sometimes this is more heroic and will bring a larger reward.

"For Thy sake." These are the wondrous words which, when they are found in the heart as well as in the mouth, turn water into wine and every base metal into gold. BAM068, 070-071

---

*Lord, whatever seemingly small thing I am called on to do today,
let me do it joyfully for Your sake. Amen.*

Worshipful Resignation

So Samuel told him everything, hiding nothing from him. Then
Eli said, "He is the LORD; let him do what is good in his eyes."
—1 SAMUEL 3:18

This idea was once expressed better by a simple-hearted man who was asked how he managed to live in such a state of constant tranquility even though surrounded by circumstances anything but pleasant. His answer was as profound as it was simple: "I have learned," he said, "to cooperate with the inevitable.". . .

Though we cannot control the universe, we can determine our attitude toward it. We can accept God's will wherever it is expressed and take toward it an attitude of worshipful resignation. If my will is to do God's will, then there will be no controversy with anything that comes in the course of my daily walk. Inclement weather, unpleasant neighbors, physical handicaps, adverse political conditions—all these will be accepted as God's will for the time and surrendered to provisionally, subject to such alterations as God may see fit to make, either by His own sovereign providence or in answer to believing prayer. BAM064-065

Lord, I determine to cooperate with the inevitable today and to accept Your will for my life, whatever that might entail. "It is the LORD: let him do what seemeth him good" (1 Sam. 3:18). Amen.

Nothing But God

So then, each of us will give an account of ourselves to God.
—ROMANS 14:12

What we need very badly these days is a company of Christians who are prepared to trust God as completely now as they know they must do at the last day. For each of us the time is surely coming when we shall have nothing but God. Health and wealth and friends and hiding places will all be swept away, and we shall have only God. To the man of pseudo-faith that is a terrifying thought, but to real faith it is one of the most comforting thoughts the heart can entertain.

It would be a tragedy indeed to come to the place where we have no other but God and find that we had not been trusting God at all during the days of our earthly sojourn. It would be better to invite God now to remove every false trust, to disengage our hearts from all secret hiding places, and to bring us out into the open where we can discover for ourselves whether or not we really trust Him. That is a harsh cure for our troubles, but it is a sure one. Gentler cures may be too weak to do the work. And time is running out on us. PON013-014

---

*Lord, may I indeed live this earthly sojourn in such a way that
I have no fear or dread of standing before You, giving account
of my life and having nothing but You. Amen.*

OCTOBER

In Case God Fails

Be strong and courageous. Do not be afraid or terrified because
of them, for the LORD your God goes with you; he will never leave
you nor forsake you.

—DEUTERONOMY 31:6

To many Christians, Christ is little more than an idea, or at best an ideal; He is not a fact. Millions of professed believers talk as if He were real and act as if He were not. And always our actual position is to be discovered by the way we act, not by the way we talk. . . .

Many of us Christians have become extremely skillful in arranging our lives so as to admit the truth of Christianity without being embarrassed by its implications. We fix things so that we can get on well enough without divine aid, while at the same time ostensibly seeking it. We boast in the Lord but watch carefully that we never get caught depending on Him. "The heart is deceitful above all things, and desperately wicked: who can know it" (Jer. 17:9)?

Pseudo-faith always arranges a way out to serve in case God fails it. Real faith knows only one way and gladly allows itself to be stripped of any second ways or makeshift substitutes. For true faith, it is either God or total collapse. And not since Adam first stood up on the earth has God failed a single man or woman who trusted Him. PON012-013

*Thank You, Father, that my faith rests in an unfailing God. Help
me remember that I don't need a backup plan, "just in case."
I rest in Your faithfulness today. Amen.*

Nothing Can Hinder God

However, if you suffer as a Christian, do not be ashamed,
but praise God that you bear that name.
—1 PETER 4:16

The essence of spiritual worship is to love supremely, to trust confidently, to pray without ceasing, and to seek to be Christlike and holy and to do all the good we can for Christ's sake. How impossible for anyone to hinder that kind of "practice." As soon as our normal churchgoing religion is interdicted by government decree or made for the time impossible by circumstances, we can retire to the sanctuary of our own hearts and worship God acceptably till He sees fit to change the circumstances and allow us to resume the outward practice of our faith. But the fire has not gone out on the altar of our heart in the meantime, and we have learned the sweet secret of submission and trust, a lesson we could not have learned any other way.

If we find ourselves irked by external hindrances, be sure we are victims of our own self-will. Nothing can hinder the heart that is fully surrendered and quietly trusting, because nothing can hinder God.

ROR148-149

Lord, I know that nothing can hinder the worship of my heart except the coldness of my heart! May I remain "fully surrendered and quietly trusting." Find me faithful today, I pray. Amen.

God Did It!

So he said to me, "This is the word of the LORD to Zerubbabel:
'Not by might nor by power, but by my Spirit,'
says the LORD Almighty."
—ZECHARIAH 4:6

He says, "I will do it for you. Why do you worry? I will do it for you. I am God. I am Jehovah. I am your righteousness. I am your provider. I am your healer. I am your banner of victory. I am your shepherd. I am your peace. I am your everything."

If God is all this to us, then there is no reason why anybody should be downhearted in this hour. If God could make a world out of nothing, why can't He make anything He wants now for His people? God invites us to see Him work. . . .

If we will unite our hearts and intentions and dare to believe it, we will see God begin to move in great strength and in great power. We will see coming down from heaven that which we so desperately struggled to bring in from the outside. We will see the great God do it and then it will not be said, "This man did it," or "That woman did it." But we can all say together, "Not by might, nor by power, but by my spirit, saith the LORD of hosts" (Zech. 4:6). RRR148, 150

Lord, may I always dare to believe that You are more than enough to provide my needs. I ask You to do great works in Your world as I trust and watch. Amen.

We Still Have God

But store up for yourselves treasures in heaven, where moths
and vermin do not destroy, and where thieves do not break in
and steal.

—MATTHEW 6:20

A s Christians we look at everything differently. . . .
People of the world, for instance, hope for life, health, financial prosperity, international peace, and a set of favorable circumstances. These are their resources—upon them they rest. They look to them as a child looks to its nursing mother.

Christians do not despise these temporal blessings, and if they come to them, they sanctify them by receiving them with prayers of gratitude to God. But they know their everlasting welfare is not dependent upon them. These blessings may come or go, but true Christians abide in God where no evil can touch them and where they are rich beyond all the power of their minds to conceive—and this altogether apart from earthly circumstances. . . .

The world's resources are good in their way, but they have this fatal defect—they are uncertain and transitory. Today we have them tomorrow they are gone. It is this way with all earthly things since sin came to upset the beautiful order of nature and made the human race victims of chance and change. . . .

If the world's foundations crumble, we still have God, and in Him we have everything essential to our ransomed beings forever.

TWP025-026

---

*Thank You, Father, for the eternal treasure that can be mine
when I serve You. Keep me from the lure of transitory treasure
and focused on that which is eternal. Amen.*

Peace Is God's Word

In your righteousness, rescue me and deliver me; turn your
ear to me and save me. Be my rock of refuge, to which I can
always go.

—PSALM 71:2–3

David did well to seek God's help in his troubles. When he faced confusion, he prayed, "Deliver me . . . and cause me to escape" (Ps. 71:2). God can deliver from confusion by establishing moral order within the life. When the eye becomes single, when the life becomes all one piece, inward antagonisms are abolished, and internal harmony is restored.

It is not a wonder that there is so little of true joy among the sons of men. With the will at a perpetual stalemate, with the heart's purposes constantly at an irritating impasse, with the mind at wit's end, and the whole life in a state of almost constant frustration, how can joy abide?

There is no way out of the woods except through full and quick surrender to the will of God. When such a surrender is made, God will soon bring order out of confusion. Peace is God's word, and it follows faith and obedience as the harvest follows the seed. But the whole will of God is necessary to peace; half measures will only increase the confusion. TET048

In the midst of a confusing world, help me to find peace, Father,
in full surrender to Your whole will. Amen.

The Will of God at Any Cost

I have been crucified with Christ and I no longer live, but Christ
lives in me. The life I now live in the body, I live by faith in the Son
of God, who loved me and gave himself for me.

—GALATIANS 2:20

Few sights are more depressing than that of a professed Christian
defending his or her supposed rights and bitterly resisting any
attempt to violate them. Such a Christian has never accepted the way
of the cross. . . .

The only cure for this sort of thing is to die to self and rise with
Christ into newness of life. The man or woman who sets the will of
God as his or her goal will reach that goal not by self-defense but by
self-abnegation. Then no matter what sort of treatment that person
receives from other people, he or she will be altogether at peace. The
will of God has been done—this Christian does not care whether it
comes with curses or compliments, for he or she does not seek one or
the other, but wants to do the will of God at any cost. Then, whether
riding the crest of public favor or wallowing in the depths of obscurity, he or she will be content. If there be some who take pleasure in
holding this Christian down, still he or she will not resent them, for
he or she seeks not advancement but the will of God. TWP090

*I repeat, Lord, my first-prayed commitment to be crucified with
Christ, allowing Christ to live through me, so that You are glorified
in my life. Amen.*

No Need for Fear

For I am convinced that neither death nor life, neither angels
nor demons, neither the present nor the future, nor any powers,
neither height nor depth, nor anything else in all creation, will be
able to separate us from the love of God that is in Christ Jesus
our Lord.
—ROMANS 8:38–39

Surely Bible-reading Christians should be the last persons on earth to give way to hysteria. They are redeemed from their past offenses, kept in their present circumstances by the power of an all-powerful God, and their future is safe in His hands. God has promised to support them in the flood, protect them in the fire, feed them in famine, shield them against their enemies, hide them in His safe chambers until the indignation is past, and receive them at last into eternal tabernacles.

If we are called upon to suffer, we may be perfectly sure that we shall be rewarded for every pain and blessed for every tear. Underneath will be the Everlasting Arms, and within will be the deep assurance that all is well with our souls. Nothing can separate us from the love of God. . . .

This is a big old world, and it is full of the habitations of darkness, but nowhere in its vast expanse is there one thing of which a real Christian need be afraid. Surely a fear-ridden Christian has never examined his or her defenses. TWP005-006

---

*Lord, thank You for the assurance that I can face anything in my
life without a trace of fear! Amen.*

No Accidents

The Lord makes firm the steps of the one who delights in him.
—PSALM 37:23

To the child of God, there is no such thing as accident. He travels an appointed way. The path he treads was chosen for him when as yet he was not, when as yet he had existence only in the mind of God.

Accidents may indeed appear to befall him and misfortune stalk his way; but these evils will be so in appearance only and will seem evils only because we cannot read the secret script of God's hidden providence and so cannot discover the ends at which He aims. . . .

The man of true faith may live in the absolute assurance that his steps are ordered by the Lord. For him, misfortune is outside the bounds of possibility. He cannot be torn from this earth one hour ahead of the time which God has appointed, and he cannot be detained on earth one moment after God is done with him here. He is not a waif of the wide world, a foundling of time and space, but a saint of the Lord and the darling of His particular care. WTA003-004

Lord, it's comforting to know that today and every day You are directing my life by the preset plans that are known only to You. I'll rest in that, whatever may come my way today. Amen.

The Power of Right Thinking

I have considered my ways and have turned my steps
to your statutes.
—PSALM 119:59

What we think about when we are free to think about what we will—that is what we are or will soon become. . . .

The Psalms and Prophets contain numerous references to the power of right thinking to raise religious feeling and incite to right conduct. "I thought on my ways, and turned my feet unto thy testimonies" (Ps. 119:59). "While I was musing the fire burned: then spake I with my tongue" (Ps. 39:3). Over and over the Old Testament writers exhort us to get quiet and think about high and holy things as a preliminary to amendment of life or a good deed or a courageous act. . . .

Thinking about God and holy things creates a moral climate favorable to the growth of faith and love and humility and reverence. We cannot by thinking regenerate our hearts, nor take our sins away, nor change the leopard's spots. Neither can we by thinking add one cubit to our stature or make evil good or darkness light. So to teach is to misrepresent a scriptural truth and to use it to our own undoing. But we can by Spirit-inspired thinking help to make our minds pure sanctuaries in which God will be pleased to dwell. BAM044-046

Lord, my mind will be inundated with thoughts today—some necessary, some impure, some wasteful, some covetous, some neutral. Take control of my mind, that my thoughts throughout may be pleasing to You. Amen.

Proud of Our Humility

For I know that good itself does not dwell in me, that is, in my
sinful nature. For I have the desire to do what is good,
but I cannot carry it out.
—ROMANS 7:18

Three considerations should destroy pride forever within our breasts: the majesty of God, the enormity of our sins, and the wonder of Christ's redeeming death. But so tenacious is the root of Adam that we are often proud even of our want of pride. It is not uncommon to see holy men defending their holiness with positive violence and resenting any doubt cast upon their perfections.

For a Christian to claim credit for any good work is a violation of the most elementary teachings of the New Testament. Two things are taught clearly there: that I can of myself do no good thing; and if any good deed is done, it is the Lord Himself who has done it. That should settle our pride of service for good, but in fact it is not so. We still love to bask in the praise that our Christian efforts bring us.

For a Christian to revel in the praise he is accorded for some good work is as logically askew as for a singer to rush out and take a bow for another singer's solo. It is a cheap form of robbery and must be exceedingly hateful to God. TET077-078

*Father, forgive me for the pride that is so ugly, yet so close to
the surface. Remind me today that I can do all things through
Christ—but nothing of myself. Amen.*

Saintliness and Holiness

Then he said to them all: "Whoever wants to be my disciple must
deny themselves and take up their cross daily and follow me."
—LUKE 9:23

If anyone should wonder what I mean by godliness, saintliness, holiness, I'll explain. I mean a life and a heart marked by meekness and humility. The godly soul will not boast or show off. I mean reverence. The godly man will never take part in any religious exercise that shows disrespect for the Deity. The cozy, cute terms now applied to God and Christ will never pass his lips. He will never join in singing religious songs that are light, humorous, or irreverent. He will cultivate a spirit of complete sincerity and discuss God and religion only in grave and reverent tones.

Further, I mean separation from the world unto God in an all-out, irrevocable committal. The holy man will not envy the world, nor will he imitate it or seek its approval. His testimony will be, "I am crucified unto the world and the world unto me." He will not depend upon it for his enjoyments, but will look above and within for the joy that is unspeakable and full of glory.

In short, any true work of God in the churches will result in an intensified spirit of worship and an elevated appreciation of the basic Christian virtues. It will make men Christlike, will free them from a thousand carnal sins they did not even know were sins before. It will free them from earthly entanglements and focus their whole attention upon things above. PON092-093

*Lord, help me live a life of virtue, forsaking all else, so I can
experience freedom and communion with You. Amen.*

Where Is Mary?

She had a sister called Mary, who sat at the Lord's feet listening
to what he said.
—LUKE 10:39

Today the Christian emphasis falls heavily on the "active" life. People are more concerned with earth than with heaven; they would rather "do something" than to commune with God. The average Christian feels a lot nearer to this world than to the world above. The current vogue favors "Christian action." The favorite brand of Christianity is that sparked by the man in a hurry, hardhitting, aggressive, and ready with the neat quip. We are neglecting the top side of our souls. The light in the tower burns dimly while we hurry about the grounds below, making a great racket and giving the impression of wonderful devotion to our task. . . .

It is time that we prayerfully test the flavor of present Christianity and compare its spiritual quality with that of the New Testament. I think we shall find the element of mystic worship all but absent from it. . . .

It is to our lasting reproach that we cannot live full, rounded and symmetrical lives, embodying in our redeemed personalities the practical service of Martha and the adoring vision of Mary. We would appear to be unwilling to have both sisters present at once. Just now Martha is all over the premises, but where is Mary? I wish someone would find her soon.TET046-047

Lord, forgive me for neglecting the important aspects of worship and adoration. Quiet my heart as I sit at Jesus' feet to hear what He has to say to me. Amen.

As Much Like God As Possible

Whoever wants to become great among you must be your servant, and whoever wants to be first must be your slave.
—MATTHEW 20:26–27

From these words we may properly conclude (and the context strongly supports the conclusion) that there is nothing wrong with the desire to be great provided (1) we seek the right kind of greatness; (2) we allow God to decide what is greatness; (3) we are willing to pay the full price that greatness demands; and (4) we are content to wait for the judgment of God to settle the whole matter of who is great at last. . . .

No one whose heart has had a vision of God, however brief or imperfect that vision may have been, will ever consent to think of himself or anyone else as being great. The sight of God, when He appears in awesome majesty to the wondering eyes of the soul, will bring the worshiper to his knees. and fill him with such an overwhelming sense of divine greatness that he must spontaneously cry "Only God is great!" . . .

Obviously there are two kinds of greatness recognized in the Scriptures—an absolute, uncreated greatness belonging to God alone, and a relative and finite greatness achieved by or bestowed upon certain friends of God, who by obedience and self-denial sought to become as much like God as possible. BAM048-049

Lord, help me to emulate You, the model of true greatness, today. Amen.

The Work of the Hammer

Woe to those who quarrel with their Maker. . . . Does the clay say
to the potter, "What are you making?" Does your work say,
"The potter has no hands"?
—ISAIAH 45:9

It was the enraptured [Samuel] Rutherford who could shout in the midst of serious and painful trials, "Praise God for the hammer, the file and the furnace."

The hammer is a useful tool, but the nail, if it had feeling and intelligence, could present another side of the story. For the nail knows the hammer only as an opponent, a brutal, merciless enemy who lives to pound it into submission, to beat it down out of sight and clinch it into place. That is the nail's view of the hammer, and it is accurate except for one thing: The nail forgets that both it and the hammer are servants of the same workman. Let the nail but remember that the hammer is held by the workman, and all resentment toward it will disappear. The carpenter decides whose head shall be beaten next and what hammer shall be used in the beating. That is his sovereign right. When the nail has surrendered to the will of the workman and has gotten a little glimpse of his benign plans for its future, it will yield to the hammer without complaint. ROR155-156

---

*Lord, You are indeed sovereign and have every right to hammer
me and shape me and mold me and use me any way You want.
I yield today to Your plans for my life. Amen.*

The File and the Furnace

But he knows the way that I take; when he has tested me,
I will come forth as gold.
—JOB 23:10

The file is more painful still, for its business is to bite into the soft metal, scraping and eating away the edges till it has shaped the metal to its will. Yet the file has, in truth, no real will in the matter, but serves another master as the metal also does. It is the master and not the file that decides how much shall be eaten away, what shape the metal shall take, and how long the painful filing shall continue. Let the metal accept the will of the master, and it will not try to dictate when or how it shall be filed.

As for the furnace, it is the worst of all. Ruthless and savage, it leaps at every combustible thing that enters it and never relaxes its fury till it has reduced it all to shapeless ashes. All that refuses to burn is melted to a mass of helpless matter, without will or purpose of its own. When everything is melted that will melt and all is burned that will burn, then and not till then the furnace calms down and rests from its destructive fury. . . .

How could [Samuel] Rutherford find it in his heart to praise God for the hammer, the file, and the furnace? The answer is simply that he loved the Master of the hammer, he adored the Workman who wielded the file, he worshiped the Lord who heated the furnace for the everlasting blessing of His children. ROR156

Lord, let me, like Job and like Rutherford, see that after the trial is the gold, that after the hammer, the file, and the furnace is the everlasting blessing of Your children. Amen.

Satisfied with Second Violin

Do you not know that in a race all the runners run, but only one gets the prize? Run in such a way as to get the prize.
—1 CORINTHIANS 9:24

There was a celebrated Englishman who sat with a friend once, watching and listening to a philharmonic orchestra. As they listened, the Englishman watched a man playing second violin. He was playing it well, but he was second violin. The Englishman said to his friend, "See that man there playing second violin? If I were playing second violin in that orchestra, do you know what I would do? I would never rest day or night until I was playing first violin. And then I would never give myself rest day or night until I was directing that orchestra. When I got to be director, I would never rest until I had become a composer. And when I got to composing music for the orchestra, I would never give myself rest until I was the best composer in England."

The children of the world are sometimes wiser than the children of light. We have been offered not the directorship of a great orchestra, but glory and truth unsearchable. We have been offered the face of God and the glory of Christ. We have been offered holiness and righteousness and indwelling by the Spirit. We can have our prayers answered and have hell fear us because we have a hold on God who invites us to draw on His omnipotence. We are offered all this, and yet we sit and play second violin without ambition. RRR021

Lord, don't let me be satisfied with second fiddle. Strengthen me to run in such a way that I might be all that You want me to be, for Your glory. Amen.

Lord, Send the Oil

How good and pleasant it is when God's people live together
in unity! It is like precious oil poured on the head, running down
on the beard, running down on Aaron's beard, down on the collar
of his robe.

—PSALM 133:1–2

And just as Aaron's body had the oil dripping down around it, onto his clothing, so that he smelled like the oil that had been put on his head, so this living together in unity among the Lord's people brings a blessing of oil, an anointment that comes down upon us. It's the same ointment that ran on the head of Jesus, even the Holy Spirit, and comes down all over His people. You and I are members of that Body of which He is the Head, and the oil that flowed on His head can flow down over His Body, which is you and me, and we can keep an unbroken continuity of life from the Jordan River. The life of the Holy Spirit came upon the head of Jesus, and it comes now upon you and me and upon all the people of God that dwell together in unity.

Are we such that God can bless us? Do we have this unity of determination to glorify the Lord alone . . . of a determination to see the Lord work, of oneness in present expectation, of submission to the Lord and of resolution to put away everything that hinders? If we are, then we're a united people and we may expect any time the oil that flowed on the head of Jesus to flow down over us and bring oil and blessing and life for evermore. SAT101

Lord, give us that unity, that absorption, that resolution to put away anything that hinders. Let us feel the oil. Amen.

God Is . . .

God is love.
—1 JOHN 4:8

When the Scripture says, "God is love," it is not defining God. It does not tell us what God is in His metaphysical being. In the first place, the Bible never tells us what God is in His deep, essential being. No one can conceive what God is (except God), because God is inconceivable. Even if anyone could conceive it, it couldn't be expressed because God is ineffable. And if it could be expressed, it couldn't be understood because God is incomprehensible.

Therefore, to equate love with God is to go way off in your theology. If God is love in His metaphysical being, then God and love are equal to each other—identical. We could worship love as God! Thus, we would be worshiping an attribute of personality and not the person Himself, thereby destroying the concept of personality in God and denying in one sweep all the other attributes of the deity. Don't forget that it also says, "God is light" (1 John 1:5) and "This is the true God, and eternal life" (5:20), but we don't try to limit His nature to just light or life! AOGII196-197

Holy Father, You are supremely loving and far beyond my comprehension. I praise You today for who You are—wholly unlike any other. Amen.

Purified by Fire

With it he touched my mouth and said, "See, this has touched
your lips; your guilt is taken away and your sin atoned for."
—ISAIAH 6:7

We like Isaiah's vision and awareness. But we do not like to think of the live coal out of the fire being placed on the prophet's lips.

Purification by blood and by fire. Isaiah's lips, symbolic of all his nature, were purified by fire. God could then say to him, "Thine iniquity is taken away" (Isa. 6:7).

That is how the amazed and pained Isaiah could genuinely come to a sense of restored moral innocence. That is how he instantly found that he was ready for worship and that he was also ready and anxious for service in the will of God.

With each of us, if we are to have that assurance of forgiveness and restored moral innocence, the fire of God's grace must touch us. It is only through the depths of the forgiving love of God that men and women can be so restored and made ready to serve Him. WHT077

Thank You, Father, that the fire of Your grace includes all the suffering of our Lord Jesus Christ. Cleanse me, purge me, purify me by His blood. Amen.

We Have Lost God

Let us then approach God's throne of grace with confidence,
so that we may receive mercy and find grace to help us in our
time of need.
—2 CHRONICLES 21:20

The average person in the world today, without faith and without God and without hope, is engaged in a desperate personal search throughout his lifetime. He does not really know where he has been. He does not really know what he is doing here and now. He does not know where he is going.

The sad commentary is that he is doing it all on borrowed time and borrowed money and borrowed strength—and he already knows that in the end he will surely die! It boils down to the bewildered confession of many that "we have lost God somewhere along the way." . . .

Man, made more like God than any other creature, has become less like God than any other creature. Created to reflect the glory of God, he has retreated sullenly into his cave—reflecting only his own sinfulness.

Certainly it is a tragedy above all tragedies . . . that man, made with a soul to worship and praise and sing to God's glory, now sulks silently in his cave. Love has gone from his heart. Light has gone from his mind. Having lost God, he blindly stumbles on through this dark world to find only a grave at the end. WHT065-066

*Lord, may I not live and then "depart without being desired."
Instead, may I find fulfillment and purpose in You. Direct me
to that end, I pray. Amen.*

God Was Forced Out

Then Jesus said to his disciples, "Whoever wants to be my disciple must deny themselves and take up their cross and follow me."

—MATTHEW 16:24

Before the Lord God made man upon the earth, He first prepared for him a world of useful and pleasant things for his sustenance and delight. In the Genesis account of the creation, these are called simply "things." They were made for man's use, but they were meant always to be external to the man and subservient to him. In the deep heart of the man was a shrine where none but God was worthy to come. Within him was God; without, a thousand gifts which God had showered upon him. . . .

Our woes began when God was forced out of His central shrine and things were allowed to enter. Within the human heart things have taken over. Men have now by nature no peace within their hearts, for God is crowned there no longer, but there in the moral dusk, stubborn and aggressive usurpers fight among themselves for first place on the throne. . . .

The roots of our hearts have grown down into things, and we dare not pull up one rootlet, lest we die. Things have become necessary to us, a development never originally intended. God's gifts now take the place of God, and the whole course of nature is upset by the monstrous substitution. POG021-022

Lord, deliver me from this dependence on material things. If You need to completely remove some things from me, help me to be willing to give them up in complete submission to You. Amen.

Little Need for God

And I'll say to myself, "You have plenty of grain laid up for many years. Take life easy; eat, drink and be merry."
—LUKE 12:19

It does not take great wisdom to perceive that we live in a generation of completely self-confident men and women. We are doing so well and flourishing in so many ways that we feel little need for God. . . .

It is my judgment that every one of us should be sure we have had that all-important encounter with God. It is an experience that leaves us delighted in our love for Him. Like Abraham, we become satisfied with the revelation that only God matters.

If you are living only to buy and sell and get gain, that is not enough. If you are living only to sleep and work, that is not enough. If you are living only to prosper and marry and raise a family, that is not enough.

If you live only to get old and die, and never find forgiveness and the daily sense of God's presence in your life, you have missed God's great purpose for you. MMG030, 032

Oh, Lord, give me a sense not only of my own mortality, but of the importance of an eternal perspective. Give me a keen sense of forgiveness and of Your presence in my life today. Amen.

God As Honored Guest

The kings of the earth rise up and the rulers band together
against the LORD and against his anointed, saying, "Let us break
their chains and throw off their shackles."
—PSALM 2:2-3

The old world of fallen nature is the world of human will. There, man is king, and his will decides events. So far as he is able in his weakness, he decides how and what and when and where. He fixes values: what is to be esteemed, what despised, what received, and what rejected. His will runs through everything. . . .

Yet in their pride men assert their will and claim ownership of the earth. Well, for a time it is true, that this is man's world. God is admitted only by man's sufferance. He is treated as visiting royalty in a democratic country. Everyone takes His name upon his lips, and (especially at certain seasons) He is feted and celebrated and hymned. But behind all this flattery, men hold firmly to their right of self-determination. As long as man is allowed to play host, he will honor God with his attention, but always He must remain a guest and never seek to be Lord. Man will have it understood that this is his world; he will make its laws and decide how it shall be run. God is permitted to decide nothing. Man bows to Him, and as he bows, manages with difficulty to conceal the crown upon his own head. POM034-035

---

*Lord, I want to heed the admonition of God through the psalmist,
"Kiss the Son, lest he be angry" (Ps. 2:12). Help me to give You
today the supremacy, the throne, the absolute authority that
You deserve. Amen.*

The Problem with Science

The Lᴏʀᴅ looks down from heaven on all mankind to see if there
are any who understand, any who seek God.
—PSALM 14:2

When God spoke out of heaven to our Lord, self-centered men
who heard it explained it by natural causes, saying, "it thundered" (John 12:29). This habit of explaining the Voice by appeals
to natural law is at the very root of modern science. In the living,
breathing cosmos, there is a mysterious Something, too wonderful,
too awful for any mind to understand. The believing man does not
claim to understand. He falls to his knees and whispers, "God." The
man of earth kneels also, but not to worship. He kneels to examine,
to search, to find the cause and the how of things. Just now we happen to be living in a secular age. Our thought habits are those of the
scientist, not those of the worshiper. We are more likely to explain
than to adore. "It thundered," we exclaim, and go our earthly way.
But still the Voice sounds and searches. The order and life of the
world depend upon that Voice, but men are mostly too busy or too
stubborn to give attention. POG073-074

*Lord, I don't claim to understand, but I fall to my knees and
whisper, "God." Give me increasingly the mind of the worshiper,
I pray. Amen.*

Nature Worship

The earth is the Lord's, and everything in it, the world, and all
who live in it.
—PSALM 24:1

Then there is nature worship. That is the worship of the natural man, only on a very poetic and philosophical level. It is an appreciation for the poetry of religion. It's a high enjoyment of the contemplation of the sublime. . . .

Such are the poets; they like to look at trees and write sonnets. Well, there's a good deal of religion and supposed worship that is no higher than that. It's simply the enjoyment of nature. People may mistake the rapt feeling they have in the presence of trees and rivers for worship. Ralph Waldo Emerson said that he had at times—on a moonlit night walking across a meadow after a rain and smelling the freshness of the ground and seeing the broken clouds with the moon struggling through—he said he had often been glad to the point of fear. Yet Emerson was not a regenerated man. He did not claim to be.

I want to warn you against the religion that is no more than love, music, and poetry. I happen to be somewhat of a fan of good music. I think Beethoven's nine symphonies constitute the greatest body of music ever composed by mortal man. Yet I realize I'm listening to music; I'm not worshiping God necessarily. There's a difference between beautiful sound beautifully put together and worship. Worship is another matter. WMJ013-014

---

*Lord, help me remember that everything of beauty is from the
Creator, who alone is worthy of my worship. Amen.*

Idolatry

You shall not make for yourself an image in the form of anything in heaven above or on the earth beneath or in the waters below.
—EXODUS 20:4

Idolatry is of all sins the most hateful to God because it is in essence a defamation of the divine character. It holds a low opinion of God, and when it advertises that opinion, it is guilty of circulating an evil rumor about the Majesty in the heavens. Thus it slanders the Deity. No wonder God hates it.

We should beware of the comfortable habit of assuming that idolatry is found only in heathen lands and that civilized people are free from it. This is an error and results from pride and superficial thinking. The truth is that idolatry is found wherever mankind is found. Whoever entertains an unworthy conception of God is throwing his or her heart wide open to the sin of idolatry. Let that person go on to personalize his or her low mental image of the Deity and pray to it, and he or she has become an idolater—and this is regardless of his or her nominal profession of Christianity.

It is vitally important that we think soundly about God. Since He is the foundation of all our religious beliefs, it follows that if we err in our ideas of God, we will go astray on everything else. TWP104

Lord, forgive me for insidious idolatry that portrays You as anything less than You are. Even to try to picture You in my mind tends to distort Your image. I fall on my knees to worship the incomprehensible God. Amen.

A King on a Throne

My ears had heard of you but now my eyes have seen you.
Therefore I despise myself and repent in dust and ashes.

—JOB 42:5-6

Everything comes out from God and returns to God again. The great God Almighty, the Lord God omnipotent, reigneth. He has now the same amount of power that He had when He made the heaven and the earth and called the stars into being. He will never have any less power than He has now, nor will He ever have any more since He has all the power there is. That is the God we serve! . . .

The great God Almighty stretches forth His broad wings and moves upon the wind. God will hold you up. He'll keep you if you turn yourself over to Him! He'll hold you when nothing else can; nothing will be able to destroy you.

God contains, perpetuates, and sustains all things. He is "upholding all things by the word of his power" (Heb. 1:3). It is God that holds all things together. Do you ever wonder why you don't cave in from fourteen pounds of air pressure on every square inch of your body? Have you ever wondered why you don't blow up from internal pressure? Because the great God Almighty has spoken His power into His universe, and everything runs according to that power. AOGII80-81

Lord, throughout this year I have been confronted with Your majesty. May this cause me to recognize my own sinfulness, to repent and to allow You to have the throne. Amen.

Our Sovereign Lord

The Most High does not live in houses made by human hands. . . .
Heaven is my throne, and the earth is my footstool.
—ACTS 7:48-49

How can you be a Christian and not be aware of the sovereignty of the God who has loved us to the death?

To be sovereign, God must be the absolute, infinite, unqualified ruler in all realms in heaven and earth and sea. To be Lord over all the creation, He must be omnipotent. He must be omniscient. He must be omnipresent.

With all that is within me, I believe that the crucified and risen and glorified Savior, Jesus Christ, is the sovereign Lord. He takes no orders from anyone. He has no counselors and no advisers. He has no secretary to the throne. He knows in the one effortless act all that can be known, and He has already lived out our tomorrows and holds the world in the palm of His hand.

That is the Lord I serve! I gladly own that I am His; glory to God! The Christ we know and serve is infinitely beyond all men and all angels and all archangels, above all principalities and powers and dominions, visible and invisible—for He is the origin of them all!

MWTJune22

Lord, to begin to understand Your attributes is totally overwhelming. That such an Almighty God would care so much for His creation is truly humbling.

The Seeking Heart Finds God

You will seek me and find me when you seek me with all your heart.

—JEREMIAH 29:13

God being who He is must have obedience from His creatures. Man being who he is must render that obedience. And he owes God complete obedience whether or not he feels for Him the faintest trace of love in his heart. It is a question of the sovereign right of God to require His creatures to obey Him. Man's first and basic sin was disobedience. When he disobeyed God, he violated the claims of divine love with the result that love for God died within him. Now, what can he do to restore that love to his heart again? The answer to that question is given in one word: Repent.

The heart that mourns its coldness toward God needs only to repent its sins, and a new, warm and satisfying love will flood into it. For the act of repentance will bring a corresponding act of God in self-revelation and intimate communion. Once the seeking heart finds God in personal experience, there will be no further problem about loving Him. To know Him is to love Him, and to know Him better is to love Him more. ROR165

Lord, I mourn my coldness toward You and repent, that I may enter into a loving, intimate relationship with You. Amen.

Worship in Spirit and Truth

God is spirit, and his worshipers must worship in the Spirit
and in truth.

—JOHN 4:24

Worship must be in spirit and in truth! It must be the truth of God and the Spirit of God. When a person, yielding to God and believing the truth of God, is filled with the Spirit of God, even his faintest whisper will be worship.

The stark, tragic fact is that the efforts of many people to worship are unacceptable to God. Without an infusion of the Holy Spirit, there can be no true worship. This is serious. It is hard for me to rest peacefully at night knowing that millions of cultured, religious people are merely carrying on church traditions and religious customs and they are not actually reaching God at all.

We must humbly worship God in spirit and in truth. Each one of us stands before the truth to be judged. Is it not now plain that the presence and the power of the Holy Spirit of God, far from being an optional luxury in our Christian lives, is a necessity? WHT046

Lord, fill me with Your Spirit as I worship You today. I don't want just to carry on church traditions and religious customs. Send the Spirit today, that my worship might be more real. Amen.

The Self-Existent God

The LORD reigns, let the nations tremble; he sits enthroned
between the cherubim, let the earth shake.
—PSALM 99:1

In this context, I confess a sadness about the shallowness of Christian thinking in our day. Many are interested in religion as a kind of toy. If we could make a judgment, it would appear that numbers of men and women go to church without any genuine desire to gear into deity. They do not come to meet God and delight in His presence. They do not come to hear from that everlasting world above! . . .

Compared to Him, everything around us in this world shrinks in stature and significance. It is all a little business compared to Him— little churches with little preachers; little authors and little editors; little singers and little musicians; little deacons and little officials; little educators and little statesmen; little cities and little men and little things!

Brethren, humankind is so smothered under the little grains of dust that make up the world and time and space and matter that we are prone to forget that at one point God lived and dwelt and existed and loved without support, without help, and without creation.

Such is the causeless and self-existent God! CES038-039

---

*Lord, as I enter the church service this next Sunday, help me
to come expectantly. I'm little; You are big. Let me wait in silence
before You. Amen.*

NOVEMBER

Monday Morning

The LORD is in his holy temple; let all the earth be silent
before him.
—HABAKKUK 2:20

As God's people, we are so often confused that we could be
known as God's poor, stumbling, bumbling people. That must
be true of a great number of us, for we always think of worship as
something we do when we go to church.

We call it God's house. We have dedicated it to Him. So we continue with the confused idea that it must be the only place where we
can worship Him.

We come to the Lord's house, made out of brick and wood and
lined with carpeting. We are used to hearing a call to worship: "The
Lord is in His holy temple—let us all kneel before Him."

That is on Sunday and that is in church. Very nice!

But Monday morning comes soon. The Christian layman goes to
his office. The Christian school teacher goes to the classroom. The
Christian mother is busy with duties in the home. . . .

Actually, none of us has the ability to fool God. Therefore, if we
are so engaged in our Saturday pursuits that we are far from His
presence and far from a sense of worship on Saturday, we are not in
very good shape to worship Him on Sunday. WHT121-122

---

*Lord, I want to kneel before You in worship not only on Sunday,
but on Saturday and the rest of the week as well. Accept my
entire life as a sacrifice of worship to You, I pray. Amen.*

In His Holy Temple

So whether you eat or drink or whatever you do, do it all for the glory of God.
—1 CORINTHIANS 10:31

On Monday, as we go about our different duties and tasks, are we aware of the Presence of God? The Lord desires still to be in His holy temple, wherever we are. He wants the continuing love and delight and worship of His children, wherever we work.

Is it not a beautiful thing for a businessman to enter his office on Monday morning with an inner call to worship: "The Lord is in my office—let all the world be silent before Him"?

If you cannot worship the Lord in the midst of your responsibilities on Monday, it is not very likely that you were worshiping on Sunday! . . .

I guess many people have an idea that they have God in a box. He is just in the church sanctuary, and when we leave and drive toward home, we have a rather faint, homesick feeling that we are leaving God in the big box.

You know that is not true, but what are you doing about it? WHT122

Lord, may I today—whatever day it happens to be—go about my tasks with an overlying sense of worship, that You would be glorified in everything I do, say, or think today. Amen.

The Inner Sanctum

Here I am! I stand at the door and knock. If anyone hears my
voice and opens the door, I will come in and eat with that person,
and they with me.
—REVELATION 3:20

O ne of the most liberating declarations in the New Testament
is this:

The true worshippers shall worship the Father in spirit and
in truth: for the Father seeketh such to worship him. God is a
Spirit: and they that worship him must worship him in spirit
and in truth. (John 4:23–24)

Here the nature of worship is shown to be wholly spiritual. True
religion is removed from diet and days, from garments and ceremo-
nies, and placed where it belongs—in the union of the spirit of men
with the Spirit of God.

From man's standpoint, the most tragic loss suffered in the Fall
was the vacating of this inner sanctum by the Spirit of God. At the
far-in hidden center of man's being is a bush fitted to be the dwelling
place of the triune God. There God planned to rest and glow with
moral and spiritual fire. Man by his sin forfeited this indescribably
wonderful privilege and must now dwell there alone. For so intimately private is the place that no creature can intrude; no one can
enter but Christ, and He will enter only by the invitation of faith.

MDP004-005

*Lord, fill the inner sanctum of my heart, I pray. Come in and fill
me with Your holy fire, that I might uniquely sense Your presence
today. Amen.*

Because He Is God

Whom have I in heaven but you? And earth has nothing I desire
besides you.
—PSALM 73:25

The teaching of the Bible is that God is Himself the end for which
man was created. "Whom have I in heaven but thee?" cried the
psalmist, "and there is none upon earth that I desire beside thee"
(Ps. 73:25). The first and greatest commandment is to love God with
every power of our entire being. Where love like that exists, there
can be no place for a second object. If we love God as much as we
should, surely we cannot dream of a loved object beyond Him which
He might help us to obtain.

Bernard of Clairvaux begins his radiant little treatise on the love of
God with a question and an answer. The question: Why should we love
God? The answer: Because He is God. He develops the idea further,
but for the enlightened heart little more need be said. We should love
God because He is God. Beyond this the angels cannot think. MDP060

---

*Father, I do indeed love You simply because You are God. May You
continue to be the focus of my dreams and desires as I go about
my ordinary day. Amen.*

Too Familiar with God

Glorify the LORD with me; let us exalt his name together.
—PSALM 34:3

Worship rises or falls in any church altogether depending upon the attitude we take toward God, whether we see God big or whether we see Him little. Most of us see God too small; our God is too little. David said, "O magnify the LORD with me," and "magnify" doesn't mean to make God big. You can't make God big. But you can see Him big.

Worship, I say, rises or falls with our concept of God; that is why I do not believe in these half-converted cowboys who call God the Man Upstairs. I do not think they worship at all because their concept of God is unworthy of God and unworthy of them. And if there is one terrible disease in the Church of Christ, it is that we do not see God as great as He is. We're too familiar with God. WMJ021

Oh, God, may my concept of You be worthy of Your majesty.
Forgive me for being too familiar and for seeing You so small.
I magnify You and fall on my face in worship. Amen.

The True Meaning of Worship

Wealth and honor come from you; you are the ruler of all things. In your hands are strength and power to exalt and give strength to all. Now, our God, we give you thanks, and praise your glorious name.
—1 CHRONICLES 29:12–13

A ctually, basic beliefs about the Person and the nature of God have changed so much that there are among us now men and women who find it easy to brag about the benefits they receive from God—without ever a thought or a desire to know the true meaning of worship!

I have immediate reactions to such an extreme misunderstanding of the true nature of a holy and sovereign God.

My first is that I believe the very last thing God desires is to have shallow-minded and worldly Christians bragging about Him.

My second is that it does not seem to be very well recognized that God's highest desire is that every one of His believing children should so love and so adore Him that we are continuously in His presence, in Spirit and in truth.

That is to worship, indeed. WHT023-024

Lord, help me, in the midst of all the blessings You shower upon me, to keep my focus on the Giver and not on the gifts. Teach me to love and adore You in genuine worship. Amen.

We Belong to God

You are worthy, our Lord and God, to receive glory and honor
and power, for you created all things, and by your will they were
created and have their being."
—REVELATION 4:11

Every soul belongs to God and exists by His pleasure. God being who and what He is, and we being who and what we are, the only thinkable relation between us is one of full Lordship on His part and complete submission on ours. We owe Him every honor that is in our power to give Him. Our everlasting grief lies in giving Him anything less.

The pursuit of God will embrace the labor of bringing our total personality into conformity to His. And this not judicially, but actually. I do not here refer to the act of justification by faith in Christ. I speak of a voluntary exalting of God to His proper station over us and a willing surrender of our whole being to the place of worshipful submission which the Creator-creature circumstance makes proper. . . .

Made as we were in the image of God, we scarcely find it strange to take again our God as our All. God was our original habitat, and our hearts cannot but feel at home when they enter again that ancient and beautiful abode. POG096, 098

---

*Father, I am Your creation, and I owe You every honor I can give.
I bow in complete submission to Your Lordship. How can I do any
less? Amen.*

Some Things Must Go

Through these he has given us his very great and precious
promises, so that through them you may participate in the divine
nature, having escaped the corruption in the world caused
by evil desires.
—2 PETER 1:4

I repeat my view of worship—no worship is wholly pleasing to
God until there is nothing in me displeasing to God. . . .

There is nothing in either of us that can be made good until Jesus
Christ comes and changes us—until He lives in us and unites our
nature with God, the Father Almighty. Not until then can we call
ourselves good.

That is why I say that your worship must be total. It must involve
the whole you. That is why you must prepare to worship God, and
that preparation is not always pleasant. There may be revolutionary
changes which must take place in your life.

If there is to be true and blessed worship, some things in your life
must be destroyed, eliminated. The gospel of Jesus Christ is certainly
positive and constructive. But it must be destructive in some areas,
dealing with and destroying certain elements that cannot remain in
a life pleasing to God. WHT125

---

*Search me, O God, and know my heart. May there be nothing
in me displeasing to You, that I may worship You totally. If there
is anything to be destroyed within me, I yield myself to the Holy
Spirit's work. Amen.*

Evil in Our Nature

Cleanse me with hyssop, and I will be clean; wash me, and I will
be whiter than snow.
—PSALM 51:7

Why should we delude ourselves about pleasing God in worship? If I live like a worldly and carnal tramp all day and then find myself in a time of crisis at midnight, how do I pray to a God who is holy? How do I address the One who has asked me to worship Him in spirit and in truth? Do I get on my knees and call on the name of Jesus because I believe there is some magic in that name?

If I am still the same worldly, carnal tramp, I will be disappointed and disillusioned. If I am not living in the true meaning of His name and His nature, I cannot properly pray in that name. If I am not living in His nature, I cannot rightly pray in that nature.

How can we hope to worship God acceptably when these evil elements remain in our natures undisciplined, uncorrected, unpurged, unpurified? Even granted that a man with evil ingredients in his nature might manage through some part of himself to worship God half-acceptably. But what kind of a way is that in which to live and continue? WHT126-127

*Lord, it is the longing of my heart that I might worship You
acceptably. Purge me and cleanse me, that the evil nature within
me might be subdued. Amen.*

NOVEMBER 10

Saved to Worship

But you are a chosen people, a royal priesthood, a holy nation,
God's special possession, that you may declare the praises of
him who called you out of darkness into his wonderful light.
—1 PETER 2:9

I believe a local church exists to do corporately what each Christian believer should be doing individually—and that is to worship God. It is to show forth the excellencies of Him who has "called [us] out of darkness into his marvellous light" (1 Peter 2:9). It is to reflect the glories of Christ ever shining upon us through the ministries of the Holy Spirit.

I am going to say something to you which will sound strange. It even sounds strange to me as I say it, because we are not used to hearing it within our Christian fellowships. We are saved to worship God. All that Christ has done for us in the past and all that He is doing now leads to this one end. . . .

If we are willing to confess that we have been called out of darkness to show forth the glory of Him who called us, we should also be willing to take whatever steps are necessary to fulfill our high design and calling as the New Testament Church. WHT093-094, 097

---

*Lord, I acknowledge today that my highest calling and my
purpose for existence is to worship You. May I and my church
glorify You through our worship. Amen.*

In Need of Worshipers

And [we] will give our attention to prayer and the ministry
of the word.
—ACTS 6:4

Well, we have great churches and we have beautiful sanctuaries and we join in the chorus, "We have need of nothing." But there is every indication that we are in need of worshipers.

We have a lot of men willing to sit on our church boards who have no desire for spiritual joy and radiance and who never show up for the church prayer meeting. These are the men who often make the decisions about the church budget and the church expenses and where the frills will go in the new edifice. . . .

It seems to me that it has always been a frightful incongruity that men who do not pray and do not worship are nevertheless actually running many of the churches and ultimately determining the direction they will take.

It hits very close to our own situations, perhaps, but we should confess that in many "good" churches, we let the women do the praying and let the men do the voting.

Because we are not truly worshipers, we spend a lot of time in the churches just spinning wheels, burning the gasoline, making a noise but not getting anywhere. WHT016-017

Lord, give us men who are willing to lead in the Church, in prayer and in true worship, of which You are so deserving. Amen.

With a Loud Voice

The whole crowd of disciples began joyfully to praise God in loud
voices for all the miracles they had seen: "Blessed is the king
who comes in the name of the Lord! Peace in heaven and glory
in the highest!"
—LUKE 19:37-38

This does not mean, and I am not saying, that we must all worship alike. The Holy Spirit does not operate by anyone's pre-
conceived idea or formula. But this I know: When the Holy Spirit of
God comes among us with His anointing, we become a worshiping
people. This may be hard for some to admit, but when we are truly
worshiping and adoring the God of all grace and of all love and of
all mercy and of all truth, we may not be quiet enough to please
everyone. . . .

First, I do not believe it is necessarily true that we are worshiping
God when we are making a lot of racket. But not infrequently worship is audible. . . .

Second, I would warn those who are cultured, quiet, self-possessed,
poised, and sophisticated that if they are embarrassed in church when
some happy Christian says "Amen!" they may actually be in need of
some spiritual enlightenment. The worshiping saints of God in the
Body of Christ have often been a little bit noisy. WHT014-015

*Lord, may my worship be genuine and heartfelt, whether it be
in quiet meditation or in loud exaltation! Amen.*

Religious Extroversion

The LORD does not look at the things people look at. People look
at the outward appearance, but the LORD looks at the heart.
—1 SAMUEL 16:7

The accent in the Church today," says Leonard Ravenhill, the
English evangelist, "is not on devotion, but on commotion."
Religious extroversion has been carried to such an extreme in evangelical circles that hardly anyone has the desire, to say nothing of the courage, to question the soundness of it. Externalism has taken over. God now speaks by the wind and the earthquake only; the still small voice can be heard no more. The whole religious machine has become a noisemaker. The adolescent taste which loves the loud horn and the thundering exhaust has gotten into the activities of modern Christians. The old question, "What is the chief end of man?" is now answered, "To dash about the world and add to the din thereof." . . .

We must begin the needed reform by challenging the spiritual validity of externalism. What a man is must be shown to be more important than what he does. While the moral quality of any act is imparted by the condition of the heart, there may be a world of religious activity which arises not from within but from without and which would seem to have little or no moral content. ROR084-085

---

*Lord, yesterday I saw the need for loud exaltation at times; today
I am reminded of the importance of internal meditation, and of
guarding myself from mere external noise. Give me the right
balance in my worship, I pray. Amen.*

The One Thing Missing

You say, "I am rich; I have acquired wealth and do not need a
thing." But you do not realize that you are wretched, pitiful, poor,
blind and naked. . . . Those whom I love I rebuke and discipline.
So be earnest and repent.
—REVELATION 3:17, 19

Christian churches have come to the dangerous time predicted long ago. It is a time when we can pat one another on the back, congratulate ourselves, and join in the glad refrain, "We are rich, and increased with goods, and have need of nothing!"

It certainly is true that hardly anything is missing from our churches these days—except the most important thing. We are missing the genuine and sacred offering of ourselves and our worship to the God and Father of our Lord Jesus Christ. . . .

We have been surging forward. We are building great churches and large congregations. We are boasting about high standards, and we are talking a lot about revival.

But I have a question, and it is not just rhetoric: What has happened to our worship? WHT009-010

Lord, may we not become caught up in all we have and yet be
found wanting in the most important element in our church life!
May we understand that true success comes from the intimacy
with You that we experience in true worship. Amen.

NOVEMBER 15

Set Aside the Agenda

The whole assembly became silent as they listened to Barnabas
and Paul telling about the signs and wonders God had done
among the Gentiles through them.

—ACTS 15:12

When we compare our present carefully programmed meetings with the New Testament, we are reminded of the remark of a famous literary critic after he had read Alexander Pope's translation of Homer's Odyssey: "It is a beautiful poem, but it is not Homer." So the fast-paced, highly spiced, entertaining service of today may be a beautiful example of masterful programming—but it is not a Christian service. The two are leagues apart in almost every essential. About the only thing they have in common is the presence of a number of persons in one room. There the similarity ends and glaring dissimilarities begin. . . .

Throughout the New Testament after Pentecost, one marked characteristic of all Christian meetings was the believers' preoccupation with their risen Lord. Even the first Church Council . . . was conducted in an atmosphere of great dignity and deep reverence. It is of course unthinkable that such a meeting could have been held without some kind of agenda. Someone had to know what they had gathered to discuss. The important point to be noticed, however, is that proceedings were carried on in an atmosphere of Christian worship. They lost sight of the program in the greater glory of a Presence. ROR105-107

*Thank You, Father, for the commitment to excellence in many
churches. But don't let us lose sight of the glory of Your
presence, which is so much more important. Amen.*

The Program Instead of the Presence

With great power the apostles continued to testify to the resurrection of the Lord Jesus. And God's grace was so powerfully at work in them all.

—ACTS 4:33

N ow, I freely admit that it is impossible to hold a Christian service without an agenda. If order is to be maintained, an order of service must exist somewhere. If two songs are to be sung, someone must know which one is to be sung first, and whether this knowledge is only in someone's head or has been reduced to paper, there is indeed a "program," however we may dislike to call it that. The point we make here is that in our times the program has been substituted for the Presence. The program rather than the Lord of glory is the center of attraction. So the most popular gospel church in any city is likely to be the one that offers the most interesting program—that is, the church that can present the most and best features for the enjoyment of the public. These features are programmed so as to keep everything moving and everybody expectant. . . .

We'll do our churches a lot of good if we each one seek to cultivate the blessed Presence in our services. If we make Christ the supreme and constant object of devotion, the program will take its place as a gentle aid to order in the public worship of God. If we fail to do this, the program will finally obscure the Light entirely. And no church can afford that. ROR107-109

Like the apostles, Lord, I want to see the resurrected Christ in all His glory. Help us to focus not on the program of our worship but on the Lord of glory, who is the object of our worship. Amen.

Religious Entertainment

Let the message of Christ dwell among you richly as you
teach and admonish one another with all wisdom through
psalms, hymns, and songs from the Spirit, singing to God
with gratitude in your hearts.
—COLOSSIANS 3:16

Religious entertainment has so corrupted the Church of Christ that millions don't know that it's a heresy. . . . They don't know that it's as much a heresy as the counting of beads or the splashing of holy water or something else. To expose this, of course, raises a storm of angry protest among the people. . . .

When you raise your eyes to God and sing, "Break Thou the bread of life, dear Lord, to me," is that entertainment—or is it worship? Isn't there a difference between worship and entertainment? The church that can't worship must be entertained. And men who can't lead a church to worship must provide the entertainment. That is why we have the great evangelical heresy here today—the heresy of religious entertainment. SAT006-007

*Lord, help me to be aware of the dangers of religious entertain-
ment, and fill me to overflowing with psalms and hymns and
spiritual songs to Your glory! Amen.*

Wasted Religious Activity

Yet you, LORD, are our Father. We are the clay, you are the
potter; we are all the work of your hand.

—ISAIAH 64:8

There is probably not another field of human activity where there is so much waste as in the field of religion. . . .

In the average church, we hear the same prayers repeated each Sunday year in and year out with, one would suspect, not the remotest expectation that they will be answered. It is enough, it seems, that they have been uttered. The familiar phrase, the religious tone, the emotionally loaded words have their superficial and temporary effect, but the worshiper is no nearer to God, no better morally, and no surer of heaven than he was before. Yet every Sunday morning for twenty years, he goes through the same routine and, allowing two hours for him to leave his house, sit through a church service and return to his house again, he has wasted more than 170 twelve-hour days with this exercise in futility. . . .

I need only add that all this tragic waste is unnecessary. The believing Christian will relish every moment in church and will profit by it. The instructed, obedient Christian will yield to God as the clay to the potter, and the result will be not waste but glory everlasting.

BAM100-101, 103

I don't ever want to waste another hour just going through the motions, Father. As I worship, may I do so with an attitude of obedience, expectancy, and yielding—as the clay before the potter. Amen.

Quality Matters to God

Yet a time is coming and has now come when the true worshipers will worship the Father in the Spirit and in truth, for they are the kind of worshipers the Father seeks.

—JOHN 4:23

To God quality is vastly important, and size matters little. . . . Man's moral fall has clouded his vision, confused his thinking, and rendered him subject to delusion. One evidence of this is his all but incurable proneness to put size before quality in his appraisal of things. The Christian faith reverses this order, but even Christians tend to judge things by the old Adamic rule. How big? How much? and How many? are the questions oftenest asked by religious persons when trying to evaluate Christian things. . . .

The Christian faith engages a spiritual kingdom where quality of being is everything.

The hour cometh, and now is, when the true worshippers shall worship the Father in spirit and in truth: for the Father seeketh such to worship him. God is a Spirit: and they that worship him must worship him in spirit and in truth. (John 4:23–24)

With these words Jesus showed how far both Jews and Samaritans were astray in their argument over the proper place to worship. Not the beauty of a city nor the size of a mountain matters to the Father; truth and spirit and all the wealth of moral qualities that gather around them: these are all in all. BAM072-074

Lord, deliver me from the "size matters" mentality. Renew my worship, I pray. Amen.

Divine Sacredness

The commander of the Lord's army replied, "Take off your
sandals, for the place where you are standing is holy." And
Joshua did so.
—JOSHUA 5:15

D o you quietly bow your head in reverence when you step into
the average gospel church?

I am not surprised if your answer is no.

There is grief in my spirit when I go into the average church, for
we have become a generation rapidly losing all sense of divine sacredness in our worship. Many whom we have raised in our churches
no longer think in terms of reverence—which seems to indicate they
doubt that God's Presence is there.

In too many of our churches, you can detect the attitude that anything goes. It is my assessment that losing the awareness of God in
our midst is a loss too terrible ever to be appraised. WHT117

*Lord, I pray that we might restore to our worship a real sense
of the divine sacredness of Your Presence in our churches and in
our lives. Amen.*

No Wonder, No Holy Fear

Fire came out from the presence of the LORD and consumed the
burnt offering and the fat portions on the altar. And when all the
people saw it, they shouted for joy and fell facedown.
—LEVITICUS 9:24

We of the nonliturgical churches tend to look with some disdain upon those churches that follow a carefully prescribed form of service, and certainly there must be a good deal in such services that has little or no meaning for the average participant—this not because it is carefully prescribed but because the average participant is what he is. But I have observed that our familiar impromptu service, planned by the leader twenty minutes before, often tends to follow a ragged and tired order almost as standardized as the Mass. The liturgical service is at least beautiful; ours is often ugly. Theirs has been carefully worked out through the centuries to capture as much of beauty as possible and to preserve a spirit of reverence among the worshipers. Ours is often an off-the-cuff makeshift with nothing to recommend it. Its so-called liberty is often not liberty at all but sheer slovenliness. . . .

In the majority of our meetings there is scarcely a trace of reverent thought, no recognition of the unity of the body, little sense of the divine Presence, no moment of stillness, no solemnity, no wonder, no holy fear. GTM004-005

We need, oh Lord, a renewed sense of the awe, the wonder, and the beauty of worship. Grant that I might begin to sense Your awesome presence in my worship today. Amen.

A Worshiper First

Ask the Lord of the harvest, therefore, to send out workers
into his harvest field.
—MATTHEW 9:38

The work of Christ in redemption, for all its mystery, has a simple and understandable end: it is to restore men to the position from which they fell and bring them around again to be admirers and lovers of the triune God. God saves men to make them worshipers.

This great central fact has been largely forgotten today, not by the liberals and the cults only, but by evangelical Christians as well. By direct teaching, by story, by example, by psychological pressure we force our new converts to "go to work for the Lord." Ignoring the fact that God has redeemed them to make worshipers out of them, we thrust them out into "service," quite as if the Lord were recruiting laborers for a project instead of seeking to restore moral beings to a condition where they can glorify God and enjoy Him forever. . . .

Our Lord commands us to pray the Lord of the harvest that He will send forth laborers into His harvest field. What we are overlooking is that no one can be a worker who is not first a worshiper. Labor that does not spring out of worship is futile and can only be wood, hay, and stubble in the day that shall try every man's works. BAM125

*Make me a fervent, passionate worshiper, Lord, that I may
become a worthy and effective worker. Amen.*

Worshipers Out of Rebels

For you were once darkness, but now you are light in the Lord.
Live as children of light.
—EPHESIANS 5:8

Something wonderful and miraculous and life-changing takes place within the human soul when Jesus Christ is invited in to take His rightful place. That is exactly what God anticipated when He wrought the plan of salvation. He intended to make worshipers out of rebels; He intended to restore to men and women the place of worship that our first parents knew when they were created.

If we know this result as a blessed reality in our own lives and experience, then it is evident that we are not just waiting for Sunday to come so we can "go to church and worship."

True worship of God must be a constant and consistent attitude or state of mind within the believer. It will always be a sustained and blessed acknowledgement of love and adoration, subject in this life to degrees of perfection and intensity. WHT024

Forgive me, Father, when I fall into the old patterns of darkness. May I remember that I have been made a child of light and consequently have every reason to worship You, not just when I go to church but throughout every week. Amen.

My First Priority

I rejoiced with those who said to me, "Let us go to the house
of the Lord."
—PSALM 122:1

What are we going to do about this awesome, beautiful worship that God calls for? I would rather worship God than do any other thing I know of in all this wide world. . . .

I cannot speak for you, but I want to be among those who worship. I do not want just to be a part of some great ecclesiastical machine where the pastor turns the crank and the machine runs. You know—the pastor loves everybody and everybody loves him. He has to do it. He is paid to do it.

I wish that we might get back to worship again. Then when people come into the church they will instantly sense that they have come among holy people, God's people. They can testify, "Of a truth God is in this place." WHT018, 020

---

*Lord, I pray that Your Church would discover a renewed passion
for worship, that we would become a people who make Your
presence known through our very actions, attitudes, and presence
in the world. Amen.*

Work and Worship

For we are God's handiwork, created in Christ Jesus to do good
works, which God prepared in advance for us to do.
—EPHESIANS 2:10

To understand the relative importance of work and worship, it is
necessary to know the answer to the familiar question, "What is
the chief end of man?" The answer given in the catechism, "To glorify God and to enjoy Him forever," can scarcely be improved upon,
though of course it is an outline only and needs to be enlarged somewhat if it is to be a full and satisfying answer.

The primary purpose of God in creation was to prepare moral
beings spiritually and intellectually capable of worshiping Him. . . .

Without doubt the emphasis in Christian teaching today should
be on worship. There is little danger that we shall become merely
worshipers and neglect the practical implications of the gospel. No
one can long worship God in spirit and in truth before the obligation
to holy service becomes too strong to resist. Fellowship with God
leads straight to obedience and good works. That is the divine order,
and it can never be reversed. BAM123, 126

---

*Draw me deeper into fellowship with You, Father. Lead me to
focus on worship so that I can then, as a result, be useful in
service. Amen.*

Designed for a Single Purpose

Then God said to Abraham, "As for you, you must keep my covenant, you and your descendants after you for the generations to come."

—GENESIS 17:9

We are surrounded throughout our lifetime by a multitude of things designed for specific purposes. Without argument, most things are at their best when they are fulfilling their purpose and design.

For instance, a piano is made with a specific purpose: to produce music. However, I happen to know that someone once stood on a piano in order to put a fastener of some kind in the ceiling, I have seen piano tops that were cluttered filing cabinets or wide library shelves.

There is an intelligent design in the creation of a piano. The manufacturer did not announce: "This is a good piano. It has at least nineteen uses!" No, the designer had only one thought in mind: "This piano will have the purpose and potential of sounding forth beautiful music!" . . .

Do not miss the application of truth here. God was saying to Abraham, "You may have some other idea about the design and purpose for your life, but you are wrong! You were created in My image to worship Me and to glorify Me. If you do not honor this purpose, your life will degenerate into shallow, selfish, humanistic pursuits."

MMG022-023

May I be faithful, Lord, to the purpose for which You have created me. Life is too short and too futile to waste on anything other than worship of my Creator. Amen.

Tragic Blindness

*What good will it be for someone to gain the whole world,
yet forfeit their soul? Or what can anyone give in exchange for
their soul?*
—MATTHEW 16:26

This is my position: Let the scientist stay in his field and I will stay in mine. I am as glad and thankful as anyone for the benefits of research, and I hope scientists will soon find the cure for heart disease, for I have lost many good friends from sudden heart attacks.

But listen to me now about the difference in meaning between the short-term matters of our physical beings and the eternal relationships between the believer and his God.

If you save a person from diphtheria when he is a baby, or save him in his teens from smallpox, or save him in his fifties from a heart attack, what have you done?

If that man lives to be ninety and still is without God and does not know why he was born, you have simply perpetuated the life of a mud turtle. That man who has never found God and has never been born again is like a turtle, with two legs instead of four and no shell and no tail, because he still does not know what life has been all about. WHT060

---

*Thank You, Heavenly Father, that You opened my eyes to see the
purpose for my existence and the importance of focusing foremost
on the things of eternity. May I be faithful to share the message of
salvation today with others who are yet in blindness. Amen.*

The Bottom Line

After he drove the man out, he placed on the east side of the
Garden of Eden cherubim and a flaming sword flashing back
and forth to guard the way to the tree of life.
—GENESIS 3:24

Yes, worship of the loving God is man's whole reason for existence. That is why we are born and that is why we are born again from above. That is why we were created and that is why we have been recreated. That is why there was a genesis at the beginning, and that is why there is a re-genesis, called regeneration.

That is also why there is a church. The Christian church exists to worship God first of all. Everything else must come second or third or fourth or fifth. . . .

Sad, sad indeed, are the cries of so many today who have never discovered why they were born. It brings to mind the poet Milton's description of the pathetic lostness and loneliness of our first parents. Driven from the garden, he says, "they took hand in hand and through the valley made their solitary way." WHT056-057

Lord, use me today to point someone to the way out of the wilderness. Sad, sad indeed is the fact that so many of my own acquaintances may not yet know why they were born. Speak through me today. Amen.

NOVEMBER 29

The Chief End of Man

Through Jesus, therefore, let us continually offer to God
a sacrifice of praise—the fruit of lips that openly profess his name.
—HEBREWS 13:15

One of the greatest tragedies that we find, even in this most enlightened of all ages, is the utter failure of millions of men and
women ever to discover why there were born. . . .

Those who have followed the revelation provided by the Creator
God have accepted that God never does anything without a purpose.
We do believe, therefore, that God had a noble purpose in mind
when He created us. We believe that it was distinctly the will of God
that men and women created in His image would desire fellowship
with Him above all else.

In His plan, it was to be a perfect fellowship based on adoring
worship of the Creator and Sustainer of all things.

If you are acquainted with the Shorter Catechism, you know
that it asks an age-old, searching question: "What is the chief end
of man?"

The simple yet profound answer provided by the Catechism is
based upon the revelation and wisdom of the Word of God: "The chief
end of man is to glorify God and to enjoy Him forever." WHT049, 051

*May You be pleased, Father, as I seek to fulfill my chief aim
today—to glorify You and enjoy You forever. Amen.*

God Always Has a Purpose

*Everyone who is called by my name, whom I created
for my glory, whom I formed and made.*
—ISAIAH 43:7

God never acts without purpose—never. People act without purpose. I feel that a great deal of what we do in the church today is purposeless. But God never acts without a purpose. Intellect is an attribute of the deity. God has intellect, and this means that God thinks; and so God never does anything without an intelligent purpose. Nothing in this world is without meaning.

God put the universe together with a purpose, and there isn't a single useless thing anywhere—not any spare parts; everything fits into everything else. God made it like that. . . .

Now, these plain people of whom I speak believe that God created things for a purpose. He created the flowers, for instance, to be beautiful; He created birds to sing; He created the trees to bear fruit and the beasts to feed and clothe mankind. And in so saying, these people affirm what the Holy Scriptures and Moses and the prophets and the apostles and saints since the world began have all said. God made man for a purpose, and that purpose is given by the catechism. The answer is, "To glorify God and to enjoy Him forever." God made us to be worshipers. That was the purpose of God in bringing us into the world. WMJ001-003

Lord, may I never forget that You brought me into the world that I might be a worshiper. May I joyfully worship You every day of my existence on this earth. Amen.

DECEMBER

God's Desire

So God created mankind in his own image, in the image
of God he created them; male and female he created them.
—GENESIS 1:27

I believe there is good sound reasoning back of all this. I believe that He created man out of no external necessity. I believe it was an internal necessity. God, being the God He was and is, and being infinitely perfect and infinitely beautiful and infinitely glorious and infinitely admirable and infinitely loving, out of His own inward necessity had to have some creature that was capable of admiring Him and loving Him and knowing Him. So God made man in His own image; in the image and likeness of God made He him; and He made him as near to being like Himself as it was possible for the creature to be like the Creator. The most godlike thing in the universe is the soul of man.

The reason God made man in His image was that he might appreciate God and admire and adore and worship—so that God might not be a picture, so to speak, hanging in a gallery with nobody looking at Him. He might not be a flower that no one could smell; He might not be a star that no one could see. God made somebody to smell that flower, the lily of the valley. He wanted someone to see that glorious image. He wanted someone to see the star, so He made us and in making us made us to worship Him. WMJ003

*Lord, I can't completely comprehend how or why You created me
in Your image, as much like You as a creature could be. But I'll
respond today with admiration for Your creation and with worship
for my Creator. Amen.*

We Were Made to Worship

This is what the LORD says: "What fault did your ancestors find
in me, that they strayed so far from me?"
—JEREMIAH 2:5

Now we were made to worship, but the Scriptures tell us something else again. They tell us that man fell and kept not his first estate, that he forfeited the original glory of God and failed to fulfill the creative purpose, so that he is not worshiping now in the way that God meant him to worship. All else fulfills its design: flowers are still fragrant and lilies are still beautiful and the bees still search for nectar amongst the flowers, the birds still sing with their thousand-voice choir on a summer's day, and the sun and the moon and the stars all move on their rounds doing the will of God.

And from what we can learn from the Scriptures, we believe that the seraphim and cherubim and powers and dominions are still fulfilling their design—worshiping God who created them and breathed into them the breath of life. Man alone sulks in his cave. Man alone, with all of his brilliant intelligence, with all of his amazing, indescribable, and wonderful equipment, still sulks in his cave. He is either silent, or if he opens his mouth at all, it is to boast and threaten and curse, or it's nervous ill-considered laughter, or it's humor become big business, or it's songs without joy. WMJ006-007

---

*Lord, somehow do today the much-needed work of bringing us
out of our caves that we might be drawn to once again do what
we were created to do. Amen.*

Why Such Idiots?

For God did not send his Son into the world to condemn
the world, but to save the world through him.
—JOHN 3:17

Without worship, we go about miserable; that's why we have all the troubles we have. . . . I'm not angry with people when I see them go off the deep end, because I know that they have fallen from their first estate along with Adam's brood and all of us together. They haven't been redeemed. And so they have energy they don't know what to do with; they have capacity they don't know how to use. They have skills and don't know where to put them, and so they go wild. . . . If they had been taught that they came into the world in the first place to worship God and to enjoy Him forever and that when they fell, Jesus Christ came to redeem them, to make worshipers out of them, they could by the Holy Ghost and the washing of the blood be made into worshiping saints, and things would be so different. WMJ008-009

Lord, it's so easy to condemn people who "act like such idiots."
Thank You that in Your grace, You don't condemn, but reach out
to save! Amen.

Pick Up the Harp

Ascribe to the LORD the glory due his name; bring an offering
and come before him. Worship the LORD in the splendor
of his holiness.
—1 CHRONICLES 16:29

Man was made to worship God. God gave to man a harp and said, "Here above all the creatures that I have made and created, I have given you the largest harp. I put more strings on your instrument, and I have given you a wider range than I have given to any other creature. You can worship Me in a manner that no other creature can." . . .

The purpose of God in sending His Son to die and rise and live and be at the right hand of God the Father was that He might restore to us the missing jewel, the jewel of worship—that we might come back and learn to do again that which we were created to do in the first place: worship the Lord in the beauty of holiness, to spend our time in awesome wonder and adoration of God, feeling and expressing it, and letting it get into our labors and doing nothing except as an act of worship to Almighty God through His Son, Jesus Christ. I say that the greatest tragedy in the world today is that God has made man in His image and made him to worship Him, made him to play the harp of worship before the face of God day and night, but he has failed God and dropped the harp. It lies voiceless at his feet. WMJ007-008

*Help me, Father, to pick up the harp and bring You the glory
due to Your name. I've come to know You in a deeper way; may I
respond with heartfelt worship. Amen.*

Admiring Awe and Sincere Humility

Humble yourselves, therefore, under God's mighty hand,
that he may lift you up in due time.
—1 PETER 5:6

Those of us who have been blessed within our own beings would not join in any crusade to "follow [our] feelings." On the other hand, if there is no feeling at all in our hearts, then we are dead! . . .

Real worship is, among other things, a feeling about the Lord our God. It is in our hearts. And we must be willing to express it in an appropriate manner.

We can express our worship to God in many ways. But if we love the Lord and are led by His Holy Spirit, our worship will always bring a delighted sense of admiring awe and a sincere humility on our part.

The proud and lofty man or woman cannot worship God any more acceptably than can the proud devil himself. There must be humility in the heart of the person who would worship God in spirit and in truth. WHT084

Lord, I bring to You a heart filled with adoration and humility.
Accept my worship as something that brings joy to You. Amen.

An Awesomeness About God

Praise be to the Lord God, the God of Israel, who alone does marvelous deeds. Praise be to his glorious name forever; may the whole earth be filled with his glory. Amen and Amen.

—PSALM 72:18–19

Worship also means to "express in some appropriate manner" what you feel. Now, expressing in some appropriate manner doesn't mean that we always all express it in the same way all the time. And it doesn't mean that you will always express your worship in the same manner. But it does mean that it will be expressed in some manner.

And what will be expressed? "A humbling but delightful sense of admiring awe and astonished wonder." It is delightful to worship God, but it is also a humbling thing, and the man who has not been humbled in the presence of God will never be a worshiper of God at all. He may be a church member who keeps the rules and obeys the discipline, and who tithes and goes to conference, but he'll never be a worshiper unless he is deeply humbled. "A humbling but delightful sense of admiring awe." There's an awesomeness about God which is missing in our day altogether; there's little sense of admiring awe in the Church of Christ these days. WMJ004-005

Great God, I do indeed stand in admiring awe at the wondrous things You do. Remind me today of that awesomeness about You that I so often forget in my hurried life. Amen.

A Consistent State of Mind

I will extol the LORD at all times; his praise will always be
on my lips.
—PSALM 34:1

Worship must always come from an inward attitude. It embodies a number of factors, including the mental, spiritual, and emotional. You may not at times worship with the same degree of wonder and love that you do at other times, but the attitude and the state of mind are consistent if you are worshiping the Lord.

A husband and father may not appear to love and cherish his family with the same intensity when he is discouraged, when he is tired from long hours in business, or when events have made him feel depressed.

He may not outwardly show as much love toward his family, but it is there, nonetheless, for it is not a feeling only. It is an attitude and a state of mind. It is a sustained act, subject to varying degrees of intensity and perfection. WHT083

Whether I feel like it or not, whether I see Your hand in my circumstances or not, whatever enters my life today, "I will bless the LORD at all times" (Ps. 34:1). Amen.

The Essence of Worship

Jesus replied: "Love the Lord your God with all your heart
and with all your soul and with all your mind."
—MATTHEW 22:37

In worship several elements may be distinguished, among them love, admiration, wonder and adoration. Though they may not be experienced in that order, a little thought will reveal those elements as being present wherever true worship is found.

Both the Old and the New Testaments teach that the essence of true worship is the love of God. "Thou shalt love the Lord thy God with all thy heart, and with all thy soul, and with all thy mind" (Matt. 22:37). Our Lord declared this to be the sum of the Law and the Prophets. . . .

It is quite impossible to worship God without loving Him. Scripture and reason agree to declare this. And God is never satisfied with anything less than all: "all thy heart . . . all thy soul . . . all thy mind." This may not at first be possible, but deeper experience with God will prepare us for it, and the inward operations of the Holy Spirit will enable us after a while to offer Him such a poured-out fullness of love. TIC126

Lord, weed out of my life any conflicting interests, that I might indeed love You with all my heart, soul, and mind. Amen.

A Personal Love Experience

You, God, are my God, earnestly I seek you; I thirst for you,
my whole being longs for you, in a dry and parched land where
there is no water.
—PSALM 63:1

They can change the expressions in the hymnals, but whenever men and women are lost in worship, they will cry out, "O God, thou art my God; early will I seek thee" (Ps. 63:1). Worship becomes a completely personal love experience between God and the worshiper. It was like that with David, with Isaiah, with Paul. It is like that with all whose desire has been to possess God.

This is the glad truth: God is my God.

Brother or sister, until you can say God and I, you cannot say us with any meaning. Until you have been able to meet God in loneliness of soul, just you and God—as if there were no one else in the world—you will never know what it is to love the other persons in the world.

In Canada, those who have written of the saintly Holy Anne said, "She talks to God as if there were nobody else but God and He had no other children but her." That was not a selfish quality. She had found the value and delight of pouring her personal devotion and adoration at God's feet. WHT089

May I know today that personal love experience with You, my God.
I will seek You early, for You are my God. Amen.

To Perfectly Love and Worthily Praise

My heart, O God, is steadfast; I will sing and make music
with all my soul.
—PSALM 108:1

I will refer to one of God's great souls of the past and his book, *The Cloud of Unknowing*. We do not know the name of the devoted saint who more than 600 years ago wrote in his pre-Elizabethan English for the purpose, as he declares it, "that God's children might go on to be 'oned' with God."

At the beginning of his book, he breathed a brief prayer of longing and devotion, and I come back to it often for the good of my own spirit.

He said, "Oh God, under whom all hearts be open, and unto whom all will speaketh, and unto whom no privy thing is hid, I beseech Thee, so for to cleanse the intent of my heart with the unspeakable gift of Thy grace, that I may perfectly love Thee and worthily praise Thee!" . . .

I can discern no trace of theological fault or error in this prayer of devotion and desire breathed long ago by this saint of God.

"Oh God, fix my heart so I may perfectly love Thee and worthily praise Thee!" Nothing extreme and fanatical there. The true child of God will say "Amen" to this desire within the being to perfectly love God and worthily praise Him. ITB033-034

---

*Father, may I love You and praise You with the same devotion;
may I be one with You. Amen.*

Growing Admiration for God

Your right hand, Lord, was majestic in power. Your right hand, Lord, shattered the enemy. In the greatness of your majesty you threw down those who opposed you. You unleashed your burning anger; it consumed them like stubble.

—EXODUS 15:6–7

Then there is admiration, that is, appreciation of the excellency of God. Man is better qualified to appreciate God than any other creature because he was made in His image and is the only creature who was. This admiration for God grows and grows until it fills the heart with wonder and delight. "In our astonished reverence we confess Thine uncreated loveliness," said the hymn writer. "In our astonished reverence." The God of the modern evangelical rarely astonishes anybody. He manages to stay pretty much within the constitution. Never breaks over our bylaws. He's very well-behaved God and very denominational and very much one of us, and we ask Him to help us when we're in trouble and look to Him to watch over us when we're asleep. The God of the modern evangelical isn't a God I could have much respect for. But when the Holy Ghost shows us God as He is, we admire Him to the point of wonder and delight.

WMJ022-023

Maybe it's time, Lord, for You to show us a new and unusual vision of Your majesty and power! Come among us in power and restore to us a sense of wonder, astonishment, and delight. Amen.

Where Are the Admirers?

Know that the LORD is God. It is he who made us, and we are
his; we are his people, the sheep of his pasture.
—PSALM 100:3

The dictionary says that to admire is "to regard with wondering esteem accompanied by pleasure and delight; to look at or upon with an elevated feeling of pleasure." According to this definition, God has few admirers among Christians today.

Many are they who are grateful for His goodness in providing salvation. At Thanksgiving time the churches ring with songs of gratitude that "all is safely gathered in." Testimony meetings are mostly devoted to recitations of incidents where someone got into trouble and got out again in answer to prayer. To decry this would be uncharitable and unscriptural, for there is much of the same thing in the book of Psalms. It is good and right to render unto God thanksgiving for all His mercies to us. But God's admirers, where are they?

The simple truth is that worship is elementary until it begins to take on the quality of admiration. Just as long as the worshiper is engrossed with himself and his good fortune, he is a babe. We begin to grow up when our worship passes from thanksgiving to admiration. As our hearts rise to God in lofty esteem for that which He is ("I AM THAT I AM"), we begin to share a little of the selfless pleasure which is the portion of the blessed in heaven. TIC127

*Lord, I praise You for the wonderful things You have done for me
and for the awesome God that You are. Amen.*

Delighted Wonder

Let us acknowledge the LORD; let us press on to acknowledge
him. As surely as the sun rises, he will appear; he will come
to us like the winter rains, like the spring rains that water
the earth.
—HOSEA 6:3

God always acts like Himself, wherever He may be and whatever He may be doing; in Him there is neither variableness nor shadow of turning. Yet His infinitude places Him so far above our knowing that a lifetime spent in cultivating the knowledge of Him leaves as much yet to learn as if we had never begun. . . .

So imperfectly do we know Him that it may be said that one invariable concomitant of a true encounter with God is delighted wonder. No matter how high our expectation may be, when God finally moves into the field of our spiritual awareness, we are sure to be astonished by His power to overwhelm the mind and fascinate the soul. He is always more wonderful than we anticipate, and more blessed and marvelous than we had imagined He could be. TIC038

---

*Great God of wonder, help me to know You well enough to be
awed by that knowledge. Help me to have the type of encounter
with You today that would leave me in speechless wonder. Amen.*

Astonished Wonder

They recognized him as the same man who used to sit begging at the temple gate called Beautiful, and they were filled with wonder and amazement at what had happened to him.

—ACTS 3:10

We find much of spiritual astonishment and wonder in the book of Acts. You will always find these elements present when the Holy Spirit directs believing men and women.

On the other hand, you will not find astonished wonder among men and women when the Holy Spirit is not present.

Engineers can do many great things in their fields, but no mere human force or direction can work the mysteries of God among men. If there is no wonder, no experience of mystery, our efforts to worship will be futile. There will be no worship without the Spirit.

If God can be understood and comprehended by any of our human means, then I cannot worship Him. One thing is sure. I will never bend my knees and say, "Holy, holy, holy," to that which I have been able to decipher and figure out in my own mind! That which I can explain will never bring me to the place of awe. It can never fill me with astonishment or wonder or admiration. WHT085

Renew in me a sense of wonder, Lord—wonder that comes only when I really see Your Holy Spirit at work in the midst of Your people, doing the unexplainable. Amen.

Where Is the Awe?

But you, Israel, my servant, Jacob, whom I have chosen,
you descendants of Abraham my friend.
—ISAIAH 41:8

Yes, Abraham was lying face down in humility and reverence, overcome with awe in this encounter with God. He knew that he was surrounded by the world's greatest mystery. The presence of this One who fills all things was pressing in upon him, rising above him, defeating him, taking away his natural self-confidence. God was overwhelming him and yet inviting and calling him, pleading with him and promising him a great future as a friend of God!

This is God's way and God's plan. This is God!

As we examine the nature of believing faith in our day, we find ourselves asking, "Where is the mystery? Where is the reverence, the awe, the true fear of God among us?" MMG021-022

Where, indeed, O Lord, is the awe and fear of Your power? Restore it to Your people and bring us to our knees before You, we pray. Amen.

The Wonder, the Mystery, the Majesty

When the disciples heard this, they fell facedown to the ground, terrified.

—MATTHEW 17:6

A wesome wonder and overpowering love" in the presence of that ancient Mystery, that unspeakable Majesty, which the philosophers call the Mysterium Tremendum, but which we call our Father which art in heaven. . . .

The evangelical rationalism which tries to explain everything takes the mystery out of life and the mystery out of worship. When you have taken the mystery out you, have taken God out, for while we may be able to understand Him in some measure, we can never fully understand God. There must always be that awe upon our spirits that says, "Ah, Lord God, Thou knowest!"—that stands silent and breathless or kneels in the presence of that awful Wonder, that Mystery, that unspeakable Majesty, before whom the prophets used to fall, and before whom Peter and John and the rest of them fell down as if dead, before whom Isaiah recoiled and cried, "I am a man of unclean lips" (Isa. 6:5). WMJ005-006

Lord, the disciples heard Your voice and fell on their faces before You, as did Isaiah when he caught a glimpse of Your glory. May I be overwhelmed today with a glimpse of the Mysterium Tremendum. Amen.

Silent Adoration

Come, let us bow down in worship, let us kneel before
the Lord our Maker; for he is our God and we are the people
of his pasture, the flock under his care.

—PSALM 95:6–7

Next is adoration, to love God with all the power within us. To love God with fear and wonder and yearning and awe. To yearn for God with great yearning, and to love Him to a point where it is both painful and delightful. At times this will lead us to breathless silence. I think that some of the greatest prayer is prayer where you don't say one single word or ask for anything. Now God does answer, and He does give us what we ask for. That's plain; nobody can deny that unless he denies the Scriptures. But that's only one aspect of prayer, and it's not even the important aspect. Sometimes I go to God and say, "God, if Thou dost never answer another prayer while I live on this earth, I will still worship Thee as long as I live and in the ages to come for what Thou hast done already." God's already put me so far in debt that if I were to live one million millenniums I couldn't pay Him for what He's done for me. WMJ024

Lord, You have given me so much. Today I ask nothing but Your Presence as I bow before You in silent adoration. Amen.

Adoration for Only One

Love the Lord your God with all your heart and with all your soul
and with all your mind and with all your strength.
—MARK 12:30

The admonition to "love the Lord thy God with all thy heart . . . and with all thy mind" (Matt. 22:37) can mean only one thing. It means to adore Him.

I use the word "adore" sparingly, for it is a precious word. I love babies and I love people, but I cannot say I adore them. Adoration I keep for the only One who deserves it. In no other presence and before no other being can I kneel in reverent fear and wonder and yearning and feel the sense of possessiveness that cries, "Mine, mine!" . . .

Consecration is not difficult for the person who has met God. Where there is genuine adoration and fascination, God's child wants nothing more than the opportunity to pour out his or her love at the Savior's feet. WHT088-089

Father, may I indeed sense that genuine adoration and fascination that leads me to pour out my heart in love for You. Amen.

The Reverential Fear of God

Serve the LORD with fear and celebrate his rule with trembling.
—PSALM 2:11

When we come into this sweet relationship, we are beginning to learn astonished reverence, breathless adoration, awesome fascination, lofty admiration of the attributes of God and something of the breathless silence that we know when God is near.

You may never have realized it before, but all of those elements in our perception and consciousness of the divine Presence add up to what the Bible calls "the fear of God." . . .

The fear of God is that "astonished reverence" of which the great Faber wrote. I would say that it may grade anywhere from its basic element—the terror of the guilty soul before a holy God—to the fascinated rapture of the worshiping saint. There are very few unqualified things in our lives, but I believe that the reverential fear of God mixed with love and fascination and astonishment and admiration and devotion is the most enjoyable state and the most purifying emotion the human soul can know. WHT030-031

Lord, teach me today something of that astonished reverence, that combination of frightening and wonderful feelings that make up true knowledge of You. Amen.

The Art of True Worship

Give thanks to the LORD, for he is good; his love endures forever.
—1 CHRONICLES 16:34

It remains only to be said that worship as we have described it here is almost (though, thank God, not quite) a forgotten art in our day. For whatever we can say of modern Bible-believing Christians, it can hardly be denied that we are not remarkable for our spirit of worship. The gospel as preached by good men in our times may save souls, but it does not create worshipers.

Our meetings are characterized by cordiality, humor, affability, zeal, and high animal spirits; but hardly anywhere do we find gatherings marked by the overshadowing presence of God. We manage to get along on correct doctrine, fast tunes, pleasing personalities, and religious amusements.

How few, how pitifully few are the enraptured souls who languish for love of Christ. . . .

If biblical Christianity is to survive the present world upheaval, we shall need to recapture the spirit of worship. We shall need to have a fresh revelation of the greatness of God and the beauty of Jesus. We shall need to put away our phobias and our prejudices against the deeper life and seek again to be filled with the Holy Spirit. He alone can raise our cold hearts to rapture and restore again the art of true worship. TIC130-131

Father, help me to recapture the spirit of worship, that passion for Christ of which Paul speaks, through a fresh revelation of Your awesome presence. Amen.

Something Beyond Song

*I remembered my songs in the night. My heart meditated
and my spirit asked.*
—PSALM 77:6

Both the Bible and the testimony of a thousand saints show that there is experience beyond song. There are delights which the heart may enjoy in the awesome presence of God which cannot find expression in language; they belong to the unutterable element in Christian experience. Not many enjoy them because not many know that they can. The whole concept of ineffable worship has been lost to this generation of Christians. Our level of life is so low that no one expects to know the deep things of the soul until the Lord returns. So we are content to wait, and while we wait we are wont to cheer our hearts sometimes by breaking into song. . . .

The Bible is a musical book and, next to the Scriptures themselves, the best book to own is a good hymnbook. But still there is something beyond song. . . .

Where the Holy Spirit is permitted to exercise His full sway in a redeemed heart, the progression is likely to be as follows: First, voluble praise, in prose speech or prayer or witness; then, when the crescendo rises beyond the ability of studied speech to express, comes song; when song breaks down under the weight of glory, then comes silence where the soul, held in deep fascination, feels itself blessed with an unutterable beatitude. ROR168-169

---

*Lord, as I "commune with mine own heart" (Ps. 77:6), let me in
that silence find that something which is beyond song. I worship
You now in the stillness. Amen.*

DECEMBER 22

Silence in the Presence of God

Tremble and do not sin; when you are on your beds,
search your hearts and be silent.
—PSALM 4:4

The Bible and Christian biography make a great deal of silence, but we of today make of it exactly nothing. . . .

At the risk of being written off as an extremist or a borderline fanatic, we offer it as our mature opinion that more spiritual progress can be made in one short moment of speechless silence in the awesome presence of God than in years of mere study. While our mental powers are in command, there is always the veil of nature between us and the face of God. It is only when our vaunted wisdom has been met and defeated in a breathless encounter with Omniscience that we are permitted really to know, when prostrate and wordless the soul receives divine knowledge like a flash of light on a sensitized plate. The exposure may be brief, but the results are permanent.

ROR168-169

Today, Lord, I long for that moment of silence in Your majestic presence. Speak, Lord, in this stillness. Amen.

Levity in Addressing God

How great you are, Sovereign LORD! There is no one like you, and there is no God but you, as we have heard with our own ears.
—2 SAMUEL 7:22

Those who heard Luther's prayers have told us of the tremendous effect they often had upon the listeners. He would begin in moving humility, his spirit facedown in utter self-abnegation, and sometimes rise to a boldness of petition that would startle the hearers.

There is among us today a pseudo-mysticism which affects a tender intimacy with God but lacks that breathless awe which the true worshiper must always feel in the presence of the Holy God. This simpering spirit sometimes expresses itself in religious baby talk wholly unworthy of those who are addressing the Most High.

To hear a so-called Christian . . . addressing words of saccharine sweetness to one whom he or she calls "Jesus dear," is a shocking experience for anyone who has once seen heaven opened and stood speechless before the Holy Presence. No one who has ever bowed before the Burning Bush can thereafter speak lightly of God, much less be guilty of levity in addressing Him.

When Horace Bushnell prayed in the field under the night sky, his friend who knelt by his side drew in his arms close to his body. "I was afraid to stretch out my hands," he said, "lest I touch God." TET069-070

God, I come to You in intimacy, but also with the awe and reverence of a subject before a majestic King. Amen.

Becoming What We Love

Do not love the world or anything in the world. If anyone loves
the world, love for the Father is not in them.

—1 JOHN 2:15

We are all in process of becoming. We have already moved
from what we were to what we are, and we are now moving
toward what we shall be. . . .

Not only are we all in the process of becoming, we are becoming
what we love. We are to a large degree the sum of our loves and we
will of moral necessity grow into the image of what we love most; for
love is among other things a creative affinity; it changes and molds
and shapes and transforms. It is without doubt the most powerful
agent affecting human nature next to the direct action of the Holy
Spirit of God within the soul.

What we love is therefore not a small matter to be lightly shrugged
off; rather it is of present, critical, and everlasting importance. It is
prophetic of our future. It tells us what we shall be, and so predicts
accurately our eternal destiny. . . .

This furnishes in part (but only in part) a rational explanation for
the first and greatest commandment: "Love the Lord thy God with all
thy heart, and with all thy soul, and with all thy mind" (Matt. 22:37).

To become like God is and must be the supreme goal of all moral
creatures. This is the reason for their creation, the end apart from
which no excuse can be found for their existence. GTM195-197

*Lord, wean me from unworthy loves, and give me a pure, full love
for You, that I might become like You. Amen.*

Thou Art Worthy

And they sang a new song, saying: "You are worthy to take the
scroll and to open its seals, because you were slain, and with
your blood you purchased for God persons from every tribe and
language and people and nation."
—REVELATION 5:9

D id you ever stop to think about the rapture? It's going to be
something that's never happened before. You might be walking
around on the street and hear the sound of the trumpet—and suddenly you're transformed! You won't know what to do or how to act.
And the people lying in their graves, what'll they do? I know what
they'll do—they'll sing! There's going to be singing at the consum-
mation, on that great day!

"Thou art worthy to take the book, and to open the seals thereof: for thou wast slain, and hast redeemed us" (Rev. 5:9)—that's the
theme of the new song. The theme of the new song isn't "I am"; it's
"Thou art." Notice the difference! When you look at the old hym-
nody of Wesley, Montgomery, and Watts, it was, "Thou art, O God,
Thou art." But when you look at the modern hymns, it is, "I am, I am,
I am." It makes me sick to my stomach. Occasionally a good hymn
with testimonies is all right, but we've overdone it. The song of the
ransomed is going to be, "Thou are worthy, O God." AOG014

---

*I long for that day, Lord, when I can join in the singing. I await
Your return, Lord Jesus. Amen.*

A New Order

See, I will create new heavens and a new earth. The former
things will not be remembered, nor will they come to mind.
—ISAIAH 65:17

Amid all the world religions, only Christianity is able to proclaim
the Bible's good news that God, the Creator and Redeemer, will
bring a new order into being! Indeed, that is the only good news
available to a fallen race today. God has promised a new order that
will be of eternal duration and infused with eternal life.

How amazing!

It is a promise from God of a new order to be based upon the
qualities the exact opposite of mankind's universal blight—temporality and mortality. God promises the qualities of perfection and
eternity—qualities that cannot now be found anywhere on this earth.

What a prospect! . . .

God's revelation says that Jesus Christ is the eternal Victor, triumphant over sin and death. That is why He is the Head of the new
creation, which has upon it the banner of eternity rather than of
temporality and the mark of life forevermore rather than the mark
of death. TRA139-140, 142

What a prospect, indeed! Thank You, Father, for the eternal
victory of Jesus Christ. I worship You now and long for that day
of completion. Amen.

Around the Throne of God

The twenty-four elders fall down before him who sits on the throne and worship him who lives for ever and ever. They lay their crowns before the throne.

—REVELATION 4:10

All of the examples that we have in the Bible illustrate that glad and devoted and reverent worship is the normal employment of moral beings. Every glimpse that is given us of heaven and of God's created beings is always a glimpse of worship and rejoicing and praise because God is who He is.

The Apostle John in Revelation 4:10–11 gives us a plain portrayal of created beings around the throne of God. . . .

I can safely say, on the authority of all that is revealed in the Word of God, that any man or woman on this earth who is bored and turned off by worship is not ready for heaven. WHT013

Lord, revive my worship so that it may indeed be a foretaste of the worship I will enjoy for all eternity. Amen.

Bored in Heaven

Each of the four living creatures had six wings and was covered
with eyes all around, even under its wings. Day and night they
never stop saying: "Holy, holy, holy is the Lord God Almighty,
who was, and is, and is to come."
—REVELATION 4:8

I have been at funerals where the presiding minister preached the
deceased right into heaven. Yet the earthly life of the departed
plainly said that he or she would be bored to tears in a heavenly en-
vironment of continuous praise and adoration of God.

This is personal opinion, but I do not think death is going to
transform our attitudes and disposition. If in this life we are not really
comfortable talking or singing about heaven, I doubt that death will
transform us into enthusiasts. If the worship and adoration of God
are tedious now, they will be tedious after the hour of death. I do not
know that God is going to force any of us into His heaven. I doubt
that He will say to any of us, "You were never interested in worshiping
Me while you were on earth, but in heaven I am going to make that
your greatest interest and your ceaseless occupation!"

Controversial? Perhaps. But I am trying to stir you up, to encour-
age you to delight in a life of praise and spiritual victory! JIV067-068

*May my worship on earth prepare me for the enthusiastic
celebration that will be heaven. May I learn to delight in a life
of praise. Amen.*

He's Pleased

Father, I want those you have given me to be with me where I am, and to see my glory, the glory you have given me because you loved me before the creation of the world.

—JOHN 17:24

Gerhard Tersteegen wrote a song.

Midst the darkness, storm and sorrow, One bright gleam I see.
Well I know that blest tomorrow, Christ will come for me.

And then he writes six stanzas and the last four lines are these:

He and I in that bright glory, One deep joy shall share.
Mine to be forever with Him, And His that I am there.

Did you ever stop to think that God is going to be as pleased to have you with Him in heaven as you are to be there? The goodness and mercy of God, the loving kindness of the Lord—it's wonderful! He can bring us into such a relationship with Him that He can please us without spoiling us. He pleases us, and He's pleased when we're pleased. And when we're pleased with him, He's pleased. . . .

Thank God, thank God! Let us praise the lovingkindness of God forever, for of His goodness there is no end. Amen! AOG056-057

How amazing to know that You take delight in me, Lord! I delight in my communion with You. Amen.

Walking in the Presence of His Lord

Then I heard every creature in heaven and on earth and under
the earth and on the sea, and all that is in them, saying: "To him
who sits on the throne and to the Lamb be praise and honor
and glory and power, for ever and ever!"
—REVELATION 5:13

One of the purest souls ever to live on this fallen planet was Nicholas Herman, that simple-hearted Christian known throughout the world as Brother Lawrence. . . .

Early in his life Brother Lawrence found Christ as his own Savior and Lord and entered into what he called "the unspeakable riches of God and of Jesus Christ." He was a common cook, but he learned to turn the modest service into a kind of worship. . . .

He spent his long life walking in the presence of his Lord, and when he came to die, there was no need for any particular change in his occupation. At the last hour someone asked him what was going on in his thoughts as death approached. He replied simply: "I am doing what I shall do through all eternity—blessing God, praising God, adoring God, giving Him the love of my whole heart. It is our one business, my brethren, to worship Him and love Him without thought of anything else." PON022-023

*Lord, may I live now as I will for all of time, praising and adoring
You with my whole heart. Amen.*

The Transcendence of God

As the heavens are higher than the earth, so are my ways
higher than your ways and my thoughts than your thoughts.
—ISAIAH 55:9

When we say that God is far above, we're using an analogy.
We're thinking about a star that's way above, way out yonder
in space—but that isn't what we really mean when we think about
the transcendent God.

If you miss this point, you might as well stop reading, because this
is critical to understanding what follows. When we say that God's
transcendence is "farness above," we are not thinking about astronomical distances or physical magnitude. God never thinks about
the size of anything, because God contains everything. He never
thinks about distance, because God is everywhere. . . .

God is the uncreated One who had no beginning, the self-existent
One who was never created, but who was simply God, who made all
things. . . .

There is a vast gulf, an all but infinite gulf, fixed between that
which is God and that which is not God—between the great I AM
and all created things, from the archangel down to the tiniest virus
that cannot be seen with the naked eye. God made all that and is just
as high above one as the other. God's uncreated quality of life causes
Him to be transcendent, to rise high above all creatures. AOGII037-040

---

*Father, the knowledge of your transcendence gives me great
hope in Your power, yet it also humbles me, knowing that I am
nothing compared to You. Help me to understand more fully just
how great You are. Amen.*

Reference Codes for Books and Booklets by A. W. Tozer

CONTINUE WORSHIPING ALONGSIDE TOZER WITH THE REST OF HIS TRINITARIAN DEVOTIONS

Spend a year dwelling on the awesomeness of God with A. W. Tozer. He will expand your faith in a God so great that words fall short to describe Him. He will nourish you with truth. Encounter Tozer's heart and wisdom like never before in this newly revised edition.

978-0-8024-1968-2

Spend a year encountering the Son of God alongside A. W. Tozer. In this 365-day devotional, you can intentionally pursue Christ daily. Encounter the character of Christ, His work on the cross, and His limitless love for you. With each page, may your heart be filled and your worship increased.

978-0-8024-1970-5

Spend a year unearthing the wonder of the Holy Spirit alongside A. W. Tozer. This devotional explores many of the defining characteristics of the Holy Spirit. Each day seeks to stoke the believer's internal desire to hunger and thirst after the Spirit of God.

978-0-8024-1969-9

MOODY
Publishers®

"I am looking for the fellowship of the burning heart—for men and women of all generations who love the Savior until adoration becomes the music of their soul."

—A. W. Tozer

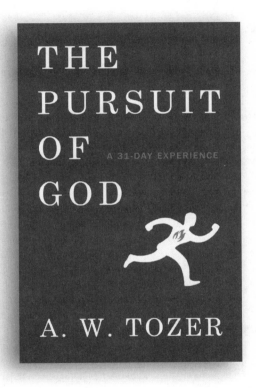

MOODY
Publishers®

om the Word to Life®

The Pursuit of God is an enduring favorite—over a million copies are now in print in 20 languages. The complete text of this classic has been divided into 31 daily meditations. Quotations from some of Tozer's forty-plus works, contemporary authors, and even classic authors enhance the text.

978-0-8024-2195-1

"What comes into our minds when we think about God is the most important thing about us."
—A. W. Tozer

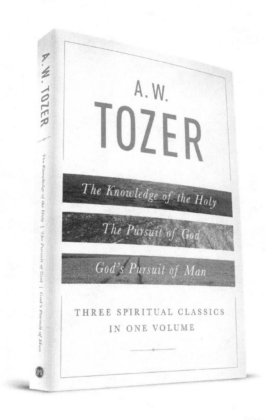

Considered to be Tozer's greatest works, *The Knowledge of the Holy*, *The Pursuit of God*, and *God's Pursuit of Man* are now available in a single volume. Discover a God of breathtaking majesty and world-changing love, and find yourself worshiping through every page.

978-0-8024-1861-6

A.W. TOZER

ABOUT   QUOTES   MEDITATIONS   BOOKS   MEDIA

NEW TO TOZER?   PODCAST

"REFUSE TO BE AVERAGE. LET YOUR HEART SOAR AS HIGH AS IT WILL."

A. W. Tozer

DISCOVER MORE: Watch the mini-documentary or browse the Tozer resources

STAY ENCOURAGED: Listen to the *Mornings With Tozer* podcast

STAY UPDATED: Sign up for the Tozer newsletter

Visit AWTOZER.com